HORSING
AROUND

Humor in Life and Letters

Sarah Blacher Cohen, *General Editor*

Advisory Editors

HORSING AROUND

CONTEMPORARY COWBOY HUMOR

**Edited by Lawrence Clayton
and Kenneth W. Davis**

 Wayne State University Press
Detroit

Library of Congress Cataloging-in-Publication Data

Horsing around : contemporary cowboy humor / edited by
  Lawrence Clayton and Kenneth W. Davis.
        p.   cm.—(Humor in life and letters)
    Includes bibliographical references.
      ISBN 0-8143-2143-7 (alk. paper).—ISBN 0-8143-2144-5 (pbk. :
  alk. paper)
      1. Cowboys—West (U.S.)—Humor.   2. West (U.S.)—Social
  life and customs—Humor.   3. Cowboys' writings, American—
  West (U.S.)   4. Cowboys—West (U.S.)—Literary collections.
  5. American wit and humor—West (U.S.)   6. American
  literature—20th century.   7. American literature—West (U.S.)
  8. Cowboys—West (U.S.)—Folklore.   I. Clayton, Lawrence,
  1938-   .   II. Davis, Kenneth W., 1932-   .   III. Series.
  F596.H686   1991
  978—dc20   90-21452

Grateful acknowledgment is made to Ace Reid for permission
to use the cartoons that appear throughout this volume.

Book design by Mary Krzewinski

For Everett A. Gillis
Mentor and Friend

CONTENTS

ACKNOWLEDGMENTS

Grateful acknowledgment is made to the following for permission to reprint copyrighted material: The University of Illinois Press for "My Brother Is a Cowboy" by Carolyn Osborn; to Doubleday for "The Coyote Hunt" by Elmer Kelton; to Maverick Books for "Thoroughbreds," "The Mad Hatter," "Republican to the Death," "LBJ Was Here," "The Devil in Texas," and "Confessions of a Cowdog" by John R. Erickson; to the University of Nebraska Press for "Wild Cattle" and "A Bitter Lesson" by John R. Erickson; to the Texas Folklore Society for "Night Horse Nightmare" by Paul Patterson; to *Livestock Weekly* for "A True Story about Cats: How Not to Get Rich Quick," "Windmiller or Windmillie: There's Ample Fun for All," and "Do Gooders Don't Always Do That Much Good" by Curt Brummett and "Summer Cowboys Sometimes Welcome Advent of Autumn" and "Boxing Gloves Are Cheaper than a Broken Hand" by John R. Erickson; to Coyote Cowboy Company for "The Vanishing Breed?" "Crossbred Stew," "Hello, I'm from the Government . . . I'm Here to Help You," "The Cow Committee," and "A Rider, a Roper, and a Hell'uva Windmill Man" by Baxter Black; to Coyote Cowboy Press for "The Oyster," "The Defense of the Chicken," and "The #2 Hairball" from *Croutons on a Cow Pie* by Baxter Black (1988); to Ace Reid of Ace Reid Enterprises, Kerrville, Texas for the cartoons; and finally, to *Red Neck Review of Literature*, in which an early version of the Introduction appeared.

Special thanks go to Carol Donald, Joy Cron, and Charlene Archer for their efforts on the word processor to prepare this material for publication.

INTRODUCTION

The American cowboy has long been known for his brand of rowdy, even abrasive humor and his ability to laugh in the face of crisis and danger. Collections of that humor have been provided in Ramon Adams's *The Cowboy and His Humor*[1] and Stan Hoig's *The Humor of the American Cowboy*.[2] Both of these collections, however, deal with the humor of the old-time cowboy, the cowboy who flourished before the modern age of mechanization.

The examples of humor we have gathered for this collection are from the contemporary world of cowboys who work with pickups, helicopters, and well-trained horses. A sight common these days in the ranching country is a group of horses tethered at the tailgate of a pickup and a helicopter in the air. The helicopter pilot spots strays in thick brush or obscure ravines and helps cowboys on horseback round them up. This relationship of man, beast, and machine provides the context for the humorous pieces in this collection. As the expansion of the railroads across the Great Plains and on to the West ushered in an earlier era of ranching, so the personal automobile brought about the modern era of ranching in the Southwest, the geographic setting for the materials in this collection. After World War I, the increased availability of cars and small trucks made frequent contact with city life easy. Large trucks made the feed wagons pulled by mules or horses obsolete. Later, giant trucks eliminated the need for long cattle drives; their smaller cousins—pickups, vans, and four-by-fours—brought an end to camping out around the chuckwagon. Other mechanical inventions of the twentieth century—the airplane, radio, and of course, television—further expanded the lives of cowboys and ranchers by making information about the world quickly accessible. Today's cowboy with a small transistor radio in his shirt pocket and a

13

satellite dish in his backyard gets the Dow-Jones average and latest episodes of the hottest television series as quickly as do the city dwellers.

The humor of modern cowboys is the humor of a traditional occupational group that continues to adapt to change yet maintains its strong ties with the old methods of doing its work. The quality of this humor is likewise modern and adaptive. Although the physical world of the contemporary cowboy is heavily mechanized, cowboy humor contains elements that link it to traditional motifs in European and American folklife and literature. Cowboys in conflict with ranch foremen or owners are sometimes similar to scheming servant figures in the comedies of Plautus and Terence. Stories of cowboys who delight in sometimes harsh practical jokes exemplify the survival of the sorts of humor Mark Twain and Bret Harte so well understood. Common also in modern cowboy humor are accounts of anguish and exasperation stemming from conflicts with cattle that rebel against transportation on cattle trucks and run about wildly through city streets terrorizing citizens and vexing city policemen. Using battery-powered prods to encourage market-bound cattle into waiting transport trucks, cowboys enjoy all the benefits of modern technology. Yet to survive the indignities, irritations, and bone-crushing agonies of their vocations, they still resort to that timeless device for venting spleen, the humorous story. Now, this humor mirrors the age of technology; the cowboy's nineteenth-century predecessor told tales about cattle drives, not yarns about pulling horse trailers through downtown traffic. But despite shifts in content and despite some obvious television influence, the cowboy oral tradition is not dying; the long hours to fill with conversation persist in the cowboy's daily routine.

This tradition of oral storytelling deserves some comment. Although the practice is lacking in or absent from some segments of modern ranching life, it continues among cowboys. The physical demands of the cowboy's work keep him away from radio and television entertainment for long periods of time. Around the saddle house or toolshed on rainy days, in the branding pens, around the campfire or cook house at mealtimes, or waiting at the far side of the pasture for daylight to come so that the roundup can begin—here the men tell and retell stories that form the loosely structured saga of life on that particular ranch. This cycle reflects the unique makeup of the crew at that time, the history of that ranch, and its famous—or infamous—cowboys, horses, bad cattle, and mean-spirited cooks, foremen, or owners.

The humor of this collection stems from present-day cowboy life in the American West, principally in Texas, New Mexico, Oklahoma, and Colorado. The material proves that although the life and work of the cowboy may have altered over time, his sense of humor—what Adams called "one of the outstanding traits of the old-time cowboy"[3] is intact. The comment made in 1985 by George Peacock, a third-generation cowboy and manager of the ninety-nine-section Nail Ranch in Shackelford County in West Texas, is revealing": A cowboy's life is so lonely that he has to pull a trick or a joke along to keep himself going."[4] Curt Brummett, a fresh talent in cowboy storytelling, elaborates on this point: "Cowboy humor comes from two sources, boredom and revenge. Boredom has to be broken up some way or another. And I might add, some of the plots to stir things up can get pretty complicated. These acts come in the form of practical jokes, and for the most part are fairly exciting, and seldom harmful. Of course, when some idiot gets bored and then does something to get unbored, the victim has a tendency to want to even the score. The plot for revenge can end it once and for all, if the payback is good enough. If the payback is inflicted with only a mild interest, the boredom is broken up for quite a while, because revenge follows revenge. But should the initial payback come in the form of a well-planned and well-executed trick, boredom is sure to set in once again. Of course, the telling of these tricks keeps them alive in the memories of the poor guys involved in the first place."[5]

Cowboys can find a time and a place—any time and any place—to promote humor. This outlet may take the form of tricks or pranks, stories or anecdotes of dangerous working conditions, or even tall tales. A cowboy bucked off a feisty mount is apt to hear a wisecrack rather than a kind inquiry. A cowboy kicked by a cow in the cutting alley at separating time is more apt to be jibed for being such a klutz than to get any special sympathy. Narratives of the more spectacular or dangerous of these actions go into oral tradition and spice up the life of the men as they repeat and embellish the tales. The stories have the effect of reinforcing the verve and will of the men who engage in this demanding life.

Although some observers are ready to declare the contemporary cowboy nonexistent, studies such as *Buckaroos in Paradise*[6] and *The American Cowboy*[7] as well as the photography by Martin Schreiber's *Last of a Breed*,[8] prove that in parts of the modern American West the cowboy is alive and well. Unfortunately, however, these studies suggest that cowboy life is in a state of transition and is nearly at its end. Bob Anderson, a cowboy from Breckenridge, Texas, refutes such a notion when he says, "As long as there are cows, there will be cowboys. Only time will tell how the cowboy will live and do his work."[9] In characteristic humor, one old-timer reportedly said, "There will always be cowboys. No one will ever invent a machine that can take as much abuse as a cowboy can."[10]

The language of the modern cowboy may suggest that his character is undergoing change. In contrast with the language of the old-time cowboy, the language of today's cowboy seems less loaded with cow-country metaphor. But the language of today's cowboy is not less salty or effective than that of his predecessors. The modern cowboy's abilities at swearing have declined not at all, and he remains as reluctant as ever to use such language when women—especially those he deems "ladies"—are present. He still admires "the fairer sex" and, if lucky, has either admired from a distance or found a companion who understands the life a cowboy has to lead in order to be himself. Even so, he tones down his colorful phrases in his wife's presence. But whatever his marital situation, the modern cowboy continues to use witty language that is penetrating, perceptive, and highly effective in his yarn-spinning, swearing, boasting, teasing, and bemused descriptions. His language is sometimes spare, sometimes grandly prolix.

Fortunately, some of the humor of modern cowboy life is finding its way into print. The following collection is arranged into three parts. Part 1, "From the Horse's Mouth," consists of stories related by those who experienced them firsthand. Such are the stories by cowboys Curt Brummett and Paul Patterson, and ex-ranch manager John Erickson, and in poetry of cowboy and veterinarian Baxter Black and cowboy Sam Brown. These talented folk artists have shaped events and actions into well-ordered, humorous reminiscences. Part 2, "Collectors' Items," reflects the work of the folklorist, the collector, who then retells cowboy material. The work of Kenneth Davis and Lawrence Clayton and the stories of John Erickson recorded from cartoonist Ace Reid reflect that particular viewpoint. In Part 3, "Belles Lettres," Benjamin Capps, Carolyn Osborn, and Elmer Kelton incorporate humorous cowboy material in fictional literary works. The pieces are not mainly humorous in intent. Rather, their purpose is simply to tell a good story.

The artistic level of modern cowboy humor is a moot point. Without doubt, its function is to entertain. Much of the effectiveness of pieces that still circulate in the oral tradition stems from the skill with which the folk narrator relates the newest jokes or offers a variant of a familiar oral narrative. This teller of tales may be a cowboy who has joined the spit-and whittle crowd on the courthouse lawn or a cap-wearing, pickup-driving operator of a small ranch, a man who delights in swapping yarns over coffee at the local Dairy Queen when he has time to get away from the long hours of making a living. The narrator may be fresh from the open range, and still clad in the customary leather chaps, vest, boots, ten-gallon hat, spurs, denim pants, and durable shirt, or someone more familiar with a word processor monitor and keyboard. Of whatever lifestyle, the authors of the pieces in this volume together demonstrate that humor can be subtly ironic or bluntly intense, that is can be bawdy or scatological, that it can be redemptive. Some narrators are conscious of all of these qualities and more; the best users of humor, however, just do it spontaneously.

In words and pictures, the examples of humor in this collection treat a wide variety of recurrent themes common in the life of today's cowboy. With his accounts of growing up in the Southwest Curt Brummett joins a familiar group of American writers who captured the sometimes hilarious, sometimes bittersweet humor and *angst* of childhood and early adult initiations involving conflicts with authority figures: parents, school teachers, older cowboys. Brummett is also a wise commentator on the difficulties of maintaining a marriage in a world that still lacks some of the amenities commonly expected by most wives. John Erickson focuses on the humor of men in conflict with strong-willed cows and horses. Like Brummett, he knows the appeal of humorous initiatory experiences; his youthful protagonists sometimes show their kinship to the greenhorn in the penny dreadfuls and in the novels of B. M. Bower and her more famous contemporary, Owen Wister. Like many of his fellow writers, and like cartoonist Ace Reid, Erickson is a folklorist: his story "The Devil in Texas" is a clever retelling of the ancient story of a human being in conflict with the Devil. In pictures with spare, acerbic captions, Ace Reid memorializes the everyday, the ordinary as well as the major conflicts in the life of the working cowboy. Paul Patterson, an old-time storyteller in the grand tradition of oral narration, offers self-deprecating humor as well as broad, grandly comic accounts of his experiences as a working cowboy. Baxter Black, a satirist in the tradition of Pope and Lord Byron, examines the response of cattlemen to the government, outsiders, health faddists, and the overly squeamish. He demolishes the notion that the cowboy is a vanishing breed. Novelist and poet Sam Brown demonstrates the modern cowboy humorist's keen sense of the ridiculous and supports Bax-

ter Black's argument that the modern working cowboy, warts and
all, carries on traditions which are nearly two hundred years old in
America.

Lawrence Clayton and Kenneth Davis, folklorists and collectors, preserve incidents and accounts which link present day
cowboy humor with ancient traditions in Anglo-American and His-
panic folk narratives. Clayton's accounts of saga material from the
north central Texas short grass ranching country, and Davis's stories of colorful characters and situations in which uppity folks get
their proper chastisements, demonstrate the rich traditional basis
of much modern humor in the American West. Clayton's narratives
stress conflicts cowboys and sometimes their womenfolk have with
each other, with nature, with technology, with animals: these elements and more provoke conflicts which are often fraught with
physical danger but which give rise to comedy. Davis's tales survey
a variety of facets of life in the American West; they treat eccentric
sorts who in almost all cultures are fair game for comic narratives;
they record language that reveals much about the world views of
modern southwesterners and westerners; they support ancient delight in quick-thinking characters who cope with large and small
challenges more with mental agility than with physical prowess.

The fiction writers included here, Elmer Kelton, Benjamin
Capps, and Carolyn Osborn, are moderns whose views are shaped,
as is the humor of the West shaped generally, by traditional elements
and themes. Kelton's account of a coyote hunt shows the influence
of a chase scene such as the one in Chaucer's "The Nun's Priest's
Tale" in which an entire small community turns out to run after a
chicken-stealing fox. Kelton's chase is more detailed than Chaucer's,
but it has the same comic intensity, the same revelation of the
folkways of a people. In "Slim Wilkinson," Benjamin Capps also
finds humor in a coyote hunt. Capps's focus is on family traditions
and the promise of their continuation. Like Kelton and other fiction
writers and storytellers, Capps understands the humor as well as
the pathos of a distinctive way of life: the cowboy life.

Carolyn Osborn's detailed verbal portrait of the modern
cowboy in "My Brother Is a Cowboy" gives a composite view of a
character who is in many way an anachronism yet is the exemplar
of the spirit that keeps the cowboy alive. With wisdom and grace as
well as thoroughly satiric humor, Osborn uses first person narration to tell of the life of a quasi-mythical cowboy—the brother in
the story—and of women and family who must cope with this
unique person. Not all cowboys have all the traits of Osborn's

character, but she manages to give him characteristics common to many contemporary cowboys. Osborn's story provides a feminine perspective of modern cowboy life and humor.

Whatever uses the contemporary cowboy's humor is put to, it still mirrors a way of life involving basic elements of the human condition: close contact with a sometimes beneficent, sometimes uncaring nature: exposure to the beauty as well as the stubbornness of different animals; and personal isolation. Cowboy humor may be stinging or abrasive, but its intent is seldom to malign. To some modern readers, facets of the cowboy's humor may seem sexist, or callously indifferent to animals, but few occupational groups have as much regard for humans and animals as do today's cowboys. Contemporary cowboy humor still serves as humor has long done—to correct, to encourage, but most of all to entertain.

Listed in the bibliography are sources that elaborate upon and elucidate this long tradition of humor, especially in the United States. Particular attention has been given to the folk tradition of the tall tale, for the culture that provides the context for the present collection is definitely that of a particularly colorful folk group.

The glossary contains terms that the uninitiated might find obscure. Geographic distribution, particularly in the Southwest, may cause trouble for those in other areas of the American West, for some of these terms are admittedly in the dialect of the region indicated. The broad similarity, however, in the life and work will make the intent as clear as that in a good revenge prank.

Ace Reid

The collection of printed material is interspersed with cartoons by Ace Reid, by common consent the premier cowboy cartoonist in the Southwest if not in the world. His success is due to the creative expression Reid gives to the interpretation of the plight of today's cowboys. The situations in his cartoons are just so typical of the real cowboy that the appeal is universal. His principal cartoon character, Jake, may well be the archetypal humorous, down-and-out cowboy; and his support characters—Zeb, Maw, Banker Tufernal, and Wilbur the Horse Trader—represent well-known types in the world of today's cowboys.

Born at Lelia Lake in the Texas Panhandle, Ace Reid, Jr., grew up near Electra, Texas, a town named for the daughter of the founder of the famous Waggoner Ranch. He left Electra in 1952,

COW POKES

By Ace Reid

"Wul, if the boss don't like this gate, tell him I'm a $5.00 a day cowboy doin' the job of $4.50 an hour carpenter!"

joined the navy, and toured the world. Then for a time he was a rancher and tried to get rich in the oil business. Because he had a penchant for drawing and humor, he decided to capitalize upon his talent and became widely known for his efforts in cartooning and humor in general. He now lives at the Draggin' S Ranch in the Texas hill country near Kerrville, where his studio is located.

In his biography of Reid, *Ace Reid: Cow Poke*, John Erickson says that Reid describes himself as "a damn good artist . . . a writer, a painter, a cartoonist, and a storyteller," for, "I just don't know of anything I could leave out, 'cause I am doing a little bit of all of it and have been fairly successful at every bit of it" (p. 129). Reid's cartoons have appeared in the *Livestock Weekly*, the *San Angelo Standard Times*, the *San Antonio Express*, and five hundred other newspapers. A veteran of the banquet circuit as well as a public speaker and entertainer, he also has had his own radio show. His humorous calendars featuring Jake and his friends are much sought.

Notes

1. Ramon Adams, *The Cowboy and His Humor* (Austin: Encino Press, 1968).
2. Stan Hoig, *The Humor of the American Cowboy* (1958; reprint, Lincoln: University of Nebraska Press, 1970).
3. Adams, *Cowboy*, p. 3.
4. George Peacock, interview by Lawrence Clayton, Albany, Texas, 1985.
5. Curt Brummett to Lawrence Clayton, April 19, 1986, in Clayton's possession.
6. Howard W. Marshall and Richard E. Ahlborn, *Buckaroos in Paradise: Cowboy Life in Northern Nevada,* (1980; reprint, Lincoln: University of Nebraska Press, 1981).
7. Lonn Taylor and Ingrid Maar, *The American Cowboy* (Washington: Library of Congress, 1983).
8. Martin Schreiber, *Last of a Breed* (Austin: Texas Mongthly, 1982).
9. Bob Anderson, interview by Lawrence Clayton, Albany, Texas, 1985.
10. John Erickson, interview by Lawrence Clayton, Abilene, Texas, 1987. The originator is unknown to us.

★ 1 ★

From the Horse's Mouth:
Cowboy-Writers

CURT BRUMMETT

A gifted spinner of yarns about ranch life, Curt Brummett was born in Clovis, New Mexico and grew up in eastern New Mexico. His schooling came in Forrest and Clovis. He graduated from Clovis High School in 1966, "much to the relief of several aunts, uncles, and an assortment of teachers. My mother always said I would graduate; she just didn't know when" (to Lawrence Clayton, April 19, 1986). Brummett's well-developed humor is based on his experiences in school and his work as a cowboy. He went to the oil fields to make a living, but when the oil crash of 1986 came, he returned to cowboying. His comment on the cowboy life is worth recounting here: "There is no way you can compare the cowboy's lifestyle to any other, no matter how hard you try. But it seems that everyone else has tried to compare themselves to the cowboy. It just won't work, because unless you have known the hardships of being on horseback in a blizzard, or been so hot you couldn't breathe, or been so stove up you could barely walk, you just can't understand why a cowboy comes back for more. The good Lord knows that it ain't the wages. I think it is the fact that a cowboy knows or at least thinks that he is doing something very few others can do. Whether it's breaking horses, or fixing a windmill, or calving a bunch of heifers, or gathering some old renegade cows or bulls. For the most part it is a thankless job. And the ones who still do it, do it because they love it and do so with the hope that they are keeping alive a way of life that few others could withstand and absolutely cannot understand" (ibid.).

Brummett's keen ear for the sentence patterns, the cadences, and the idioms of his home territory gives his writing the freshness, the appeal of gifted oral narration—even though his words are reduced to print. His work is much in the tradition of Mark Twain.

24

A True Story about Cats: How Not to Get Rich Quick

One form of humor involves physical abuse. Here that treatment is administered to a variety of people and one tomcat, whose misfortune sparks rebellion from his neighborhood friends. The scratches to the youngsters are severe, but two pool hall hangers-on also learn a valuable lesson. This anecdote reveals that all of the young cowboy's experience may not come from working cattle on the open range. These days a youngster gets his experience and earns his keep where he can and takes his lumps—and his scratches—as they come.

One spring day as Terry, Larry, and I, three school kids, were hanging around the pool hall on our lunch hour, we were discussing our financial crisis.

We had just spent our allowance for the next 200 years replacing an outhouse that had disintegrated due to careless handling of four stolen sticks of dynamite, three blasting caps, one can of black powder and five gallons of kerosene. We didn't blow it up on purpose. But no one seemed to believe us.

After we got beat dang near to death, we had to make arrangements to pay for it. It didn't matter that it hadn't been used in fifteen years. It had to be replaced.

It wasn't our fault that lightning hit our storehouse. And we never did figure out how they knew it was us that got the explosives. But the situation was we were dead broke and everyone in town was watching us like we had the plague.

We had decided there was no way to get ahead money-wise, so we planned to learn how to play 42 for fun and profit. We were watchin' ever so close when Elmo Carstead casually mentioned there were just too many damn cats around the store, the garage, and pool hall. He also stated that if he killed 'em off the mice and rats would soon take over. So there he was; he just didn't know what he was gonna do.

Buel Addelman came up with the perfect solution:

"Elmo, that ain't no problem; all you got to do is castrate the Toms an' that way you don't lose any cats but you don't gain any cats either." Buel never missed a play. Elmo came back by stating he didn't have time to catch and castrate those Toms, 'cause when he wasn't waiting for an important phone call he had to be at the

pool hall defending his championship. But he admitted that the
idea was sure worth thinking on.

Buel bid 84 and mentioned that since everyone at the pool
hall would benefit from such good animal control, they could all
chip in some money and pay fifty cents per Tom. That is if the job was
done right. You know, no excessive bleeding and things like that.

Terry and I had done started figuring. We figured there must
be sixty or sixty-five Toms out of that whole town full of cats. Larry,
being the only one showing any sense, started slipping towards
the door. Terry got him stopped and started convincing him about
how easy it would be. After all, we had all helped castrate calves,
colts, pigs, and sheep. And besides, how else could three school
kids get rich quicker?

Terry was busy with Larry while I was busy trying to get us
hired on as custom cat cutters. It took quite a bit of talking. Buel
wasn't real sure we had the experience to handle a job as important
as this, and Elmo wanted it done right. After some pretty hard
talking on my part, Elmo and Buel finally gave in, and we sealed
the deal.

Elmo said he would put out some scraps in an old cement
silo of his. Since it only had one door, he could trap maybe thirty-
five or forty cats. The next day we could skip lunch and come right
on over and make $10 or $15 right quick. He winked at Buel and
the deal was set.

We went on back to school and never said a word about our
new money making business. That night we all got our pocket
knives sharpened to perfection. We knew that the sharper the knife
the quicker the cut, and the quicker the cut, the more money we
could make.

The next morning at recess we got together and decided that
a business of this importance deserved our full-time attention. We
skipped out and headed for the pool hall.

We found Elmo and Buel hard at work, keeping their championship, and convinced them that we wouldn't get in trouble for
skipping class. After all, school was for kids too dumb to make any
money. And besides, we already had our own business. We had
decided that after we cut all the local cats, we might just go from
town to town, as professionals.

Well, we followed Elmo and Buel out to that old silo. When
they opened that door, I never saw so many cats in my life. It
looked like there were a hundred in that room, and we guessed
there must be at least half of 'em Toms. Elmo and Buel were grinning. We thought they were happy 'cause they had found someone
to do the job. Not so.

Elmo said that part of the silo top was gone, and when he shut us in there would be plenty of light to see by. And when we got done cuttin' all those Toms, just holler and they would come let us out.

When we stepped into that silo and they closed the door, it dawned on all three of us that we didn't know beans about cuttin' cats.

Now these cats were a long ways from being gentle house-cats, and there probably weren't two in the whole place that had ever been touched by a human. But we didn't think about that, cause we were too busy listening to all that hissing and growling. You will never know what stark cold fear is until you are locked in a silo with a bunch of cats as scared as you are.

We seriously discussed going back to school, but we changed our minds on that, because if we went back failures we were sure to get in trouble. So we would just go ahead and get started.

Since I had the sharpest knife, it was decided that Terry and Larry would do the flanking. We started by Terry grabbing a big yellow Tom. And from there things just went to hell.

We figured that holding cats was probably like holding calves; once you get a hold of one, don't turn him loose. But we also discovered that turning a mad, scared cat loose wasn't all that easy. I didn't realize a cat could wreck so much stuff with two stout kids holding him.

They got him stretched out, and I cut him. Did you know when you cut a scared cat that it changes his voice immediately and at the same time his kidneys go crazy? The sound from that cat made our hair stand on end, but all that water flying around made it lay back down. I announced that I was through with the surgery and they could turn 'im loose. I'll guarantee you one thing. Turning that cat loose took a lot longer than it did to catch him. Seemed like he was holding a grudge. Did you know a fresh castrated cat can scratch three kids (each one tryin' to escape) ninety-six times apiece while screaming and never draw a breath?

Now three kids tryin' to get away from a cat in a silo is a pretty fair wreck, but trying to run from one cat and stay away from ninety-nine more (which by this time had gone as crazy as the one just cut) is disastrous. I don't know if it was Terry or Larry that ran through the door, but I'll love him forever. Relief comes in strange forms!

When it was all said and done, we gathered ourselves up and took stock. There wasn't a place on any of us that didn't have a cat track of some kind on it. None of us had a shirt left; they were just threads hanging around our necks and off our shoulders.

When we finally calmed down a little, we looked back at the silo and there were cats still coming out that door.

We decided to call our folks instead of going back to school. The way we were hurting from those cat tracks, it wasn't gonna make any difference who whipped us 'cause there was no way we were gonna hurt any more than we already were.

We had to do a ton of explaining to our folks about the scratches and why we didn't have any shirts left and why we skipped school. Elmo and Buel not only had to explain to three mad moms, they had to give up their chairs in the pool hall for a while. Seems a couple of mothers threatened to kill 'em if they were seen around town for a while.

Terry, Larry, and I didn't get a whipping. Our dads figured the cat tracks would be punishment enough.

But they did offer to beat us to death if we ever skipped school again.

The next time Larry and Terry and I got together we decided that we would store our next batch of explosives behind the pool hall and hope for another electrical storm.

Come to think of it, we never got our fifty cents for cuttin' that cat.

 The Good Jobs I Always Get

"Wrecks" grow out of the most innocent situations, as several selections in this collection reveal. In the following story, the author and his buddy see a bad situation and try to remedy it, much to their distress, and their humiliation by a cross-bred heifer. They may have been just a little "gun shy" of the situation.

Many times I have asked myself, Self, why is it always the youngest of the crew, the newest member of the team, or the most gullible guys who always get the nasty, dirty, or even dangerous jobs that nobody else wants? I'm speaking from experience, 'cause when I was a kid, I was instructed, more than once, to do things that even a seasoned green beret would have backed off from.

Kinda like the time my dear old dad's most favorite yearling heifer got into the steer pasture. As far as my dad was concerned, this Brahma-cross heifer was the sole solution to the making of a perfect breed. He commented once that if he had to, he would pawn Maw and me off on the neighbors and sell his favorite cutting horse just to feed her. Me and a buddy of mine had been checking some water gaps on the northwest side of the steer pasture and was on our way back to the house when we spotted this heifer about two hundred yards from the gate. The only problem was she was two hundred yards into the wrong pasture. The gate was closed, so we figured she just crawled through somewhere and we just needed to put her back.

Well, the first thing we thought of was to stretch her out a time or two and then show her the home pasture. But us being the sensible-type ranch kids we were, we decided to drive her to the gate and put her back in the gentle way. Boy, Dad would sure be proud of us. From the second that decision was made, things just kinda went to hell.

First off, in the country I was raised in there are certain things that are learned at a very early age. One of which is, the only thing dumber than a cow is a black cow, whether it's crossed with any other color or not. And the only thing dumber than a black cow is somebody (anybody) that tries to work just one. That's one rule that has held true all my life.

We knew where we wanted her to go; she knew where we wanted her to go. The problem was she didn't care nothin' about goin', least not where we wanted her. She left out with only one thing in mind, and that was to go anywhere but there.

Now my little bay horse was pretty fast, and he would cow better than most. Terry's horse was some better than mine in the cow department but not quite so fast. But even with the combination of us and our horses, we couldn't get her to drive. After about five minutes of cut, slash, and run we had succeeded in several things: we had lost about a half mile of country, we had made ourselves and our horses mad, and we had a black cross-bred heifer mad enough to fight anything that moved.

I remembered another rule: if it don't drive, pen, or pay attention, then rope it, choke it, and show it home is a nice place to be. Terry and I had our ropes down and was fixin' to attack, when three of the cowboys that were working for my dad came over the hill and saw us. It was a couple of minutes later that I figured out being a kid had its drawbacks. Well, one of them, an experienced hand named Bob, saw what was going on and figured right quick what the trouble was. Then he explained in pretty harsh terms that a couple of dumb kids shouldn't be messin' with something they didn't know anything about. Now me being the quiet type then, as I am now, I took my chewing out and then told him since he knew so damned much about it, he could put her back in the heifer pasture. Terry and I would just sit back and learn.

The only thing those boys got done that we didn't was to get her mad enough to fight everyone. Course, we got the blame for this, too. They finally decided to rope her and lead her home.

After Terry and I were told to stay the hell out of the way, Bob and his helper named Andy roped her and started for the gate. Yep, after that chewing out I got, the only thing I could hope for was for my Dad to show up and catch Bob with his rope on that special heifer. Yea, I could just picture Bob agreeing with Dad about how sorry cowboys really are. All they want to do is rope a man's cattle instead of workin'. And they would rather run the fat off a good cow instead of tending to ranch work. And all this time I would just sit back and agree and grin. Yep, I sure would like to see someone else get chewed out besides me. We got her through the gate, got the gate closed, and turned her loose. From there things kinda went downhill. That mutton-headed idiot went plumb crazy. She jumped up, ran under one horse, and headed for the gate. Seems she had it in mind to jump it instead of run through it. That was the only sensible thing she had done all afternoon. It was kinda pretty, for a minute anyway. She left the ground about five feet too soon. But while she was in the air she looked like a deer. But when she hit the gate, she looked kinda like a wet tow sack that had been thrown against a wall.

I guess all the excitement screwed up her eyesight and her ability to judge distance. When I realized she had broken her neck and was permanently dead, I got a very clear picture of my future. I would be locked in the cellar, fed bread and water, and set to sleeping on the hide of the finest cow critter that ever lived. I'd have to sleep on that hide so's I would be constantly reminded that I caused the prevention of the advancement of the entire cattle industry.

Bob cut her throat right quick, and as he started dressing her out, he told me and Terry to go get the pickup and explain to my dad how we caused her to get excited and commit suicide. And since she was so excited and hot, the meat probably wouldn't be any good.

Now if you want to talk suicide, that's what it is just to walk up and break some bad news to my dear old dad. I figured my life expectancy was about two minutes longer than it would take to ride to the house and tell my dad the story of the suicidal heifer. I'm not sayin' my old man was rough on me, but I'd sooner pregnancy-test a mountain lion than to get him mad at me.

Dad saw us riding in and met us at the barn. He greeted us cheerful enough and asked how our day went. When I tried to tell him, he cut in. "You know that heifer I was so high on? Well, I rode out this morning and looked at her real close and you know what I decided to do? She's too goofy to make a mamma out of, so I put her in the steer pasture. The next time we're out there and she's handy, we can bring her into the pens and fatten her up for beef. I sure was right about her being goofy. I had to rope her and drag her through the gate. Then I had to lay her down three or four times just so's I could get my rope off. She was plenty mad, so I decided to leave her in the steer pasture till she calmed down. Yep, she's a little dingy."

Just hearing how he had changed his mind about her was a little bit of relief on our nerves, and we did get some confidence back. So we told our story. The chewing out we got wasn't near as bad as we thought it would be, but it still hit four on the Richter scale. I guess it was sorta like steppin' out of the fire back into the fryin' pan.

We butchered her out, and she made pretty good beef, but every time I took a bite of that old silly thing, I swore if I ever got old enough and anything went wrong, I was gonna see to it that the nearest kid got the blame for it.

 ## Old Tom Was a Good Old Cat

Here is an example of a cat that turned out to be a good helper to a very independent young cowboy who didn't like the way his father was treating him. The youngster seems to resemble John Erickson's Hank the Cowdog in some ways— misunderstood, abused, vindictive, and careless. Brummett's Old Tom, a literary cousin of Erickson's Pete the Barn Cat, serves as the means of revenge, but he gives his all to help his master, who does not mind seeing some cowboys get bucked off.

It seems as though, over the years, cats have played an important role in my life, from a not-so-profitable birth control enterprise to a situation of impromptu revenge.

Me and Old Tom had a lifestyle similar to that of the Hindenburg. It seemed that every time something went wrong, it was

COW POKES   By Ace Reid

**"There goes ole Gimpey - outside of a horse
breakin' his leg and hip, a steer rope cuttin' off
two of his fingers, a mean cow cracking his arm
and shoulder, he's never had a sick day in his life!"**

blamed on him or me or both of us. And after being unjustly
accused, we would generally crash and burn.

Like the time the old man was shoeing his favorite horse,
Old Spooks. At the same time, Old Tom and I were doin' our part
to rid the world of disease-carrying rodents; we were killin' mice.

Dear old Dad had Spooks cross-tied in the hallway of the
barn. And just about had 'im calmed down, I might add. I guess
when Tom and I came tearing into the hallway from the feed room,
hot on the trail of a marauding mouse, we kinda startled dear old
Dad. Of course, when we spooked Dad, Dad spooked Spooks, and
Spooks came unglued.

I caught a glancing blow from something that knocked me
plumb out of the barn door. By the time I quit rolling, got up, and
looked inside, all I could see was cat hair, horse hair, and dust.
After the hair and dust started to settle, I could see dear old Dad
and Old Tom holed up in the back of a stall. Each one was trying to

get behind the other, in order to avoid the kicking feet of Spooks. I had never heard a cat growl like that before, and I didn't recognize many of the things that dear old Dad was calling Old Tom. Since I didn't see any blood, I left.

That night at supper, as Dad was explaining the black eye and the cat tracks on his neck, he casually mentioned that if that cat hadn't made good his escape, Dad would have clubbed him to death with the hoof nippers. That was the start. Then he said, "Due to that damned cat, Old Spooks will probably never go near the barn again, and he's sure gonna be hard to put shoes on from now on."

I was sure proud the old man didn't see me get knocked out of the barn door, and he accepted my story (with a doubtful look) about me tripping and hitting my head on the barn door. And he gave me a dirty look when I asked 'im why he called Old Spooks "Old Spooks?"

Since he didn't know I was with Old Tom, I wasn't about to tell 'im. After all, what he didn't know wouldn't hurt me.

A couple of weeks later, I was doing chores before breakfast when dear old Dad called me back to the house. It seemed there was going to be a discussion on why I had moved my cactus tray and left it on the toilet seat.

I don't think he minded me moving my plants, but he sure was upset about where I left 'em. The light bulb was burnt out in the bathroom, and it was pretty dark. But since he knew where the toilet was anyway, he started to tend to business. I guess that tray of cactus kinda changed his mind. He certainly appeared to be upset. He informed me that since his rear was gonna be sore for a while, so was mine. He did not tell an untruth.

When he got through with me, I had lost all interest in breakfast, so I limped out to the barn to finish my chores. When I had finished I caught Old Tom, and we went to the barn loft. Yep, me and Old Tom understood each other.

I was standing there holding Old Tom, thinking how I got the worst end of the discussion because there wasn't any way that cactus could have raised the welts on Dad like he had raised on me. At this time I saw my chance to even up the score.

Now, I am not a violent person, and I have never had the nerve to talk back to Dad, and even though I didn't want to, I always showed respect for him. And I have no idea as to why I did what I did.

Dad and a couple of cowboys came riding around the corner of the barn, heading out to the bull pasture. One was riding a green-broke colt, the other was riding Puddin', a goof-proof old ranch horse, and even though Dad was riding Old Spooks, I did it anyway.

I gave dear old Dad Old Tom.

Old Spooks lived up to his name, 'cause he did. He jumped sideways so hard and fast, the old man lost his hat and his cigarettes and pert near lost his seat. This, in turn, caused a major disturbance with the colt. He jumped to get clear of the horse with the screaming critter on his back, and then started bucking. Now, Puddin' stopped to see what all the commotion was about just in time to get run smooth over by a horse and cowboy. The cowboy seemed to be wearing a strange sort of hat. By now Old Tom had decided that there was entirely too much action on the ground, and he would just stay up with dear old Dad. Dad had different thoughts.

I guess it's pretty tough to ride a bucking horse and try to get rid of a scared cat, all at the same time.

By now the other two cowboys were afoot, and Old Spooks was a basket case. The last time I saw 'em they went out of sight around the corner of the barn. Spooks was gaining speed, Tom was losing ground, and dear old Dad was trying to lose Old Tom.

The other two cowboys couldn't figure out what got into that goofy cat, and were discussing it as they started to catch their horses.

I eased back to the house, content with the score.

About an hour later, when Dad came back in, he herded Spooks back towards the barn. They made it to within about forty yards, and that was as close as that horse was going. Yep, Old Spooks was getting plumb paranoid about that barn.

Dad came storming into the house and headed straight for the gun cabinet. His face and shirt looked like he had been drug through a large pile of barbed wire.

I was starting to get a little worried.

As he was trying to explain to Maw, he would stop and put in another shell.

"That goofy damned cat has attacked me for the last time. For no reason at all, he jumped right out of the barn loft right on top of me and that horse. He not only clawed the hell out of me, but he got Pete and Howard bucked off. And Howard was riding Puddin'."

I started to tell 'im that Howard got off when Spooks ran over them, but again I figured what he didn't know wouldn't hurt me.

He finished up by saying, "Pete and Howard are all right, but what little brain that horse ever had is so scrambled he won't come in for water for a month. Now that cat is gonna go. Between that cat and that kid's cactus, I seem to stay a little upset." (I thought that was kinda an understatement.)

He stormed out the door with the shot gun and blood in his eyes.

After I studied the situation for a minute, I considered telling him what really happened. Then I considered the state of mind the man with the gun was in. Then I thought . . .

Tom, better you than me.

 ## Windmiller or Windmillie: There's Ample Fun for All

Windmills are widely relied on to pump precious water into tanks for cattle to drink in areas of Texas, New Mexico, and Oklahoma where there are no streams. On ranches in these areas the cowboy has an additional responsibility—to keep the windmills working. Keeping grease in the gear box and occasionally changing the leathers on the sucker rod at the bottom of the well tubing requires two workers, and help is not always easy to find in these isolated regions. Here one windmiller has to resort to using his wife—an inexperienced hand at this kind of work, at least when the job starts. She gets a lot of experience on just this one job. The cowboy gets some he would gladly have missed.

I have heard that windmillin' can be fun. And I'm sure or at least pretty sure, that it can be if you are the windmiller, and not the windmillie. I have on occasion had the pleasure of being the windmiller, instead of the windmillie, but not very often.

Of course you know the difference, but for those that don't, I'll explain. The windmillie is the poor sucker that gets to help the windmiller.

Windmillies can be any shape, size, and pert near any age. And they can be of either sex. Female windmillies are used only as a last resort.

Reprinted from *Livestock Weekly*, January 23, 1986, pp. 18–19.

By this I mean the windmiller has had to have gone through every neighbor, every wetback, tried to clean out the bars for winos, and even tried to trick an innocent tourist before he resorts to having a female windmillie help him out. And of course the female I'm talking about is the Little Woman.

Now on the few times I've had the privilege to be the windmiller, I've only had to use the female type windmillie twice. Actually both times were the same. My first and my last. I once conned two wetbacks into helping me, but due to rather informal tools, and a complete lack of Spanish, I lost 'em.

Once just before the 4th of July rodeo, I had a set of leathers go bad in a well in the west pasture. Normally I would have just moved some cattle around and fixed them after the roping. But I had just put some straightened out yearlings in there and I needed all the fresh water I could get.

Since all the neighbors were tied up with their own problems, or already gone to some of the rodeos scattered around the country, I figured that me and the Little Woman could pull the rods and have the well pumping by late afternoon. I mean it was only the second and I wasn't up in the steer roping until the afternoon of the third. And with the Little Woman helping me I had plenty of time.

Everything but the time element was bad figuring.

Now let me say this about the Little Woman. She is probably the best cook west of the Mississippi, and she can make a shirt better than any professional tailor. And at times she can have the sweetest disposition in the world. But at times she can get plum snarly.

But in spite of all the good things I can say about her I feel like I should tell you this. She don't take orders worth a damn, and she sure don't take constructive criticism. Anyway, after I rode back to the house, and got the tools loaded in the pickup, I finally convinced her to come help me.

Since it was a shallow well, I figured I could pull it by hand and all she would have to do would be to set the wrenches. I figured this out because my neighbor had all of my regular windmillin' tools. I finally get the Little Woman and old Jughead (my pitbull Queensland Heeler crossbred cowdog) loaded up. Since we had to go through eight gates, I let the Little Woman drive, mainly because her and that goofy pup had never learned to shut a gate properly.

It was about 11:30 in the morning when we got to the well. After I got everything loose and ready to go, I adjusted the wrenches and explained to her what I wanted her to do.

Jughead jumped out of the pickup and laid down in the shade. Yep, that dog was showing more and more sense all the time.

I got started pulling on the rods, and by the time I finally got the check out of the cylinder, I thought my hemorrhoids had hemorrhoids. I got to the first coupling and told her to put the wrench on the bottom rod and pull up on the handle. I set the weight of the rods on the wrench, let the wrench rest on top of the pipe, broke the top rod loose and stood it in the corner of the tower. As smooth as it went, I thought to myself, "Self, this may go a lot better than you figured."

That was about the only good thought I had for the rest of the day. Two rods later, Jughead figured he would get in on the act. He came charging into the tower and jumped on the Little Woman's leg so he could get a better look. He not only got a better look, he scared hell out of the Little Woman. She screamed, spooked me, and I dropped the rods.

I commented on the fact that Jughead was something to really be scared of. After all, he was all of eight months old and he had been known on occasion to maul a warm buttered biscuit. She casually mentioned that since I was so big and brave, and always had total control, I could run those rods back in the well and fish the other out. (Me being the type to never mouth off, I didn't tell her what I would like to do with those rods.) I started wondering if there might be any tourists at the coffee shop in town.

It was about 12:30. I ran the rest of the rods in, got tied onto the ones I dropped, and started pulling 'em out again. By now we had a pretty good audience. About 200 steers, 30 antelope and a double handful of jackrabbits. I put Jughead in the back of the pickup to avoid a major wreck with the steers. You know how aggressive a cowdog pup can be.

I unseated the top check again, and this time we had all but three rods out. That's when the Little Woman happened to look around and see the antelope. I wouldn't have minded her taking time to appreciate the local wildlife, but she happened to notice the critters at the same time I thought she had hooked the rods. Have you ever heard three rods speeding to the bottom of a 180-foot well? They didn't make near the noise I did. I kinda' raised my voice a little. The antelope ran off and the steers spooked a little. When the steers spooked, Jughead woke up.

I mentioned to the Little Woman that she had better keep her mind on her work, or things could get a little rough. When I finally got her to put the wrench down, I climbed down off the platform and started running rods back in the well.

It was about 1:45.

There is an old saying, the third time is a charm. And this time it held true. We finally got all the rods out, the new Blackjacks on, and all the rods back in the well. I think the reason we got along so good on this trip was we were so mad we didn't say hardly anything to each other.

As I started to hook up the redrod, things got clear out of hand. During the run back to bottom, the steers got to thinking they needed a closer look at what was going on. They had eased up around the windmill tower, just to watch the Little Woman and me struggle to get them some water. While they were watching us, Jughead was watching them. I was watching my step and the Little Woman was watching for more antelope.

One steer had noticed Jughead and that's all it took. It was about 3:15. When Jughead bit that steer on the end of the nose, he forgot to turn loose (the pit in 'im, I guess). Now one steer running backwards with a dog on the end of his nose is pretty spooky to the other 199 that's been standing around minding their own business, especially if the dog's growling, the steer's bellowing, and the Little Woman's screaming. When about half the steers bumped the tower, I fell off the guide boards. About the time I hit the ground, the Little Woman bailed off into the stock tank, and Jughead and the steer broke through the bottom brace on the tower and came inside with me.

I don't care what anyone says, it only takes one steer, one dog, and one mad woman to have a stampede in a 6 × 6 × 6 pasture. Somewhere between the third and eighty-second pass over my back and head, I grabbed Jughead's hind legs and pert near ripped that steer's lip off. When the steer saw me and the furry little critter that bit 'im, he turned and joined the Little Woman in the water tank. Of course the Little Woman was in the process of coming back to surface, and she didn't see her swimming companion take the dive. That crossbred steer hit the Little Woman right square in the hip pockets. Contrary to popular belief, a woman can skip across water just like a flat rock.

I didn't know what to do first, kill that damned dog or help the Little Woman out of the water tank. It only took a couple of seconds to make a decision. I turned the dog loose and ran. I could tell she wasn't hurt by the way she was chasing Jughead and swingin' that wrench. I told her if she would just calm down, I would drive her to the house. She informed me she didn't want to calm down and that she could drive herself to the house.

That was the last straw. She got in the pickup and started to leave, and that traitor of a dog jumped in the back just as she started to drive off. Yep, that dog wasn't a complete dummy. As they went out of sight, I turned the windmill on and gathered up what tools I could find and stacked them inside the tower. Then I started walking home. It wasn't all that bad, 'cause this way I could still make the roping and know for sure that all the gates were shut properly.

It was about 15 till 4.

 ## Good Groceries and Clean Dishes

An old camp joke involves the reluctant cook who warns that the first of the crew to complain about the food has to take over the cooking chores. Brummett tells a variation of that tale where he not only figures out the old cook's ploy but wins his point—and without having to lose face in exchange.

As a general rule, ranch cooks are good cooks. However, I recall one time when that rule was not only broken but so badly mutilated that the person that broke it came very close to becoming an endangered species. What I mean to say is that the cow boss had put in charge of cooking a very unfeeling person.

I had hired out to a ranch in eastern New Mexico to help gather the renegades that had escaped roundup. The cow boss sent me to a camp and told me that the man I would be working with was a good cowboy and that as long as I made a hand, everything would be OK. He also mentioned that my new partner didn't really like to talk a lot. That was an understatement.

I got to the camp about three that afternoon; and Carlton, the cowboy, was just turning his horse loose. I introduced myself, and he showed me around the pens while he explained about my half of the chores. As I settled my gear in the house, he informed me that he would do the cooking and I would do the dishes. Since he had been there longer than me and I didn't really like to cook that much, I agreed. Then he said, "The first one to gripe gets to cook and do dishes." Now, I should have suspected something at that statement; but me being the dumb kid I was I just ignored it. That was one mistake I will never make again.

My first meal was by far the best for several days to come. It consisted of reheated stew and cornbread. And I might add that I did a splendid job on the dishes. The next morning started a strange, new dining experience that has yet to be equaled. This man had found nineteen ways to screw up a bowl of cornflakes, and I soon found out that he had his own personal style of massacre that he could use on a can of tomatoes.

One evening I mentioned that the potatoes weren't quite done, and he informed me that they were scrambled eggs and if I didn't like them, I could start doing the cooking and the dishes. Now I could cook a little, but when I hired out, the chores were divided up equally, and me being the bullheaded person I am, I just smiled and said, "That's just the way I like 'em." After about a week of eating beans that rattled like bullets when they hit the plate and bacon that either slid off the plate and squealed as it went out the door or shattered into a million pieces when you touched it with a fork, I was pert near ready to start cooking. But not quite.

Then one morning after breakfast, I made up my mind that something had to be done. I mean, when a man hands you a plate of bacon, eggs, biscuits and gravy and the only thing you can recognize is the plate, it's time to do something.

But I kept quiet, chipped myself out a cup of coffee, and tried to eat. It has been said that a hungry man will eat nearly anything, but this is not always true. I know, because I was damned sure hungry, and I left a bunch of that stuff on my plate.

It is extremely difficult to eat eggs that cackle when you cut them, and I have yet to figure out how he burned just half of each piece of bacon and left the other half raw. The biscuits were so gooey that you could have used them for caulking compound and had enough salt in 'em that they weighed two pounds apiece. The gravy wasn't all that bad—I just cut it up into little bite-sized squares and put 'em in my pocket. I figured I could chew on 'em while I was riding pastures.

When I finished my dishes and started to go catch my horse, Old Carlton mentioned the fact that I didn't eat much breakfast. Since I had just finished washing and stacking all the dishes, I didn't throw anything at him. So I just smiled and told 'im that all those good groceries were starting to put weight on me and I had just made up my mind to start watching my waist line. He just smiled and said that any time I wanted to do the cooking, I could sure have it. But since he enjoyed it so much, he sure hoped I wouldn't take it away from him. The man was sure pushing his luck.

As we rode out that morning my mind was working in high gear. I just couldn't figure this man out. I had been working with Carlton for eight days, and I still didn't know his last name. And unless it was a have-to case, there was little or no conversation.

And there was no way I could figure out why he so cheerfully destroyed good groceries.

When we got in that afternoon, there was a hand there from headquarters with Carlton's mail and some supplies. As I helped unload the pickup, Carlton grained the horses and finished his outside chores. The cowboy from headquarters told me how lucky I was to get on this particular camp. All the single guys wanted to work here just for the good food. Yep, it seemed like I was living with the best cook west of the Mississippi. I thought to myself that if the food here was considered that great, them poor boys down at headquarters must be going through pure hell. Then he told me the rest of the story.

It seemed that Carlton grew up in this area and was a pretty good cowboy. But he always wanted to be a chef. No one really took him seriously about his wish to cook because he was always pulling little jokes and forever messing with someone's mind. So when he quit his job and went to cooking school, everyone figured he was just hunting new range. But after hard work and a lot of classes, Carlton finally managed to get a job in New Orleans at a big, fine restaurant. After about six years he got the job as head hashslinger. After about twelve years as the head chef, he just got tired of his job and came back home. He hadn't changed very much, just put on a little weight, and he had gotten ten times worse at messing with people's minds.

I had been had.

The hand from headquarters went on back and left Carlton and me to work out our differences. And by supper that night I had a plan. After a meal of fried stuff that couldn't be recognized even after the black was chipped away, I set my plan into action. I washed the dishes pretty much the same as always, except for the fact that I used a little extra soap, and when I rinsed the dishes off, I used cold water on half of the utensils and half of the plates. And when I put them up, I stacked them in a special order. I suffered through breakfast, lunch, supper, and breakfast again. Each time the meal was worse, and each time there was just a tad more soap left on half the dishes.

After breakfast the second day, we rode out to do our rat killing. We split up to see what we could find and planned to meet at the branding pens. From there we would see what we could gather on our way back to camp. I made it to the pens about 1:30, and I noticed that Carlton was already there. As I rode up, I saw him take his pants off of the top rail of the corral and start putting them on.

When I got to the pens, I noticed that Carlton was kinda upset. His eyes were sunk back in his head, and he was walking like he might be a little saddle-sore. When I stepped off to get a drink and roll myself a smoke, Carlton eased over to me and said, "Pard, we need to have a talk."

Carlton worked his way around so that he was standing in the sun, so his Levi's could dry some more, and took a deep breath. "Ya know kid, I don't want you to take this the wrong way or anything like that, 'cause I think you're doing one hell of a fine job of dish washing. But I got to thinking just this morning that I may have been sloughing off on my cooking duties just a mite. Now, I might just be able to come up with a few decent meals every now and then if you could just see your way clear to get just a touch more soap off of those dishes. I haven't had the scours this bad since me and my cousin drank all that home brew and ate that half bushel of wild plums. Hell, I ain't been able to ride more than a quarter of a mile without having to stop and tend to business. As you can see, I was a little slow in getting off my horse to tend to my last business and I had to wash my Levi's out at the windmill. Now since we've had this little talk, let's go on back to camp."

From that time on I ate some of the best groceries ever, and Carlton even started talking. When I quit and went looking for newer range, I had a tactic to use on the next cook that wouldn't do what he was supposed to.

 ## Do Gooders Don't Always Do That Much Good

This section opened with an outrageous piece on the castration of a tomcat. It seems fitting to close it with a follow up of that experience. Years after the incident with which the first story deals, the young man is still suffering the consequences. Here, two animal lovers find out what the cowboy's known all along, cats can take care of themselves. We also see two of the cowboys' "friends" who enjoy a good joke, something cowboys have long cultivated even before Owen Wister wrote about such antics in his classic, The Virginian.

Reprinted from *Livestock Weekly*, January 10, 1987, pp. 20–21.

"Them eagles are gittin' so bad that besides gittin' 87 lambs and 3 calves, they jist carried off a member of the Audubon Society!"

Just the other day I was confronted by two ladies from a cat club. At first, I figured they were a couple of lost people, cause no one ever pulls up to our place except bill collectors or some idiot insurance salesman. Since I can spot a bill collector a quarter a mile away, and they just didn't look like salesmen, I just naturally figured they were lost. Seems to me, that the way I have figured in the past, I would've learned to quit figuring.

So as they stopped in front of the house, I left the horse I had been shoeing and walked over to say hello and see if I could help 'em out. (I should've stayed with the horse.)

The conversation went something like this:

"Yes mam, can I help you."

"Are you Curt Brummett?"

"Yes mam; How much do I owe you?"

"Well Mr. Brummett, you don't owe us anything, but we believe you owe the animals you have abused and mistreated a great deal more than you could ever repay." Each word had enough venom dripping off of it to supply all the rattlesnakes in Eastern New Mexico and West Texas for life. I decided right quick I wouldn't invite 'em in for coffee.

I've always been pretty hot headed and prone to get myself whipped simply because I would blow smooth up and attack when I got mad. But I figured I would get in a lot more trouble from dottin' this old bat in the eye than I would if I just let her rattle on. Besides that, this was my place and I could just tell 'em to leave.

"We are not here in an official capacity; we are just here to get an explanation for the way you seem to like to treat animals, cats in particular, Mr. Brummett." She said this as she unloaded from her car.

It was one of those foreign cars and when she unloaded, the springs gave a sigh of relief as they came back to a semi-normal position. The other old gal started to get out too.

The first lady was about fifty to fifty-five and big. She had the coldest green eyes I had ever seen, and she was wearing Levi jeans and a khaki shirt. She was even wearing combat boots! (Actually they were hiking boots.) Her hair was kind of a blood bay and fixed pretty nice. But she was as big as I am and moved like a tank. I wasn't scared though because I still had my shoeing hammer in my hand. I figured if things got plumb out of hand, I could always use it on myself to end all the pain this old gal looked like she could inflict on me.

Her partner came around the front of the car.

She looked like she could be twenty to thirty-five and stood about five feet six. She was dressed about the same way as her friend, and her hair was cut short. Now I'm not saying the woman was ugly, but if she had been inclined to a military career, she could have been a three-star general in the Canine Corps.

I gripped the hammer a little tighter.

They introduced themselves and then started demanding explanations.

During all of this I was racking my brain trying to figure out what the hell they were talking about. I finally got 'em shut down and told 'em to talk one at a time and tell me just what it was I was supposed to have done that was so terrible.

The big one, I'll call her Moose, took a step toward me and pointed her finger.

I raised the hammer a little.

"We heard about your cat castrating. When we came to talk to you about it, we had to ask directions as to how to get here. We stopped at the service station to ask where you lived, and visited with two very nice men. They not only told us how to find your house; they even explained how they have been trying for years to get you to give up your cruel ways. They even donated $5.00 apiece to our organization and told us how good they thought we were for coming out here to try and get you to stop these terrible things."

Mike and H. L. was the first two to come to my mind. I chanced a look over my shoulder and sure nuff, there was Mike's pickup settin' on top of the hill. I would've bet every thing I owned they were sittin' on the hood, each with a pair of field glasses and probably a cold beer.

Them's two sick people.

I made up my mind that if I lived through this, I would get even.

I explained or started to explain that I hadn't even touched a cat in twenty years and that the only cat I ever cut lived to scratch hell out of three kids. And as far as being cruel to animals, I would try to show them I wasn't. If they liked, I would show them around my place and let them judge for themselves.

After a quick tour of the horse pens and the chicken house and speaking to each of the eight dogs, they had calmed down considerable. Then it happened.

Three of them pups and one big brown cat made their appearance, the pups running in hot pursuit of the cat.

Now this old brown cat had been hanging around my horse pens and hay stacks for about two years. He sure helped keep the mouse problem under control and most of the birds out of the garden. But he always stayed out of sight. In fact, I hadn't even seen 'im or thought of 'im in two or three weeks. But, of course, he had to pick today to show up.

Now I knew what he was gonna do and them older dogs knew what he was gonna do. The only ones in the dark was them three pups and those two goofy women.

The general screamed "We've got to help that poor kitty. Those mean dogs will chew her to pieces."

Moose broke into a run to head off the dogs, and the general headed for the poor kitty.

Now the rest of them dogs figured if them two women could run that cat, then they might just have a chance to whup that poor kitty once and for all. And all eight dogs joined the chase.

This particular cat was probably the toughest critter in all of Eastern New Mexico, and seven counties in West Texas. He weighed about twenty to twenty-five pounds and had single hand-edly whipped every dog that had ever showed up in our little town. His favorite trick was what he was trying to work this morning.

If he happened to get bored, he would stroll around until he got the attention of some new pup or aggravate one of the older ones until he had an all out chase goin'. He would run these pups all over the place—around the horse pens, the hay stack, and the roping chute, and then he would head for the middle of the arena. When he got to his spot, he would turn and proceed to whup hell out of whatever was chasing 'im.

By the time Moose and the General had got lined out, the cat had made it to the arena. The only problem was this time when he turned around he saw a little different situation. From his reaction, I would say he wasn't really scared, just a little confused. He not only had every dog on the place coming for 'im, but he had a huge person closing in on the dogs and a two-legged pit bull closing in on him.

I know in my own mind he figured he could handle them dogs, but the Moose and the General were just too much to put up with.

He sold out, but just a hair too late.

The General had cut across, and just as the cat turned, the General grabbed 'im.

Yep! It was a terrible sight. And the sounds weren't all that pretty either.

The cat proved what I had thought ever since he had showed up—he didn't like to be handled.

About the time the General picked kitty up, she scared 'im pretty good. The first thing kitty did was to put a lip lock on the General's arm. This in turn caused a scream similar to that of a gut-shot werewolf. The scream made the dogs think the cat was hurt and could probably be whupped pretty easy, so they attacked. The Moose thought the dogs hurt the cat, and she attacked. The General knew the cat wasn't hurt, and all she wanted was loose.

Seemed from where I stood, the General had about all the rescue work she wanted.

Now as most people know, when a cat feels that his life is in danger, he climbs. It's his natural instinct. It doesn't make any difference what it is—he's gonna climb, he's just gotta climb. Well, this cat figured since he was already up off the ground, he might as well stay there. So he dug the old claws in and tried to ride the storm out.

By now, the General had developed an entirely different attitude concerning where that cat should be. She pulled 'im loose and gave 'im to the Moose.

This evidently pleased the cat because he climbed the Moose's pants leg, went up her back, and settled on her head. And I might add this was no easy accomplishment.

For a large person the Moose moved pretty good. She was kicking dogs, slappin' at that cat, and using a strange language. By the time that cat reached the top of his new tree, I was about there and was fixin' to start kickin' dogs. Then the damnest thing I ever saw happened.

The General figured she had better help the Moose and waded right into the middle of all them dogs. A brave move! The General slapped that cat so hard she not only knocked the cat loose from the Moose but she knocked the wig plumb off the Moose's head. All you could see was to big old chunks of hair fly out over the dogs and hit the ground.

Everything got quiet for about five seconds. I mean all motion stopped.

Them dogs couldn't figure where that other cat had come from; the cat couldn't figure out what kinda critter had chased it out of its make-shift tree; the General couldn't figure how she knocked the Moose's head off; and the Moose was trying to figure out why the General hit her instead of the dogs.

The cat was the first to move; he hauled freight and headed for the haystack. The dogs couldn't figure why the other cat just laid there, so they attacked.

Them two women looked at each other, started crying, and headed for their car. The Moose was a lot spookier than she had been. I don't care how you look at it, a pert-near baldheaded woman that size is spooky. As they ran past me, I noticed neither of them was hurt too bad—a couple of scratches and one or two fang marks, but nothing serious.

Hell, I know for a fact, them cat tracks will heal up. By the time they had gotten in their car and left, things had calmed down considerable. I looked around, and the cat was sitting' on top of the haystack trying to figure out why that funny little furry critter wasn't puttin up much of a fight. Mike and H. L. were rolling around on the ground, and I could hear them laughing from a quarter mile away.

The dogs had the wig divided equally, and the pups was prancing around with their trophy, each one figuring they had taught that cat a very important lesson.

I figured since everything was pert near back to normal, I would just go back to shoeing my horse. I had to wait a while.

You can't shoe a horse when you're laughing.

JOHN R. ERICKSON

John Erickson has unusual credentials for a western humorist. A native of Perryton, Texas, Erickson graduated from the University of Texas honors program and attended Harvard Divinity School for two years. He then decided to become a writer but was unsuccessful at the craft for a time. Discouraged, he returned to the Texas Panhandle and soon took a job running a ranch in Beaver County, Oklahoma. As he experienced anew the lure of the western landscape and life, he found that the shrill bitterness of his early work turned more and more to the kind of humor he presently writes.

Three books—*Panhandle Cowboy*, *The Modern Cowboy*, and *Cowboy Country*—make up one facet of his work, and he has published humorous stories in *Cattleman Magazine*, *Livestock Weekly*, and other livestock publications. Erickson and his wife Kris now run Maverick Books, the firm that published Erickson's work until 1988, when Texas Monthly Press became Erickson's publisher. He has proved that a buying public for his kind of western humor far exceeds what the New York publishing establishment estimated.

 Summer Cowboys Sometimes Welcome Advent of Autumn

The chores of the cowboy are varied. Besides branding calves, rounding up and sorting cattle and breaking horses, cowboys have to help deliver calves. Their patients are not always appreciative of their efforts, as the following segment sug-

Reprinted from *Livestock Weekly*, September 19, 1985, pp. 8–9.

"Jake, don't you know the quickest way to spoil a
good hoss is to start gittin' off over his head!"

*gests. Erickson and Andy, a summertime helper from Hou-
ston, get a lesson in unmannerly motherhood.*

It was a Sunday afternoon, "the day of rest" as they call it in the
Consumer Society, and I drove over to a windmill in the middle
pasture to check the water level in the tank. We had drained it and
cleaned it, and we'd hit a string of still days and it wasn't filling fast
enough to keep up with the cattle.

Well, after checking the tank, I noticed a Hereford cow
standing off by herself in a plum thicket. That was kind of unusual,
a cow standing alone in the heat of the day when most of the cattle
were piled three-deep around the water hole.

I drove over and checked her out. Two hundred feet away, I
knew she was in trouble. She had a sunken look in her eyes that
said she'd been in pain for several days.

The ranch had some Charolais bulls and one of them had
bred this old cow and given her a bull calf she couldn't handle. I
looked her over and guessed that she had been in labor for at least
24 hours.

The calf was long dead and the cow's nose showed that she was burning up with fever.

So much for my day of rest.

We drove back to the barn. While I caught and saddled Reno, I told Andy to gather up all our calf-pulling equipment: O.B. chains, antiseptic, water, buckets, medicine, and the calf-pulling frame with the come-along built into it.

Since I didn't know what we might be getting into, I threw in extra ropes, chains, pulleys, and fence stretchers. We hooked up the gooseneck, loaded Reno, and headed north through the sand hills. On the way, I told the wide-eyed Andy my strategy. If the cow would drive, I would take her back to the corrals. Since she was weak and suffering, I didn't know how long this would take or which route we would follow. It might take us two hours, and I would have to let her choose the itinerary.

If I got her started home, Andy would have to drive the pickup and trailer up a steep, washed-out trail and find his way back to headquarters.

What if the cow didn't go?

"Well, you'll get in on some real cowboy work before you go back to Houston."

That excited Andy but it didn't excite me. Reno was a good pasture horse in many ways, but also high-headed and iron-jawed and otherwise poorly suited for rope jobs. And he wasn't big enough to be wallowing grown stock around.

But he was the best I had at the time.

When I approached the cow on Reno, she staked out her position right away. She greeted me with that crazy look in the eyes and that way of shaking her head that tells a guy he's fixing to earn his pay.

If I wanted her, I could ride into the plum thicket and get her. She wasn't going to the house or anywhere else without a fight.

I hollered at Andy and told him to forget about driving the pickup home. Whatever doctoring we managed to do on this old sister would be done under pasture conditions.

I took down my rope and rode in to get her. Instead, she came after me.

Old Reno had been thumped around by waspy cows, and he side-stepped her horns as she blew past us. She headed for the windmill and the trailer.

I yelled at Andy: "Stay behind the trailer until I get a rope on her. She's in a nasty mood." Andy moved behind the trailer and watched the action through the slats.

If you've ever tried to pitch a loop on a fighting cow, you know it's not an easy shot. In the first place, she's facing you and that changes all the rules about jerking slack. In the second place, by the time you're within the throwing range, you're also within hooking range.

Old Reno had figured the odds in this game and he wasn't anxious to get in too close. He danced and tossed his head while I made several side arm throws at long range. At last, my loop dropped behind one ear. If I could ease around to the side and pull my slack, I would have her.

But at that very moment Andy's curiosity got the best of him. He stepped out from behind the trailer to get a better look. Maybe he thought I had the cow under control, but I didn't.

She wheeled around and went after him, leaving my loop in the dust. Andy's eyeballs got as big as boiled eggs when he saw those horns coming after him. He ducked around the back of the trailer, with the old cow breathing warm air on his hip pocket, and dived into the bed of the pickup.

I gave Andy a good scalding for not following orders, but it turned out to be a pretty good strategy. The old cow was so intent on figuring out how to get into the pickup with Andy that I was able to slip around behind her and stick a loop on her.

She fought the rope and I got her out into open ground, where she couldn't get me and Reno pinned against the pickup. Then I told Andy to take my second rope and try to catch her heels.

For the next fifteen minutes I didn't know whether to laugh or cuss. Andy would creep up behind the cow with the loop in his hand, and when she looked at him he would drop the rope and sprint to the pickup, his long hair standing straight out behind him.

He did this six times. I know because I counted, and cussed him every time he broke and ran. I was sorely tempted to ride up and give the old cow some room to work, but I didn't.

At last, when I'd just about exhausted my vocabulary, Andy pitched his loop, caught a heel, and held on. He tied the heel rope to the windmill tower and I stretched her out, ran for my equipment, and pulled the calf while she was standing up.

It was a tough delivery, and by the time I finished with her, she was ready to kill somebody. I let Andy take off the last rope. The boy had things to learn about cowboying, but by the time he went back to Houston, he'd made a pretty good windmill hand . . . and an uncommonly good sprinter.

Wild Cattle

In the account that follows, Erickson learns more about the
behavior of cattle, especially some young bulls he is trying
to load. The action also provides some insight into what
constitutes humor for a modern cowboy. The tale begins as
Erickson finds he cannot load the animal by himself.

I felt that, working alone, I had gone about as far as I dared. The
bulls were getting hot and snuffy, and the more I choused them
now the more chance there was that I would end up on the short
end of an argument. I went to the house and called Sandy Hagar.

Sandy was in his early sixties at this time and had worked
around animals all his life. In his prime, he had been—this is his
own description, not mine—a "big lard-tailed kid" who, at 210
pounds, had used muscle to solve problems. But over the years he
had been run over and thumped around enough that he had
learned to use his head. He could always figure out the easiest way
of doing a job.

When he arrived, he got right down to important business:
he rolled a Prince Albert cigarette. How he was able to perform that
delicate task with such aplomb, I never understood, for his hands
were as big as skillets. Yet he could whip up a "hot tamale" in about
sixty seconds, and, in a pinch, had been known to do it with one
hand. He rolled one for himself and then rolled one for me. I was
an abysmal failure at rolling smokes. When Sandy rolled me a
P.A., he would never lick the paper at the top, to spare me from
cold germs and such. He would hand it to me and say, "There,
hammerhead, lap the top."

We lit up, hunkered down, and talked about my problem. I
gave him my opinion of the bulls. We studied the pens and came
up with a plan. Sandy would stand behind the trailer gate, out of
sight. When I brought the bulls up the alley, I would try to push
them into the trailer with a heavy wooden crowding gate, and
when they jumped inside, Sandy would close the trailer gate behind them. We rigged up the trailer gate with a rope, so that he
could close it by pulling the rope. That way, if the bulls whirled and
came back, neither of us would be in the gate's path when it flew
open.

Reprinted from *Panhandle Cowboy*, by John R. Erickson, by permission of University
of Nebraska Press. Copyright © 1980 by the University of Nebraska Press.

"Yep, Jake, it looks hopeless, but I don't think it's serious!"

When everything was ready, Sandy took his place and I went into the pen to bring the bulls. I pelted them with rocks and sticks and horse biscuits and started them moving. When they moved out, it was a lope. They ran out the gate and into the alley toward the trailer, and I fell in behind them, yelling and waving a piece of windmill rod. When they reached the trailer, one of the bulls whirled and came back at me. I moved to the side, and he thundered right over my tracks. The other bull had stepped up into the trailer with his front feet. Sandy pulled the rope and put pressure on him. The bull didn't move. He stood there, half in and half out, sniffing the air. I made a quick assessment of the situation and decided to swing the wooden crowding gate behind him. I figured that once he felt the pressure of that heavy gate on his rump, he would hop into the trailer.

I think, had we been loading Hereford bulls, it would have worked, but with the Red Brangus, it didn't. When he felt the gate behind him, he snorted, whirled, and using his amazing quickness and acceleration, hit the crowding gate with a full head of steam. As I saw what was about to happen, my mind moved quickly, but my body reactions were a bit too slow. I knew the bull was going to hit the gate. I knew the gate was not latched to the post and that there was nothing behind it but my body. I knew that I weighed 170 pounds, and that the bull weighed half a ton. I knew exactly what would happen. A calm voice inside my head said, "John, old pal, if you put your weight against that gate when he hits it, he's going to knock you into next week. It might be a good idea for you to drop that gate and run." But my body followed instinct. When the bull whirled around, I leaned into the gate with all my strength, in effect betting my body and health that the gate would bluff him out and turn him back into the trailer. It wasn't a stupid decision. It just happened to be wrong. Most cattle can be stopped with a gate, even if it isn't latched. Most cattle can be bluffed out. Most cattle won't try to run through a heavy gate if they can see it. This bull wasn't most cattle.

When he hit the gate, he had his thousand pounds in high gear. He didn't even break stride. It was like an explosion. In a tangle of arms and legs, I flew through the air and smashed into a fence made of steel landing mats. The distance I traveled in that split second was the arc described by the gate, from closed to open position. I measured it the following day with a tape. It came to eleven feet. I don't think my feet ever touched the ground through that whole distance. That will give some indication of the brute strength of the bull—which, by the way, was only a bit more than half-grown.

I hit the steel fence with my head, and with such force that I could hear my skin and bones squish and groan. Later, when the shock began to wear off, I discovered that I had made contact with the fence in four other places: both elbows, my left shoulder, and my right shin. But at the moment of impact, my main concern was my head. I thought I was hurt, and I expected to see blood. I got to my hands and knees and crawled around in the dirt, waiting for the damage reports to come in from the various parts of my body.

I thought Sandy's reaction to the incident was odd. He laughed. Even as he asked if I was hurt, he was laughing. It irked me just a little bit, since at that moment I could hardly speak and was still not sure of the extent of my injuries. His laughter seemed in poor taste.

Since then I have noticed the same reaction among rodeo cowboys. I once saw a young bull rider get thrown completely over a hogwire fence. He missed hitting a light pole with his head by a matter of inches. His friends, who were watching from the bucking chutes, reacted with uproarious laughter. So, while laughter may seem an inappropriate response to physical danger, especially to the party most intimately involved, it is apparently a natural human response and one that does not reflect malice, meanness, or lack of feeling.

There is another explanation for Sandy's reaction, and this one doesn't require any psychology: I may have looked very funny flying through the air.

Well, I came out of the wreck with nothing more than lumps, bruises, and ruffled feelings. Sandy and I turned all four bulls back into the pasture. I never did haul them to town, and I never again tried to load one of them into a stock trailer.

I have attributed the temperament of these bulls to their Brangusness, to the three-eighths Brahma blood in their breeding. I should say, however, that when we received the Halloween bulls on the Oasis Ranch, we had no trouble handling or loading them. After I had kept them up in the pens for three days, I had no trouble loading them. But after they had run in the pasture on the Crown Ranch for two weeks, they became very difficult to handle.

What had brought about this change in only two weeks? I don't know the answer, but I can't help wondering to what extent it was a reflection of the ranch and its herd of wild cattle. You could say that it could have happened anywhere. But, as in the case of the Broken Leg Roundup, it didn't happen anywhere; it happened on the Crown ranch. At some point, what you first regard as coincidence begins to fit a pattern: every little job becomes an ordeal; nothing is easy.

 Boxing Gloves Are Cheaper than a Broken Hand

The work routine of the modern cowboy demands a cool temper and nerves of steel, which they do not always have. Here's what can happen when one loses his cool.

Most of us who have worked around cattle and horses have a few stories that need some time to age and mellow. They're about things we did in haste or anger, and they aren't very funny at the time.

Reprinted from *Livestock Weekly*, September 26, 1985, pp. 24–25.

One of the benefits of aging is that those stories get a little less painful each year, and at some point we can even laugh about them.

I guess I'm old enough now to tell this story. It happened eleven years ago.

I had recently taken a ranch job in the Oklahoma Panhandle, and I still had a lot of foolish ideas about running my outfit just so. I wanted all my fences up in top shape and I expected my cattle to stay where they belonged.

If we were running dry cows in the middle pasture and wet cows across the fence in the west pasture, I expected those cattle to stay where they belonged because . . . well, I had gone to the trouble to sort them, and by George, that's the way I wanted things to be.

Any time I found a cow in the wrong pasture, I went for a horse and moved her.

It was a matter of principle. A lot of wrecks begin as matters of principle.

Well, I was very fussy about keeping my pastures neat and orderly, so in May, when I found several stray cow-calf pairs grazing in the west pasture, I went straight to the barn and saddled a horse.

The old cows were thin and a glance across the fence told me that my neighbor was already short on grass. He had planted a field of cane for summer grazing, but it was still a long way from making a stand.

I drove the cattle north and found the place in the fence where they had gotten through. Later, I returned to the spot in the pickup and patched the hole with posts and wire.

But what makes a good fence is grass on both sides. This fence would turn a cow with a full belly, but one with hunger pains would find a hole in it. And if she couldn't find a hole, she could make one pretty quick.

For several weeks I played cat and mouse with the strays. I'd find them on my side and show up with a horse, and they would run straight to that hole in the fence. Then I would come back and cobble up another patch.

And a few days later I would find them in my pasture again.

By the first of June, I had run out of patience and was beginning to think of dirty tricks. High-life and #7 shot would get the attention of the cattle but not of the owner, the real culprit in the case.

I could get the owner's attention by hauling his stock to the sale barn and letting them stay there until he called the sheriff, at which time he would receive the good news that his cattle were safe and the bad news that he would have to pay the feed bill if he wanted them back.

But those were pretty drastic measures, and I wasn't quite ready to start a range war.

So, one very hot day in June, I decided on a compromise solution. I would take my toughest horse and run the strays around the pasture before letting them escape.

I figured a little exercise at 100 degrees might make an impression on them and leave them with a few bitter memories of my side of the fence.

I saddled Reno, a half-Arabian who didn't know the meaning of tired and could run those sand hills longer and faster than a sane man cared to stay with him.

Reno and I rode out to administer the Wrath of God.

As I recall, there were three pairs of thin cows with little rannihan calves at their sides. When they saw me coming, they headed straight for their favorite hole in the fence, only this time I spurred Reno and cut them off.

And for the next thirty minutes I ran them around and around and around, from one end of the pasture to the other.

After I'd run off two months' worth of tallow and had their tongues hanging down around their hooves, I shoved them up to the fence and let them go. They lined up like trained dogs and hopped over.

All but one calf, that is. There's always one that can't find the gate, and couldn't find it if you tore out half a mile of fence and drew him a map.

His mamma had taken him through that hole in the fence so many times that the ground on both sides was smoother than the county road in front of my house, but still he couldn't find it.

Stupidity of that magnitude would be unbelievable if it weren't so common.

The little dunce bounced off the fence three or four times and blatted for his mommie. Then he came off the wires and highballed it toward the other end of the world.

That was something I hadn't expected. I wouldn't have cared if his old lady had died of heat stroke, but separating a calf from its mother, in a country full of veal-loving coyotes . . . that sort of went against the Cowboy Code.

I was hot and tired and dripping sweat and feeling the sting of a fresh set of galls on my legs. I had every reason to let that little stupe go and find the fate he deserved, but I just couldn't bring myself to be that cold-blooded.

So I took down my rope and went after him.

There was a time in my cowboy career when I became a pretty salty pasture roper and could handle my slack well enough to zip up a loop on a squirmy little calf. Unfortunately, that moment lay some three years in the future.

A good pasture roper is a guy who's fool enough to get himself into a jam but skilled enough to get out. In 1974 I knew just enough about a rope to get myself into trouble, then to back off and get into a whole lot more.

I took after the calf, whipping and spurring and swinging that invention of the Devil, the simple twine that can hang you more ways than you have fingers and toes to count.

I don't suppose that calf had gotten more than two cups of milk out of his mamma in his whole life, and I'll never know where he got his energy, but he ran like a greyhound, dodged like a goat, and didn't have enough flesh on him to stop a good loop.

I threw and I threw and I missed and I howled and I cursed—myself and the dadgum rope and Reno and, most of all, the little snot-nosed calf that was taking my dignity apart, loop by loop.

Don't expect an honest report on how many loops I spilled. In our country, the meter shuts off at five.

I missed five loops, and finally on #6, I slopped it on. By that time, I'd seen half the ranch go by and had checked the water and salt at five windmills.

And I was so mad, so utterly humiliated, so disgusted at my sorry display of roping that I was ready to put some veal cutlets into the deep freeze.

I threw a half-hitch over my dallies, yanked a pigging string off the back of the saddle, and stormed down the rope, grabbed an ear in one hand and flank skin in the other, rolled the calf up on my knees, and threw him to the ground as hard as I could.

He bounced up before I could catch his front leg, and I had to do it all over again. This time I rammed my knee into his flank and he bounced no more. I slipped the noose of the pigging string over his front hock, gathered up the hind legs, and started to wrap.

Somehow he kicked out, and with one of those sharp little back hooves, he rolled up about six inches of skin on the inside of my forearm.

That was too much. I couldn't stand it any more. Half-blinded by sweat and half-crazy with frustration, I drew back my right fist and aimed a punch at the fleshy part of his neck.

That might have worked, if he hadn't moved just then. But he did, and instead of hitting the fleshy part of his neck, my fist slammed into the hardest, thickest part of his skull, the area right between his horns.

I'd like to say that he quivered, straightened out his legs, and died within minutes, but that ain't the way it went. He didn't even know he'd been hit, but I sure as heck did because something snapped inside my hand.

And when I went to finish my wraps, it didn't act just right. By the time I made it back to the barn, the old hand had puffed up and started pounding. But I couldn't quit. I still had a calf tied down out there in the pasture, and he'd die in the heat if I didn't do something with him.

I tied the hand in a rag, hooked up the gooseneck, and spent the next hour hauling the neighbor's rannihan calf back to its fence-busting mother—and cussing myself all the way.

By the time I made it in to Doc Harvey's office in Beaver, there wasn't much mystery about what I'd done. Doc looked at my swollen paw and said, "Yep, you busted her up pretty good. How'd you do it?"

You just don't lie to the doctor who's splinting your broken bone. I told him the whole story and he chuckled all the way through the making of the plaster cast. I think it made his day a little brighter.

Maybe he knew that as long as this world can match up a stupid calf with a stupid cowboy, the doctors won't have to advertise for business.

 ## A Bitter Lesson

The following selection speaks frankly to the erratic behavior of cattle and the sometimes only slightly less erratic—and dangerous—behavior of cowboys trying to work the cattle. The Crown Ranch is the one Erickson and his wife Kris ran

for a time in the 1970s while practicing the cowboy trade.
Evident is the cowboy's desire to build and keep a reputation
of being good at his work.

During my first months on the Crown Ranch, I learned that it was
very difficult for one man on horseback to perform the chores that
are routine on most ranches. I learned to roll with the punches.
When I had a job I didn't think I could do alone, I waited until I had
some help.

Toward the end of April I had a long list of pasture jobs that
needed attention, so I called Bill Ellzey and asked if I could hire
him for a few days' work. He said yes, and on the afternoon of
April 27 he arrived in his mud-spattered blue Chevrolet, pulling
Suds in a dilapidated old two-wheel horse trailer. It was late in the
day, but I wanted to get a few jobs out of the way before dark. We
loaded Suds and Dollarbill into my stock trailer and drove over to
the east end of the ranch.

A neighbor's steer had gotten into the big east pasture about
a month before. I had put him out of the pasture once and he had
come back. I had tried to eject him a second time, but he had fallen
in with a bunch of wild cows, and after a merry chase around the
pasture I had decided to wait until I had some help. He weighed
around six hundred pounds, and I had not wanted to try to rope
him and drag him into the trailer by myself. My trailer was covered
with a metal roof from front to back, and it was difficult for one
man to drag an animal into it by himself. It could be done, but it
required the use of two ropes, a stout horse, and some good luck.
Had the trailer been only partially covered, without a roof over the
back compartment, the job would have been fairly simple.

We found the steer on the north end of the pasture, grazing
with five or six cows near the gate we wanted to put him through.
If we could cut him away from the cows, putting him out would be
simple. We opened the gate and unloaded our horses. As soon as
the cows saw the horses, they threw their heads up, curled their
tails over their backs, and headed west at a run. We fell in behind
them, closing in from opposite sides, and cut the steer off from the
bunch. On the north end we tried to put him through the gate, but
by then he had decided that he wanted to go south. We tried to
turn him but he wouldn't turn. As a last resort, we took down our
ropes.

I took the first shot and missed. Bill moved in, made a good
shot, but couldn't fish it around the steer's neck. I loaded up again
and caught him by the horns. While I held him, Bill went for the

pickup and trailer. We dragged him into the trailer and hauled him to his home pasture. Then we loaded our horses again and drove to the little east pasture. I had some two-year-old heifers in the little east, and since there was one that was getting heavy with calf, I wanted to cut her out and take her to the house where I could watch her more closely and assist her if she had trouble delivering her first calf.

We scouted the heifers from the pickup before we unloaded our horses. We spotted the one we wanted, and I made the moronic statement that we should try to take her slow and easy.

We unloaded the horses, the heifers bolted and ran, we hit the saddles, and off we went in pursuit. Since cow brutes sometimes drive better in pairs than they do alone, we cut off the heavy heifer and took another with her and pointed them west toward the middle pens. They ran every step of the way until they reached the corral gate, which we had already opened. There they stopped. As we rode up to them, we could see that we had a pair of lunatics on our hands. Panting, ears perked, sniffing the ground, they looked in every direction for a place to run—every direction except toward the pens. All they had to do was take five steps to the west and we would be finished with them. But they weren't looking at the gate.

Bill and I knew the conventional response to this type of situation: you sit quietly on your horse and hold the cattle in front of the gate. Sooner or later, after they have milled and squirmed and sniffed for a while, they will see the gate and go through it. We waited five minutes. The heifers still had not gone into the pen. I said, "All right, that didn't work. Let's see if we can push them in." We rode toward them. When they made a move in the wrong direction, we cut them off. Finally the larger of the two threw up her head and ran into the pens. The other followed.

We sighed with relief. That wasn't so bad. The sun had dropped over the horizon and it would be dark in another thirty minutes. We had penned the cattle just in time. I fastened the gate with a piece of light chain and we started riding back to the pickup. We had accomplished our job, and we were feeling pretty good about it.

With our backs turned, we didn't notice what the heifers were doing. They ran around the pen several times, sniffing every corner and looking for an escape hole. Then, with the big one in the lead, they galloped around the pen one last time, piled into the gate, and broke the chain. The gate flew open, and we had two heifers that appeared to be heading for South Texas. I won't repeat what I said. I dug my spurs into Dollarbill's sides and off we went over the sand hills and through the sagebrush.

The heifers ran south down the fence. I didn't want to crowd them, for fear they would go through the fence into the middle pasture, so I got out in front so that I would be in a position to hold them when they came to the corner. I figured we could hold them in the corner for a few minutes, give them time to settle down, and then start them back toward the pens. If that didn't work, we would rope the big one and drag her in.

That was a sensible plan, and it should have worked. But when the heifers reached the corner, they didn't even slow down. The big one was in the lead. When she saw her path blocked up ahead, she crashed into the fence to her right. It so happened that there were some steel posts in the fence at that point, and I observed something that I had never seen before. Her front legs hit the fence with such force that sparks flew from the steel post, and it happened again when her back legs went over. Off she went in the middle pasture, with her head up in the air. A moment later the smaller heifer piled into the fence and joined her.

I rode over to where Bill was waiting. He flashed a sardonic smile. "Nice cattle."

"Yeah."

"Now what?"

I sighed. "Let's give them the night to settle down. We'll try again tomorrow."

We rode back to the trailer, grinding our teeth in silent rage. Our day had ended on a sour note of failure. We had been deprived of a feeling of accomplishment. Little did we know that the worst was yet to come.

The next morning we were in the saddle at eight-thirty and spent four hours sorting off cow-calf pairs and moving them out of the west pasture. For some odd reason the work went smoothly and we didn't have any problems. We drove the cattle into a corner of the pasture, and I sorted off the pairs while Bill held the herd.

After lunch, we were ready to go after the heifers. My wife wanted to ride with us, so I saddled Dollarbill for her and I rode Reno, the toughest horse on the ranch. As we rode toward the spot where we had last seen the heifers, we discussed our strategy. We would try to gather them quietly. If they wanted to go north, we would pen them in the middle pens. If they wanted to go west, we would take them all the way to the home corrals. If necessary and as a last resort, we would rope the big heifer.

We spotted them along the south fence, not far from the point where we had left them the night before. Some of Mark Mayo's cows were grazing on the other side of the fence. Our first objective would be to push the heifers away from the fence. They had proven the previous day that they were fence busters and we wanted to keep them away from the fence line. We spread out and closed in. We walked our horses and didn't make a sound. There is no way we could have approached them more peacefully. When the big heifer saw us, she threw up her head and bolted off to the northwest and we fell in behind her, putting ourselves between her and the fence. But after she had gone twenty-five yards, she reversed her direction and began running straight toward us. That told us something about the heifer. Any cow brute that runs toward a horse is crazy. I could see, just from the way she moved and carried her head, that we wouldn't be able to turn her to get a rope on her before she reached the fence, so I galloped away from her and told Bill and Kris to do the same. We backed off and waited to see what she would do, hoping that she would stop at the fence and give us another chance.

She plowed right into the fence, popped the staples out of five posts, and kept right on going. The second heifer, brainless dupe that she was, followed and popped out a few more staples.

I rode over to talk with Bill. He thought we should just leave the heifers alone and call it quits. They were in Mark's pasture, but they weren't hurting anything. I know now that he was right, and had this incident occurred a year later, I would have left them alone. But I was mad and frustrated, and penning those heifers had become a matter of pride. I was the manager of this ranch, and damn it, I intended to manage it, whether those heifers liked it or not.

Bill had not been defeated by these cattle as often as I and didn't understand my feelings. He grumbled that I was making a stupid decision. I replied that he could do whatever he wanted to, but I was going after the heifers. I rode to the nearest gate and started south after the outlaws.

That was a big mistake.

I thought it would be a fairly easy job, but as I rode after them, I could see that the conditions were changing fast. The heifers were running south as hard as they could go. By the time I caught up with them, they were half a mile into Mark's pasture and showing no signs of wanting to stop or go back north. And worse, they were stirring up the whole pasture. Mark's cows had started running in bunches by themselves. The pasture resembled an anthill, with cattle running in all directions. I hoped that Mark was taking a nap or reading a book and wouldn't discover the circus we had brought to his ranch. By this time I no longer cared whether we penned the heifers or not. I just wanted to get them away from Mark's cattle before their wildness rubbed off.

I had to push old Reno to catch up with them. The big heifer was out in the lead, and trailing behind her were the smaller heifer and five or six YL cows. I got out in front of them and headed them west. About a mile away there was a pasture gate that opened into our west pasture. I decided to take them there. Bill had caught up with me by this time. I told him we would take them west and cut off Mark's cows as we went. He nodded that he understood the plan, but also communicated with his facial expression what he thought about it. Dumb.

As the west fence came into view, we cut off the last of Mark's cows and were down to our two heifers again. They didn't stop running until they reached the fence. I would have been delighted if they had gone through this fence, since it would have put them back on the Crown Ranch. But of course they didn't. I held them while Bill opened the gate, then I pushed them up the fence. If we could just get them through the gate, I was ready to quit.

They walked right past the gate. Bill stopped them, turned them around, and headed them back toward the gate. They went past it again. We repeated the maneuver, and still they wouldn't go through the gate. It was incredible. We were tired, they were tired, the horses were tired. We all wanted to quit and go home. All those heifers had to do was move four steps to the west and we would be through with them. But they seemed possessed of a demonic power that would not allow them to do the right thing.

Kris came riding up on Dollarbill and the three of us held the heifers in front of the gate. Surely they would see it in a minute. They were panting for breath. Their tongues were hanging out. Yet, after they had stood in the gate for five or ten minutes, they began to mill and look to the east. We had just brought them from the east. Why would they want to go back in that direction? We held them as long as we could, and then the big one broke away.

"All right," I yelled at Bill, "let's rope them and drag them out the gate." I fell in behind the big one, and Bill got after the little one.

If I had been able to catch my heifer on the first loop, this plan would have worked, but my rope seemed to have fallen under the same evil spell that had plagued us all afternoon. The heifer was tired and was running with her head down. I couldn't see the gate or Bill or Kris. The heifer was so tired she wouldn't drive. In the best tradition of Crown-branded cattle, she wanted to fight. I tried to drag her, but Reno was out of gas. So I sat there and waited for Bill to come. I figured we could heel her, stretch her out, tie her down, and go back to the house for the stock trailer.

I waited and waited. No sign of Bill. Kris came riding up. We were wondering what had become of Bill when I heard something. I looked toward the sound and saw Bill's heifer approaching— dragging his catch rope. She trotted right past us and kept on going. I told Kris to ride back to the gate and see what had happened to Bill. If she didn't find him, she should ride back to the house and bring the pickup and trailer so we could load my heifer. She left, and I was alone again with an angry heifer on my string. I kept looking off to the north, searching for a sign of Bill. I was worried that he might have gotten into a storm. I knew that Suds would buck if he ever got a rope under his tail. I was afraid that Bill might be hurt.

About ten minutes later he came riding over a hill from the east—very slowly. Geeze, I was glad to see him.

He looked at my heifer, looked at me, and snarled, "What are you gonna do now, cowboy?"

Bill and I had ridden many miles together, had been in some tight spots, and had exchanged a few harsh words, but we had never come as close to bloodshed as we were at that moment. Right then, I understood why cowboys quit carrying six-shooters.

There was a long silence. I swallowed my anger and asked how his heifer had gotten away with his rope, and he told me. He had been chasing the heifer and was about to rope her when she stopped and charged his horse. Suds moved out of her path and she passed them on the right side. On impulse, Bill pitched the loop over his shoulder and was not even looking at her when the rope closed around her neck. Off she went, and the rope started burning through his hand. Before he could dally to the horn, she had taken it away from him and was on a romp through the pasture.

In the years since this event occurred, Bill has taken a lot of ribbing about his famous over-the-shoulder shot, and I suppose people who have heard the story have wondered why he did such a thing. I know why he did it. It was a blind response to unbearable frustration, a feeling that can be understood only by cowboys who have been beaten and humiliated by cattle. I once heard the story of a cowboy who, after missing loop after loop, threw his rope into a stock tank and rode off. Another cowboy in the same state of rage

bailed off his horse, pulled out his pocket knife, and cut his rope
into four or five pieces. Given the circumstances, Bill's response
was perfectly rational.

So there we were. We had one heifer dragging a rope
through the pasture and another on the ground. Bill asked what I
intended to do with mine. I said, "Well, let's tie her down with a
pigging string and go get the other one. To which he replied, "Fine.
I'll sit on your horse and you can tie her down." I think he was still
mad.

He got off Suds and climbed into my saddle. I took my
pigging string out of the saddlebag and walked down the rope
toward the heifer. She was lying on her side and was so tired that I
thought I could tie her down, even though she weighed seven
hundred pounds. I caught her front leg and was reaching for a
hind leg when she began to struggle. I held on as long as I could,
then she overpowered me and I had to let go. She jumped to her
feet and hit the end of the rope.

I had forgotten to mention to Bill that the rope was only
dallied (wrapped) around the horn. He thought I had thrown two
half-hitches over the horn and was tied solid, so he was not holding the rope when the heifer took out the slack. The rope spun
around the horn three times, and zing, we had another heifer loose
in the pasture. She headed east, dragging my rope behind her.

Bill slumped forward in the saddle and bowed his head. I
swallowed a sudden impulse to scream and weep. It had started
out to be such a simple job. All we had wanted to do was take one
heifer to the house.

By this time Bill and I had broken off all communication. I
hated his guts for turning the heifers loose—and for being right
that we should have left them alone—and he hated mine for getting him into this incredible mess. We cinched up our poor dripping horses and loped over the hill to see if we could get our ropes
back.

Quit? There was no chance of quitting now. We had two
wild heifers running through the neighbor's pasture, each dragging a rope that hissed through the grass and frightened every cow
brute within a quarter mile. But even worse, I was afraid that
someone driving down the county road, which ran through the
center of the pasture, would see the mess we had gotten ourselves
into—or assume that someone had a roping accident and call the
sheriff. I hoped with all my heart that we could get our ropes back,
get out of Mark's pasture, and sneak home without being observed.

We spotted my heifer in the southeast corner of the pasture and rode to her. She was so hot and snaky that she was ready to fight anything that approached her. This made it hard to get the rope off her neck, so we decided to drive her north and put her back into the middle pasture. At least then she would be away from Mark's cattle. So we started her north. Now and then she stopped and charged our horses. After she had made several razoos at Reno, I turned his hind end toward her, hoping he would kick her face in. I was very sorry he didn't.

As we approached the county road, I saw Sandy Hagar's pickup. My heart sank. Sandy and Ed Weeks, who lived in the neighborhood, had gone out for a Sunday drive and had seen one of our heifers dragging a rope. They both worked on ranches and they both knew what that meant. Fearing that someone had gotten hurt in a roping accident, they had gone looking for us. Their wives were in Ed's car, and they were scouting the north end of the pasture. I found out later that the wives ran into Kris on the road. She was bringing the pickup and trailer, and she was looking for us too.

At the very moment when Bill and I wanted nothing more than to crawl into a hole and disappear for a while, the entire neighborhood had mobilized and was trying to find us.

I told Sandy not to worry, apologized for stirring up the YL cattle, and told him what had happened. Well, I told him half the story. He and Ed had seen only one heifer dragging a rope, and I didn't tell him about the second one. Several months later, when Sandy and I were sitting around in his front yard, I told him the full story with all its gory details. He laughed.

I returned to Bill and the heifer. We continued driving her north toward the gate. Then she stopped in the shade of a little hackberry tree and wouldn't move. She put her tail to the tree and dared us to come get the rope. I rode in several times, and every time I reached for the rope she took a swipe at Reno. Finally I got the rope and we left her there and rode north to find the other heifer. The last time Bill had seen her, she had been running in that direction. Sure enough, we located her at the north end with some of Mark's cows and calves. After the wretch had gone through the fence into the middle pasture, then through the fence into Mark's pasture again, we roped her and dragged her into the middle pasture—which is exactly where we had started five and a half hours earlier.

There was a lesson in the experience, and it was branded into my memory. The lesson was that while it takes skill to rope an animal in the pasture, the real test of a cowboy comes when he has to get his rope back. Dabbing that loop on a cow brute's neck can be a lot of fun. Getting it back can be less than fun.

 The Devil in Texas

John Erickson obviously knows his classical literature. In The Hunter *he retells in novel form the old Gilgamesh epic by setting it along the Clear Fork of the Brazos River near old Ft. Griffin in the 1860s. The following tale involves the old motif of selling one's soul to the devil. In it, Erickson mentions a contemporary country song incorporating the story associated with Johann Faust, but he tells a cowboy variation of the old story. Here two cowboys meet the devil and get the best of him in true cowboy fashion. They don't tie a knot in the devil's tail. Instead, they rope him by the head and his heels and then doctor him the way they do sick cattle. Here is a unique cowboy retelling of an old story.*

After lunch, me and High Loper usually curl up on the floor of the ranch house and take a short nap. It kind of settles our grub and gives us a fresh attitude about the afternoon's work.

The other day we ate several bowls of hot spiced chili, and while we were eating, one of my favorite songs came on the radio. It was Charlie Daniels' "Devil Down in Georgia."

I don't know whether it was the chili or the song that did it, but during nap time I had an outrageous dream.

Me and Loper were ahorseback, riding through one of the pastures north of headquarters. It was a cold winter day. The prairie country was brown and bare, and the old cottonwoods reached like skeleton hands toward a brooding gray sky.

As usual, we were playing with our ropes as we rode along. Loper was mounted on a big sorrel named Happy, and I came along behind on my little Calipso mare. Loper was pitching his rope on soapweeds, and I was right behind him heeling his horse.

Old Hap was the kind of horse that was always looking for boogers. He'd shy from a cow chip, walk around a little sand rat hole, or fly over a trickle of water. So we weren't particularly sur-

Reprinted from *The Devil in Texas and Other Cowboy Tales* (Perryton: Maverick Books, 1982), pp. 75–80.

COW POKES

By Ace Reid

"I always wanted to rope an antelope, now I jist wantta git loose from one!"

prised when all at once he dropped his head, stretched out his neck, perked his ears, snorted, and started running sideways. But when Calipso did the same thing, it made us a little curious. We got our broncs under control and did some heavy spurring to get them back to the rock ledge where the runaway had started. We thought we might find a porcupine or maybe a dead calf.

What we saw was a little guy sitting on a donkey. He had his right leg thrown over the horn of his saddle, and he was rolling a Prince Albert cigarette. His face was skinny and sharp pointed, his skin as red as a hot branding iron.

He didn't wear a hat, and it was easy to see why. He had two horns coming out the sides of his bald head. He was ugly—ugly as the very devil.

Me and Loper traded glances, as if to say, "What is this?" The man lapped his cigarette and lit up. When he snapped his fingers, a flame appeared out of his thumb.

"Afternoon, boys," he said in a high, squeaky voice.

We nodded. Old Happy was pointing this guy like a bird dog. He'd spent his whole life looking for boogers, and by George he'd finally found one.

"My name's John Devil," said the man. "I come from Hell and I can out-ride, out-rope, out-cuss, and out-spit any cowboy I ever met."

Loper kind of grinned. "Well, if that's true, Mr. Devil, then you've spent too much time in Hell and Kansas. This here's the Texas Panhandle, and me and my partner have never been out-rode or out-roped. Nobody ever tried us on the spittin' and cussin'."

Old Devil laughed to himself and looked at Loper's horse. "Do you milk that thing or use him strictly for plow work?" Then he looked at my mare. "Kind of a cute little thing. If she ever grows into them long skinny legs, she's liable to stand twenty-seven hands at the withers."

Me and Loper don't mind personal insults, but bad-mouthing the horseflesh is hard to forgive, especially when it comes from a man on a donkey.

"We manage to get the work done," I said.

"I'm surprised."

Loper shifted his quid to the other cheek. "You're fixing to be more than that."

"Tell you what let's do, boys. Let's have us a little roping contest, Hell against Texas."

"Hell against Texas is a normal day around here," I said. "What else got in mind?"

"You see that steer?" Devil pointed his finger and a corriente steer suddenly appeared on the flat below. "One loop apiece, head, half-head, or horns."

"What's the stakes?"

Devil arched his brows. "Your souls, fellers, your souls. If you both miss and I catch, you got to work for me. We just can't find good help in Hell any more."

"What if we win?"

He untied his catch rope and held it up. "You get this rope. It's made of threads of pure gold, and it's worth a fortune."

It isn't every day that a cowboy gets a chance to make a fortune. We told old Devil to kiss his rope good-bye, and we went charging down the hill toward the steer, just the way we do when we're doctoring sick cattle. First man there gets first throw, and the second man stands by for a second throw or heels.

Calipso and I got there first. When the old steer saw us coming, he stuck out his tail and made a dash for the creek. He ran straight and fast, just the kind of shot I like. I knew I couldn't miss. Calipso put me right on top of him. I swung my loop and floated out a nice flat, open noose.

But at the last second, as if by magic, a gust of wind came up. My loop hit the left horn and fell into the dirt. "Get him, Loper!" I yelled over my shoulder.

Loper and Happy were hot on his tail. Loper swung and threw a pretty noose, but the same thing happened to him. A strong gust of wind came up and the loop died in the air.

We heard a squeal of laughter behind us, and here came John Devil and his donkey. "Out of the way, Texas! Here's how we do it in Hell!"

That warn't no ordinary donkey. He was as fast as a racehorse. He caught up with that Mexican steer in a hurry, and when he did, John Devil did a strange thing. He turned clear around in the saddle so that he was riding backward. When the donkey flew past the steer, Mr. Devil pitched the golden rope around his horns, put the end of the rope between his teeth, and jerked the steer plumb out of his tracks.

It wasn't the sort of thing a normal man could get by with.

"You know," I said to Loper, "there's something funny going on around here."

"Yalp. A guy might think that old Devil was cheatin'."

"A guy sure might."

"You want to work in Hell?"

"Nope."

"What do you think?"

"Let's do it."

John Devil came riding up to us, coiling up his golden rope and chuckling to himself. "Tough luck, boys. Pack your bags, we're going to . . . "

"Hell if we are," said Loper. We had our loops built.

"We're fixing to do a little pasture work."

John Devil glanced at me and then at Loper. He'd never seen such a wicked pair of faces, not in Hell or Kansas or anywhere else he'd been. "Now boys . . . " He stuck the spurs in that donkey and hauled for the caprock.

I was dallied when the slack went out of my rope. The donkey kept going, but John Devil came to a sudden stop, seeing as how I had a nice little loop fitted around his horns.

He squalled and bellered and kicked and pitched, but Loper scooted a big old circle of nylon around his middle and picked up both hocks. We stretched him out, throwed half-hitches over our dallies, and met in the middle, each of us packing a medicine bag.

"What do you reckon?" said Loper. "Pinkeye?" I said yep, so we squirted both eyes with blue drops and glued on a couple of eye patches.

"Loper, I think he's bloated too." We got the rubber hose and ran it down his guzzle.

"And he's kinder droopy in his ears." So we gave him fifteen cc's of Combiotic and a couple of big sulfa pills for good measure. Just then I felt somebody shaking my shoulder. I opened my eyes and saw High Loper and his mustache. "Wake up. What's the matter with you? You're over here gruntin' like a bunch of hogs."

I sat up and eased out a burp of garlic and chili powder. Or maybe it was gun powder. "Brother, I had a bad dream."

"About what?"

"Well, we was out roping and . . . "

"Hold it right there. I know you're lying."

"Huh?"

Loper smashed my cowboy hat down on my head. "Any dream with roping in it ain't bad. Let's go to work."

PAUL PATTERSON

As a young man, Paul Patterson saw a number of large West Texas ranches, and he trailed cattle, sheep, and horses across the unfenced stretches. In 1931, for example, he helped deliver a herd of four hundred eighty-five horses to a ranch near Orla in West Texas and worked for A. C. Hoover of Ozona, who operated four hundred sections of land on five different ranches. He bached as a single cowboy, and it was perhaps during this time that he developed his style of storytelling. Because he is now in his eighties and has practiced the art of narration most of his life, Patterson is a craftsman who has a unique style of telling dialect stories. His ability to play with words and the sounds of words is a remarkable talent. Patterson has mastered the art of understating the humor and he finds it in the everyday life and events of cowboy life, not only of an earlier day but also of the present. In addition to his cowboy credentials, Patterson has a B.A. from Sul Ross State University in Alpine and did graduate work at the University of Texas, Utah State University, the University of Madrid, and the University of Buffalo, as well as in Geneva, Switzerland. Here is "an educated feller," certainly not a greenhorn, who is also a poet. His work is available in *A Pecos River Pilgrim's Poems* from Cow Hill Press (1988) with an introduction by his good friend Elmer Kelton, whose work also appears in this collection.

Night Horse Nightmare

Cowboys still keep a night horse up to use to round up the horse herd or remuda early in the morning for the cowboys to saddle up and ride. The greatest tragedy a cowboy can face is to be afoot, and if the night horse gets loose, the whole outfit of cowboys is afoot. Patterson shows in dramatic form how this greatest tragedy—and comedy—can occur and how it affects the men involved.

Briefly, the scene, setting and stage whereon is to be enacted a drama of some thirty-six hours duration, not including time out for fretting, fixing flats, and floundering in fogs of frustration.

Cast of characters: Buster, the leading man—or, rather horse—with Bill Wyatt, Cutter Carpenter, and the horse jingler (me), playing lesser roles in this lop-sided battle of wits, wills, and wiliness.

Opening Scene: Combination kitchen–dining room–den–pantry–bedroom–semi-saddle room and semi-bathroom (i.e., out the window on cold nights) of a typical bachelor's dive on the A. C. Hoover horse ranch lying for some 263 square miles to the south and west of Buena Vista, Texas, west-of-the Pecos.

Time: Around daylight of an April Morning, 1931.

With one exception the entire cast of characters is huddled around the breakfast table, its coffee unsipped, its sowbelly unsampled, and its sorghum syrup unsopped. Though outwardly calm, inwardly pandemonium reigns supreme. Etched deep into each leathery countenance is consternation, not to say dismay. The horse jingler has just bomb-shelled them with the news that the night horse, Buster, has vamoosed, skedaddled (or, if you prefer Bill Wyatt's expression for it, consult the handwriting on the nearest outhouse wall).

As an insight into the gravity of such a situation, never in the annals of horseback history has anybody anywhere heard of an outfit without a night horse corralled and ever at the ready. An outfit without a night horse faced a calamity on the order of a croton-oiled cat on concrete. Something had to be done—and

Reprinted from *T for Texas: A State Full of Folklore*, Texas Folklore Society, Ed. F. E. Abernethy, publication no. 44 (Dallas: E-Heart Press, 1982), by permission of the Texas Folklore Society.

damned quick! But what? And how? First to mind was an idea to strike stark dread in the staunchest cowboy breast. From Cutter, the boss: "The three of us'll haf to find him and pen him afoot."

But before recounting the first futile foray, let us introduce the protagonist, Buster, lest the sudden shock of meeting him unexpectedly prove too great. Buster, a big, blood-bay with long anvil head and one little bitty shoe-button eye, was a horse whose lineage was long since lost in the mists and mysteries of time. However, the wide, flat feet and feathered fetlocks hinted of a trace of Clydesdale blood, but for the most part you could say that Buster was cold-blooded. Fact is, every move Buster makes, every step Buster takes will tend to bear this out. One consolation: Buster did not bear the proud Hoover horse brand (a triangle on the left shoulder) which bespoke of noble blood.

Why, then, this common clod, this interloper amongst all this Hoover royalty? Whence had he cometh? (Not to mention whither the hell he had goneth?) Buster had shown up in a horse roundup from the vast no man's land, the alkali flats and salt cedar jungles along the Pecos. A gelding but cut proud, Buster was here snob-nobbing. That is to say, he was here to rub shoulders—and then some—with those blue-blooded Hoover fillies. As a consequence, he wound up in serfdom jingling other but lesser geldings, work we cowboys considered too demeaning for high class Hoover horseflesh.

No noble blood to speak of, no lineage to lay hold of notwithstanding, tucked inside that long, anvil head and behind that one shoe button eye lurked a mind as cunning, as conniving as ever graced the inside of a skull, be it man, beast, bird, or bug.

We spotted Buster in the far corner of the north horse-trap, long head hung over the horse-wire fence, looking long and longingly not to say lustfully at old Kempland's manada of maidens grazing gracefully across the salt grass flat. Now, one would naturally assume that one eye no bigger than a shoe button would not be as efficient as twice as many human orbs twice as big, let alone six. Even so, with a mere corner of this one, Buster and us spotted each other about the same time and Buster was off in a cloud of clods.

This lop-sided contest of wills, wits, and wiliness lasted until 'way up in the morning, with me being the last to holler "calf rope." I would like to say it was because I was set up of sterner stuff, but in truth I had committed the ill-mannered indiscretion of relating and re-relating how I had run the mile down at the State Track Meet in Austin only a couple of summers back. ("Ain't aimin'

to brag," as they say we Texans say then go ahead and do, but I
brought that entire Memorial Stadium crowd to its collective feet. I
deem it only fair to confess, however, that I got so far behind they
thought I was ahead. That is, what they didn't know was that the
knot of runners behind me was finishing whereas I had another lap
to go.) The reason I outlasted Cutter and Bill was because Buster
was under my jurisdiction, hence my responsibility. But how was I
to know the only way to contain the likes of Buster was to keep him
under lock and key with key hidden in the bottom of Cutter's
turtle-top trunk and it likewise locked!

Some ingenious fool had whittled out a wooden peg and
stuck it into the gate's sliding latch when all Buster had to do was
clamp his teeth on it, slide it back and *adio mi chaparito*—in the
words of an Old Mexico song title. But who would have thought a
horse would have thought such thoughts? Most especially a total
nobody from nowhere when scores of night horses before him,
many of them of noble birth, had not solved the riddle.

In a sad state of disrepair we repaired to the shack to rest
and/or rant, each according to his own temperament. Bill, the
trigger-tempered one was for "grabbin' up the thirty-thirty and
creasin' the old cold-blooded, owl-headed (reflection on mother)"
but Cutter, a cooler head, counseled caution.

"Hit him a fraction low and Lord knows where we would be
at."

"Hell, I know where we would be at. Right, igod here. And
no more afooter than we, igod, are."

But the boss prevailed.

"What the hell now, then, Cutter?"

"What say you crank up your Dodge Cuepay and drive over
to headquarters? Get Lon to send Gid Redding over here a-
horseback?"

"Not me. I cain't bear to tell ol' Lon a thing like this." (Not
that Lon Freeman would have ranted, raved, snorted, and pawed
sand. But being the first boss in horseback history to let somebody
let a night horse get out would have haunted him, hounded him to
his grave.)

"Paul, you then."

"Cutter, you know I don't know nothin' about no machinery." (Which triple-negative thus interpreted means "I would not
touch this task with a twenty-foot sucker rod." Be on the order of
carrying the message to next-of-kin that the Alamo had fallen or,
say, toting those terrible tidings to the widow of General George
Armstrong Custer.)

"Then you go, Cutter," said Bill, "you know him better'n we do."

"Very reason I won't go."

"Which leaves nothin' to do but nothin'," I put in, hopefully.

"By no means," Bill said, "we're fixin' to give ol' Buster a go in my green Dodge."

"Who ever heard of rustlin' horses in a automobile?" asked Cutter, skeptically, not to mention sarcastically.

"Nobody. But nobody ever heard of a rustlin' horse flyin' the coop neither. This'll make us first both ways."

Cutter said neither yea nor nay but you could tell he was pondering it in his heart. Born with one foot planted firmly on the wild frontier, transition to the machine age was a slow, painful process. To his kind, the motor car was too complicated, too cantankerous, hence too susceptible to cold jaw, to cold shoulder, to cold-bloodedness, had maimed, mangled and mauled more of mankind in forty years than the horse had in four thousand. However, if Cutter came up with an objection it would be on religious rather than legal, technical, or sentimental grounds (having "seen the light" at B. B. Crim's cowboy camp meeting a couple of summers back).

"No, Bill. Best we stick with what the Good Lord provided for sech purposes, the beasts of the field which He give us dominion over."

"Which don't seem to have included that goddam Buster," snapped Bill cynically, not to say profanely. "So I say gettin' dominion over that (aspersion on mother) is gonna take all of them forty-odd horses under that green Dodger's hood—with us throwed in." Perceiving in Cutter a wavering of will, Bill plunged on.

"She's fresh shod, got a good mouth on 'er, shore-footed, and sound in wind and bottom. Not as apt to fall on a man as God's own . . . " Here Cutter threw both hands up in a give-in, give-up gesture.

If necessity is the mother of invention, extreme necessity is the mother of extreme measures. Bill, the ingenious one, hit upon the idea of Cutter buckling his old kack on the green Dodge's hood—like cowboys had done for years but for transporting purposes only—from job to job. Nobody had thought of buckling them on for business.

Always darkest just before dawn? In our case it was just after. A new day, a new resolve (plus forty-odd horses) notwithstanding, Buster was not allowing us within rifle range much less a lariat's length. However, to err is human. Likewise horse. Yes, even one of Buster's mental magnitude. What he had failed to take into account was (1) Bill's resolve and (2) the total and reckless abandon with which Bill was pressing Green Dodger and her forty horses. Heretofore, Buster had found Bill the most timid of horsemen. That is, Bill was the only one to top him (Buster) off and sweat him out in the corral before venturing outside. Hence a false sense of security—over-confidence on Buster's part. As a consequence the critter commenced playing off, holding something in reserve against a greater need. Or was it the opposite, so as to thumb his tail in defiance at closer range? To further humiliate us with those insultingly insinuating sounds? And cloud or windshield with clods?

But if Buster thought he was obstructing my view, he was whistling (literally as well as figuratively) in the wind. I had long since shut my eyes against the wildest ride ever taken by man, bird, beast, or being.

"To hell with Buster," I gritted through gnashed (and chattering) teeth. "Slow this damned thing down!"

"Naw. She ain't apt to step in no dog holes. Nor hub no stumps."

Given the wit, and grit, my reply would have been, "No, but we're jumpin' a hell of a bunch of 'em." Under the circumstances it came out an humble mumble: "Bill, please slow down!"

"You got the door shet. You ain't apt to fall out."

(No. But I was harboring thoughts of jumping.)

Bill's recklessness coupled with perseverance, coupled with desperation along with superior horses was beginning to tell. Buster could no longer out-run or out-dodge the Green Dodger. Fact is, we had pulled within lariat's length of Buster several times, but Cutter was always too busy riding to do any roping. One more stump-jumping, rump-bumping round did it. We coursed Buster into the corral.

"Slam the gate on him!" yelled Cutter, too tangled in his rope to dismount.

"Hell far no," Bill yelled, already in the gate with a salt-cedar stave drawed back. "I'm gonna learn him a lesson he ain't apt to fergit." Be he goof or grammarian, etymologist or ecologist, man is yet to utter a more accurate verb—learn—as regards Buster. That horse had learnt it all—now he was teaching.

Meantime Buster had almost completed his corral circle and was now headed straight for Bill, so straight, in fact, that Bill was forced to give ground. But before so doing he fetched Buster a clout atop the skull. The lick, albeit powerful, neither derailed Buster nor his unerring train of thought. The last we saw and heard of him was the haughty figure nine in his tail and the insinuating sounds emanating from thereinunder.

"Well," sighed Cutter philosophically, "at least you parted his forelock."

"Git in, we ain't done with that (expletive excluded) yet." This from Bill. Certainly not from me, or the Green Dodger. That last circle she had matched Buster drop for drop, blast for blast in the emission of gas, water, and steam, all of which she was still emitting. This plus seeping sundry oils and various greases. And the way she was giving to that left hind leg it did not take an auto doctor to diagnose it as a hip knocked down. As a consequence we were forced to repair to the shack for repairs, not to mention rest and recuperation.

Quite by accident we eventually brought Buster to book. I say accident. Actually it was Buster himself that gave us the idea though we were too small of soul to give him the glory. Since it was Cutter who made the discovery, it could have been provident instead of accident. Being the new Cutter he was at the window "lifting his eyes unto the hills from whence might cometh his help" (Here I find it apropos to point out that these hills were seventy-five miles away.) when through the darkness he caught sight of Buster inside the horse corral sneaking a water-logging bellyful, just enough to keep his speed, as he had been doing all along.

So, sad to say, it was not superior intelligence that brought Buster to book. Nor was it greater fortitude. Seeing as how he thwarted our fair means, we resorted to foul. We wired the gate shut, cut his water off all that day, opened it late that night, and then slammed it shut on him when he snuck in to water.

Buster, Bill, and Cutter have long since forded that last long river. And it is my fervent hope that they are together. I am sure of one thing. Saint Peter better leave those Pearly Gates locked and leave the keys with a higher authority. Otherwise old Buster will get out. Or in. And whichever the case might be, and wherever old Bill might be he will be "givin' that old pony a powerful good cussin'."

 Rags to Riches to Rags

Cartoonist Ace Reid is one of the bona fide characters of the contemporary western scene. In dialect fashion, Patterson

COW POKES

By Ace Reid

"Whatta you mean you're wantin' a washin' machine when you know good and well I've got to buy a new saddle?"

tells of the ups and downs of his relationship with Ace. Inherent in the tale is an old cowboy tradition of sharing, particularly clothing. This practice was prompted because the cowboys were always short on money and supplies, such as clothes and gear. But only good friends would agree to share such items.

Jist to see Ace Reid standin' around in his twenty-five-hundred-dollar boots and squinchin' out from under the brims of seven-hundred-dollar Studson hats, you would not dream he was onct as pore as I am rat now. So pore me and him have to share the same bedroll. "Cuttin beddin," us cowboys call it. Have to share a pair o' spurs; he rides with the right, me with the left, me bein' left-handed all the way down. Even have to share a saddle, which means we either ride a-bareback or walk 75 percent of the time. (Yes, 75 percent. Try hit and you'll thaink hit's more'n that.)

One suit of clothes 'tween us, and never mind the six-inch-heighth, fifty-pound-weight discrepancy. Bein' the best of buddies and constant compadres at the time, we pool our pile (four dollars and ninety-seven cents to be exack) and blow hit on a second-hand (at least) suit o' clothes that is jist as too little fer Ace as hit is too big fer me.

By the time we git used to sharin' thaings, all of a sudden (if you can call seven year sudden) Ace hits hit big with the cartoons and buys me out lock, stock, and barrel—one spur, one half a roll o' beddin, one-half a suit o' clothes, and one-half a saddle. (Make that half of a half a saddle, hit bein' only half a saddle to begin with.)

Ace Reid rich? We cain't believe hit. Me and him go around pinchin' ourselves. Only after Ace commences pinchin' the girls—and gittin' by with hit—do I know he is rich. And so do the girls, else they'd a boxed his yeres like they used to.

Yes, sir, Ace Reid's riches are fer real. Ace Reid is loaded—so loaded he pays his back taxes clear back past 1929, restocks his cow ranch and puts me on "studdy." Buys me a brand new pickup automobile to cowboy in, and hit is loaded. Air cooler blowin' pure Rocky Mountain spraing air, and hit is loaded—with pure West Texas alkali dust. CB radio, and hit is loaded—pure bull manure both a-comin' in and a-goin' out. Built-in ice box, and hit is loaded, which means so am I a right smart of the time. (Meanin' I go jist as heavy on the Coors Lite as I do on the Lone Star heavy.) Tape deck and hit is loaded with hits—Willie and Waylon, exclusive. Double gun rack in back, and hit is loaded: two thirty-ought sixes, and them loaded. Ace adds me another rack fer a double-barrel shotgun, and hit loaded with birdshot, so's me and him can stay loaded with our neighbor's exotic game birds—plovers, Indian chukars, prairie chickens, quails, turkeys, and so on.

On the sly I overhaul the shotgun. When I'm done, she is a snub-nose job, and *she* is loaded. This time, with a double dose of double-zero buck. (You simply cannot blieve what a job hit is to pertect this job I got with Ace.)

Travelin' expenses, business expenses, includin' three martini lunches three times a day, not to mention the cool Coors courses 'tween meals. Then all of a sudden Ace sells out, moves out of the cow country and downstate amongst sheep persons. Buys his self another ranch and puts me to runnin' it. Still runs cattle to maintain his dignity but runs sheep to maintain his self *with* dignity—and maintains me in the manner to which I have become accustomed (or rather addicted).

Oh, how hit sorrows me to say so, but rat then and rat there is rat when and rat where my big, ol', big-hearted buddy commences to change—commences to pinchin' pennies, to cuttin' co'ners, to what he calls *economizin'* but what I call *miserizin'*, skinflintin', short-pottin' to the *n*th degree.

(Now there is jist somethin' about a damn sheep that shrinks a man's soul, shrivels his sperit, clabbers the milk of human kindness in his breast.)

Here's what I mean: I wake up one mornin' and find my mobile icebox gone. So I would drink my Coors uncooled. I had done it. Wake up another mornin' and find my air-cooler gone. So I would sweat it out. I had done it. Wake up another mornin' and find my CB gone. So I would talk to myself, as usual. Wake up another mornin' and find my tape deck gone, long one. So I would do my own saingin'. No I wouldn't, neither. Couldn't put up with it. Neither would the coyotes. Wake up another mornin' and find my pickup gone. So I would walk. No I wouldn't, neither. Totally agin my cowboy principles.

In any case, Ace solves my problem fer me. Wake up another mornin' and find myself gone. Here are the particulars:

When Ace sells the pickup out from under me he puts me back a horseback

"Back in the saiddle agin
Back where a frien is a frien."

Amend that to "back where a frien' ain't a frien' no more," as you shall shortly see. (That's why you cain't hardly tell my saingin' from my cryin'.)

"Now, Paul, hit is customary for us ranch men to furnish you cowboys with a straing of horses but not saiddles. However, bein' hit's you, I'm furnishin' a saiddle. But be damn keerful with it. Saiddles costs money." (Yeah. Say like sebem dollars, hit being' the same ol' hull we wuz pardners in.)

Now, a man can do a lot of thaings a-horseback he cain't do in a pickup. Fun thaings. (Right around on the other hand a man can do a lot of thaings in a pickup he cain't do a-horseback. Fun thaings. All depends on what a feller *picks up*—before and after. But that's neither here nor there—and hadn't orta be.)

Now any horseback cowboy worth the salt in his sowbelly can find all kinds of cattle that need ropin' in the worst way—which is the way I rope. As a consequence I ketch this big ol' wild Ace Reid Rickety-R cow in the worst way—say like one forelaig and around the belly. As a consequence the ol' huzzy perceeds to jerk my horse down, jerk me offa my horse, and jerk a sterp offa Ace's precious saiddle. So he fars me and commences scoutin' about fer a one-laigged cowboy.

"Ace," I says, "Me fard? After all me and you have went thu together?"

"Yeah. I know, Paul. And I thaink the world and all of ye," says Ace, bursting into tears. "But putting' you back on would mean fixin' that sterp. And seventeen-fifty fer a new sterp leather! OH, MY GOD, NO!"

Onct a man is addicted to the good life, he will do anythaing to git back to it. And I tell Ace so.

"Ace, ol' frien', jist tell me what I will haf to do to git my ol' job back and I will do it."

"OK," says Ace, "Go up 'ere to my ol' doctor in Keerville ang git a laig sawed off. But you're a dam fool, Paul, much as 'at old sawbones'll charge ye."

Well sir, dogged if I don't go and git the wrong laig taken off and Ace fars me agin. Here's what he tells the Fair Employment Practice People, straight out.

"Hell far, yes, I fard 'im. A empty britches laig hangin' down over the sterp side and his good laig hangin down over the broke sterp leather, he ain't got balance enough left to head a sheep much less a cow. An', igod, I was payin' him twenty-five dollars a month and all the cornbread and molasses he could eat—plus all the clabber he could draink."

Now then, the message here, loud and clear: "Cowboy, when you sign on with a creep so cheap as to keep sheep, git ready to *read 'em an' weep!*"

 ## The Texan That Thunk Small

Texans are widely known to think big—big hats, big ranches, big state, big men. Here Patterson plays on this theme in a story reflecting an experience he had in Australia when he visited there some years back. Here he learns, to his dismay, that Australians think even bigger than Texans do.

To gain credence with an audience, especially a non-Texan audience, one must come across as frank or earnest or both. To come across as frank or earnest or both one must confess to something painful—*most* painful—in one's past or present or both.

Last year I wrung from my breast a most painful confession, which I shall do again—and find it no less painful: "I like Howard Cosell!" (Will it balance things out if I confess I hate that insufferable tennis player who suffers from tennis elbow of the mouth plus an advanced case of athlete's foot of the tongue?)

This year I shall go you one better and confess to something more painful still on the order of your old-time virgin (ex-virgin) confessing to consenting to submitting to the frontier female's fate worse than death. Here it is: as God and Glen Forbes (a chap from outback Australia) are my witnesses, I am a native-born *Texan who thinks small*! But thank the Lord, such was not always the case. In fact, this leprous affliction, this cursed curse, struck me down on the road from Alice Springs to Ayers Rock, Australia on November 21, 1979, at around 8:45 A.M.

I have no idea how it was with the Apostle Paul on the road to Damascus but to me it was like taking 220 from a cattle prod whilst under the shower. It all started when I went down under and out into the outback under pretext of gathering cowboy data for the Texas Folklore Society. In truth I was down there to brag on me and Texas and laugh to scorn "them piddling properties" them Aussies tried to palm off as ranches. (Just retribution, poetic justice for thinking more highly of me and Texas than I ought to think).

But let me start at the start and end at the ending: for my going-away-from-Texas outfit I selected a pearl-gray Texan Stetson (pronounced *Studson*) and a pair of two-tone, tan cowboy boots to go down under and out into the outback and back in in.

On this bus I was formulating my course of action. First I would ask this bus driver–guide a question. Not for an answer but as a foot in the door, that is, an opening for my autobiography, along with a lot of big geography, say like, "I been cowboyin' ever since I was seventeen-year-old. Worked on some big outfits in my time. Worked on a horse ranch acrost the Pecos that run frum eleven hundred to fifteen hundred head of hosses. Worked too with the Booger Y's, and they run arund three thousand head of cattle on two hundred and thirty sections of land—that's two hundred and thirty square miles, podner. Worked on this one outfit in Upton and Crockett Counties that run twenty-five thousand head of sheep at one time." (I had read and heard it said that there was no stigma attached to sheep down under.)

Lastly, I would tell this bloke—within earshot of the tourists, of course—how I "helped move five hundred head of hosses two hundred and fifty mile, the last hoss herd of that size to move that far acrost Texas." Then I would go into detail.

Now for the approach, the grand entry. Pearl-gray Stetson at a go-to-hell tilt, western-wear pants legs tucked inside two-tone Texas boot tops, I tromp forward and says in the proper Texas drawl, "Say, pardner, any ranches in these parts? (What he did not know and did not need to know was that a true Texan would not be caught dead saying it like this—except on TV.)

"Cattle stytion you mean, myte. Yeh, a cat-tle stytion on down the track a wys."

"How big is it?" I asked, my lips already drawed back to sneer at the piddling proportions of it.

"Ounly tew thousen squah molls," he said.

Only two thousand square miles! There went my two hundred.

Seeing my sneer starting, the bloke hurried on to inform me that Victoria River Downs to the northwest "operyted a cat-tle property of some ten thousen squah molls." By now my two hundred sections had shrunk to two acres.

"How many cattle does this Victoria River outfit run?"

"'Undred thousen beasts when the gryze is good."

My God. All of a sudden my Boogor Y three thousand shrunk to a dairy herd.

"How many cattle does this here outfit run?" I asked, anxious to get back down to my own dimensions—say like the King Ranch size.

"Bloke cawn't sie 'ow many beasts 'e's got. Aven't mustered in tew yeahs-too bloody dry."

What this Glen Forbes bloke did not know and did not need to know was that what he took to be a sneer of superiority was, in truth, sheer shock, a condition now recognized as *shrinking size syndrome*, peculiar to Texans ever since Alaska was admitted as a state—and especially when somebody else tops us in property proportions.

In another fling at superiority I enquired as to sheep stytions only to learn that the nearest one ran "eyty-seven thousen of the beasts." But you know how us Texans is not easy to put down. Way acrost yonder I spied a big red mountain, and knowin' enough joggafy to know we had 'em whupped on mountains, I felt on safe—if not superior—ground. I ast,

"How high is that mountain yonder?"

"Mountin? 'T 'ynt a mountin, myte, but a rock. Ayers Rock."

"All right. How high is that damn rock, then?" Before I thought.

"Eleven 'undred eyty-eyght feet 'igh and six and a 'awlf molls in circumference."

From here on out it is as from a glass darkly and from a great ways off. My ears heard but could scarce believe what my lips were imparting, yet I knew in my secret heart it was the God-gospel truth: "Frien's, all this time I have been putting you on. To be frank and earnest with you I am from *Rhode Island*. Never saw a cow in its natural habitat, much less a cowboy."

I wanted to lay my sleepless night in Motel Ayers Rock on the yowlings of wild dingo dogs roundabout, but knew in my secret heart it was the "syndrome" at work. For example, when I tried to visualize a dingo I could not concentrate on anything bigger than the fleas on him. (I ain't kiddin.') Then I commenced to wonder if the fleas had fleas. Then if the fleas on the fleas on the fleas had fleas—and so on. Once there, I thought I was pulling out of it when I visualized a tick in the dingo's ear. But then I commenced to wonder if the tick had ticks in his ears and so on down.

Back in the states I made straight for a shrink, slouched down on his couch, and sobbed out my story; and the *shrink shrunk*. (as God, and Tom Pepper, are my witnesses). But just before he shrunk, he collected his fee, which was one hundred dollars.

I asked him, I says, "Supposin' you had waited till now, how much would the fee be?"

"At this time, a dime."

I handed him my last dime and says, "For God sakes, do somethin'."

"First I must remind you my hours have shrunk to seconds, but I'll see what I can do."

Whether my case is terminal I cannot say. However, I do believe it is in remission, praise the Lord.

Here's what I mean. Three days later I am right here in San Antonio acting as greeter of non-Texans at the Texas Folklife Festival. Not three blocks away is playing (to full house, mind you) Larry King's *Best Little Whorehouse in Texas*. Three times a day for four days I apologize to non-Texans for us big-scale Texans ever having operated a *little* whorehouse!

 Hit's Tough Bein' a Texan

Here is a tale Patterson related to visitors at the Texas Folklife Festival held annually in August in San Antonio at

the Hemisfair grounds. The tale reflects the recollections of
an old-time-cowboy-turned-schoolteacher.

My feller folklife festivalers, my message today is mostly fer non-Texans in the crowd. Yeah, I know what you're a-thainkin'. Here's another one of them typical Texans—proud, loud, low-browed, the most bull and the least cowed of anybody in the crowd. That ain't me at all. I am quiet, polite, bright, always right, and above all *modest*. And rich. Nacherally you will want to know how I made my fortune—four fortunes, to be exact.

First fortune I made at the age of ten, herdin' sheep. Second fortune I started on at the age of seventeen, cowboyin'. Third fortune I made teachin' school (Ainglish, o'course). Fourth fortune I am in the process of right now—old age pension.

Another misconception of us Texans I want to put to rest rat now is that'un to the effect that we are hard to git along with. Nonsense. I have lived in Texas 76 years and have only been hit in the head onct with a table laig and shot at one time with a shotgun. As regards the table laig lick, you wouldn't know it happened unless you ast me a sensible question. As regards the shotgun blast, hit has stood me in good stead. Made hit possible fer me to tighten and brighten a expression expressed by Sir Winston Churchill hisself when he said, "The most exhilerating thing in loif is to be shot at without success." I say "the most accelleratin' thaing in life is to be shot at without success."

Here's what I mean: In 1931 we was movin' this herd from near Sheffield to Barnhart and our chuckwagon was camped fer dinner about a half a mile from this ranch house. I was down openin' the front yard gate of this ranch house when the shotgun went off. Hit was a matter of only a few fleetin' seconds, the boys said, until I showed up in camp. I'd a made it a damn sight sooner if I hadn't had to stop fer my horse.

Yes, hit's tought bein' a Texan. Hit's tough enough bein' a double-tough Texan. Hit's double-tough bein' a semi-tough Texan. 'Tain't the physical abuse and misuse we have to take from non-Texans tougher'n us. Hit is the snide asides we have to let ride. Say like when I'm settin' in front of two, too-tough non-Texans at the Ruidoso race track in New Mexico.

"They say lots of Texas horsus ron on this track. How will I know when they're Texas horsus?"

"Same way you'll know when they're Texans. They're always the horsus *behind*."

"*One*: Your typical Texas kaowboy will always show up with a saddle horse between his legs and *Two*, your typical Texas kaowboy will always show up with a charley horse between his ears."

"By the way, I'm moving to Texas in J'ly. What preparations should I have in mind?"

"What preparations? Preparation H. Definitely."

Stuff like this is what cuts us Texans to the quick. Pains us to the point of despair. However, as fer the physical-no sweat. Here, fer example, is a simple but ample sample of what I mean:

While back I am lopin' along 'tween the east and west lanes of Interstate 10 'tween Pecos and Van Horn when one of them ass fault cowboys is assin' along there makin' a ass out of his self on his CB—as usual—when his rig cold-jaws on him, flies the track, and rimfires me and ol' Gooseflaish (he's muh horse), bustin' a left forelaig on him and a right hinelaig on me. In other words, boogers us up a right smart. (A straight out hit-and-hightail-it job, leavin' me and muh ol' pony layin' there a-sufferin' somethin' fierce. Ol' Gooseflaish, bein a Texan thu and thu is takin' hit like a man. That is, like me. But us Texans, a independent bunch, don't ast nobody fer nothin'. But like the Good Book says, like I say to ol' Goose-flaish, "Buck up, ol' hoss, they's always a Good Samitarium comes along ever' road."

Shore nuff, up rolls one in a big long automobile, out o' state license plates—with a MD insignia thereon and with nurse at side. Providence.

"What's going on here?"

"Ol' pony's got a fore-laig busted and I got a hine one in the same shape." 'Fore I could tell them to look to ol' Gooseflaish first they had done lit in on him. "And be damn shore," I says, "you make them laigs match."

"You got it, Texas."

They put ol Goose under. Set the fracture; hit is compound. Take a couple o' hours. Then they keep the ol' pony in intensive keer another couple.

Finally, they git around to me. "Now, same as with ol' Gooseflaish, Doc," I says, "Be damn shore you make them laigs mate."

"You got my hypocritical oath on it, Texas."

He probes and pulls and pounds and pokes around there a right smart while. D'reckly he walks over to the bar ditch and picks up three flat rocks about yay size. He puts one under muh good laig, puts the other'n under the other'n. Then he raises the third un over his head, edgeways, rares back, comes down *kerwhop* and busts muh good laig exzackly to match t'othern. Next he feels around on muh person till he locates a money clip to his likin', the one with bills of ten-thousand denomination, and peels off ten of 'em fer his service. Total: hunnerd grand. (What that saw-bones don't know and don't need to know, I keep muh big money in muh hat sweat band. Take this hat here. Size seben and a half. Fools 'em ever' time. "'Thout money in the band I wear a size three.)

Next he fishes around in muh pants pocket fer some change fer his nurse, takes her by the hand, picks up his pill bag, and starts fer his car.

Jist a cotton-pickin' second here! How come you treat ol' Gooseflaish like a kaing (which is hunky-dory by me), then turn around and do me like a yeller dawg?"

"Simple, simpleton: I have nothing against an *entire horse.* Even in Texas." So sayin,' he gits in his Rolls Royce and rolls.

"Gooseflaish," I says, "Yor Good Samitarium's done come and gone, so now I'm expectin' mine along any minit now." Shore nuff. Feller pulls up, out-o'-state license plates, gits out and does the thaing I wanted most. Skins off muh boots, which are flat a-killin' me.

"Ever so much obliged to ye, stranger, relievin' me like this."

"Relieving you, yes. Relieving you of those kaowboy boots."

"Hey, feller, them boots cost me two thousan' dollars!"

"Yeah, I know. Why the hell you think I stopped in the first place?"

Compared to the treatment us Texans receive from non-Texans, ol' Rodney Dangerfield gits incense burnt in his honor and his feet kissed.

Now, like most non-Texans, naturally nosey about Texans' businesses, you'll wanta know how I made out. And you know us Texans allus make out (at least make out like we're makin' out).

I have Gooseflaish kneel down where I can take my lariat rope off the horn straing. Then I fasten one end to the saddle horn, loop the other end to the first broke laig, take holt of a salt cedar tree trunk and have old Goose pull the laig back in place. Next I take out muh pocket knife and do extensive surgery— bone surgery. Time I finish, hit is way up in the night and I have to do 'tother laig in pitch dark, which ain't no excuse fer the lousy job I do. And just how lousy I have no idear till I git up next mornin and start to walk. Dogged if I hadn't set that last laig bass ackards. And ever' time I'd start to walk away *I would do the split!*

Well, Well, Well

The cowboy hero of tall tales is Pecos Bill, the wildest cowboy ever, who rode a cyclone, ditched the Rio Grande, and performed other such feats. Here Patterson tells a tall tale that rivals the outlandish Pecos Bill stories, and he attributes the deed to his archhero, Ace Reid. Here is a moralistic tale, as well, for Patterson uses the action to illustrate a couple of cow country rules.

Now, there's still a few people on this earth who ask me, "Who is Ace Reid?" Friends, askin', "Who is Ace Reid?" is like askin', "Who is George Washington?" This is not to say George Washington *is* the father of our country and Ace Reid *ain't*. However, as a sailor in the United States Navy, with a gal in ever' port, he done all he could. Too, George Washington *could not* tell a lie, whereas Ace Reid *could*, *will*, and *does*. However, all the thaings Ace Reid has said ain't nothin' compared to all the thaings Ace Reid has done. Here's what I mean:

By the late twenties us Texas cowboys had tamed Texas down to where it was too tedious to tolerate. So, reckless, restless cowboys sech as me and Ace migrated west lookin' fer greener pastures—not only *greener* but wider, wilder, westerner ones.

Well sir, we wind up on the widest, wildest, westernist cow outfit anywheres—the Cross S in Arizona (pernounced *Rzona*, decency ferbids me to pernounce *Cross S* the way them Cross S cowboys pernounces it).

In many areas, me bein' skeered to stay by myself and all—wasn't but twenty-one years old at the time—they leave me at headquarters; and Ace, being too bashful around people, is carried on out to a lonesome line camp called Horse Camps—*horse camps* because hit's where they keep their remuda of cow ponies—one hundred seventy-five head.

"Reid," says the boss, "Knowin' how ringy you Texas cowboys are about takin' o'ders, I ain't about to shoot you any pills . . . jist a couple o' suggestions: One: I'd be ever so much obliged to ye if you'd fix up the fence around that old dry well out by the horse corrals. And see that big dun horse yonder, the one tryin' to gnaw down the barn door? That's ol Uncle. He's yore night horse—which still leaves you one hundred seventy-three head to pick yore string from . . . "

"Whadda ye mean, one hundred seventy-three head? One from one hundred seventy-five leaves one hundred seventy-four in my arithmetic."

"Mine too," says the Cross S Boss, "which braings me to suggestion number two. You ain't to ride that Roman-nose roan yonder under no circumstances—by no means."

Seein' Ace's mouth curl down and his fists come up, the boss says, "Please, in fact, make that *purty please.*"

As it turns out, Ace wouldn't a rode the roan on a bet, on a dare, or a bended-knee plea. Uncle turns out as good a all-around cowhorse as Ace is a all-around cowboy. He is the first night horse Ace ever seen that you didn't have to shut a gate on or hem up to ketch.

If Uncle does have a fault—if sech it could be called—it's an addiction to dried apples, whereas Ace hates the damn thaings. As a consequence, he feeds Uncle a hatful of dried apples ever' night, . . . and ever' mornin' the old pony reciprocates with an even dozen fraish ones stacked neatly at Ace's front door.

In fack, Ace indulges Uncle with dried apples to the extent that the old pony takes down with colic, forcin' Ace to rope out another mount—the Roman-nosed-roan—naturally. Be damned if anybody is gonna tell Ace Reid what he can or cain't do or what he *cain't* or *ain't* gonna ride. As a gesture of contempt and a indication of *muy mucho macho*, instead of saddlin' the roan inside the corral and toppin' him off—as a safety measure, Ace leads him outside, saddles him, and steps immediately upstairs. When he does, ol' Roany goes up with him, wheels in midair, rears straight up and falls over backards and commences fallin' in that damn well. Ace goes along fer the ride. Since the age of four, Ace Reid had never went anywhere's afoot—and damned if he is gonna start now.

Well sir, the fall kills ol' Roany outright but harms not a hair on our hero's head. However, this is not to say that Ace Reid is not in one hell of a fix—thirty-five feet straight down, thirty-five miles straight acrost a alkali flat to headquarters, and no chance of relief for at least thirty days.

But Ace Reid is not the type to set and fret—at least not yet—not until the old roan commences to smell and to swell—which still ain't bad—except it puts Ace in mind of them damned dried apples.

In any case, whilst the roan is layin' there a stainkin', Ace is settin' there a thainkin'. Purty soon he takes out his pocket knife, takes down his lariat rope and commences cuttin' it into varyin' lengths, each of which he then unravels into three strands, tyin' each one to his belt.

Purty soon buzzards commence settlin' in. Quick as one lights, Ace ties t'other end of a strand onto the bird's laig. Onct he harnesses enough buzzard power fer lift-off he commences, hollerin' and slappin' them birds in the face with his hat.

Well sir, I'll be a bigger liar than Tom Pepper—and he gits kicked outa hell fer lyin'—if them buzzards don't hoist our hero outa that hole smooooooooth as butter in a calf's eye.

Trouble is, them buzzards keep flappin' up, up, up till ol' Uncle down there looks like a ant. But does our hero fret? Not yet. Ace Reid would not fret on a bet. However, he finally sees fit to cut enough buzzards loose to bring the flight to a standstill—or rather a hangstill, where he hangs there a right smart while enjoyin' the view and the fraish air. "But man cannot live by view and fraish air alone." That's the Good Book's way of sayin' time to come back down to earth.

For a safe rate of descent Ace calculates leven' less buzzards—since hit taken ten fewer fer the standstill—so he cuts 'em loose and floats like a butterfly to earth.

Trouble is, he finds hisself seven mile from camp . . . and flat afoot—to a cowboy a fate worse than the frontier female's fate worse than death.

Why, oh why, didn't I leave well enough alone?" So sayin' our hero—all six foot and two hundred pound of him—bursts into tears.

Half a long, hot, dark night later we ketch sight of our hero limpin', lurchin', falterin', fallin' his last few steps to camp. All of a sudden he feels hisself fallin' further faster, said fall endin' in the loudest explosion ever to assail the year drum of man.

But most nigh as loud is our hero's lament, which went: "Well, hell, I have agin fell in this dad damn well."

The Gawd-awful explosion is ol' Roany bustin' when Ace lands on top of him. To say that Ace and ol' Roany stirs up a staink is on the order of referin' to the Pacific Ocean as damp!

Let it not be said that our hero is not in another hell of a fix—amend that to hell of a mess—as you can guess. Same scene, same settin', same sad situation—only worse. Although ol Roany is still layin' there a stainkin,' Ace ain't settin' there a thainkin' . . . impossible to thaink in sech a staink. All our hero can do is pray—which he does:

"Hit is me, O Lord, *a-standin' in the need of prayer*. This time don'st thou even try to send them buzzards, fer I know they won't come—and cain't say as I blame them. But do do somethin'. Let there be light—if nothin' else—so's I kin see my way out of the staink. To the Lord—only a minute, but to Ace a thousand years. But eventually daylight does appear and with it a face framed in the top of the well.

"Well, well, well," says the face to Ace.

"You don't have to remind me. I know where the hell I'm at. Drop me a rope," says Ace—to the face.

"So you rode the roan."

"Damn wham you, drop me yer rope."

"Promise to give me a four-hundred-yard head start? Ah ain't droppin' you no rope. I'm droppin' you somethin'better'n a rope. Hit's faster. Looky here."

Ace looks up into the face and sees the fangs, and forkedy tongue of the rustiest-lookin', raunchiest-soundin' rattlesnake ever to clabber the blood of man.

"Look out below. I'm a droppin' the son of a buck," which he does, which Ace meets halfway up on his way out. By the time Ace gits out, gits up, and gits six shots off, the Cross S boss is done out of pistol shot range—but not out of yearshot, and hollers back: "Try this on the next feller, Reid. Hit'll brain 'em outta there ever time."

Glancin' down fer some rocks to throw—"*Great good gawda-nutty!*" Draped acrost his neck with hits fangs hooked in the right side of the waist band of Ace's britches and hits rattles tucked under his left suspender is that dad-damn rattlesnake!

Next thing Ace knows, he is five mile from camp and still runnin'. Strong. Next thing Ace knows, he don't know a *damn* thing. When he comes to hisself he is stretched 'longside a chaparral bush with the rattlesnake stretched 'longside of him. Hit takes the right stuff shore nuff for Ace to stuff six shells into his gun, which he empties into the head of the snake. Now he discovers hit is jist a rattler's hide stuffed with grass and rattleweed seeds—a fake snake. Ace Reid has been had and had bad; and, boy howdy, is he mad! But mad ain't in it compared to when he discovers he is within fifteen steps of where the buzzards set him down this morning—and seven miles from camp!

He w'rastles one more cotteridge in his gun with which to kill hisself. But on the prod as he is, he realizes hit will take at least three slugs to bring hisself down. But jist as he gets the hammer cocked back and a purty good bead on hisself, up puffs ol' Uncle to the rescue. Mistakin' Ace's screams fer whistles, he's been in after Ace all along but cain't ketch him.

Needless to say, ever'body lives happy ever afterwards—ol' Uncle on dried apples and Ace on fraish horse apples! Why not, if they're fraish, besides chuck full o' fiber, *high pro, low chlo,* and (from Ace Reid's own lips) "a dam sight tastier'n anythaing I ever cooked"?

A message to you would-be cowboys is two messages: 1) Allus obey at least one order from yore boss—say like fixin' up the fence around a old dug well. 2) Allus disobey a urge to disobey the old cow country safety measure of saddlin' up in a corral, then leadin' an old pony up a step or two before steppin' upstairs—and to hell with that *muy mucho macho* image.

Baxter Black

Baxter Black is unique among contemporary cowboy humorists. He understands the life and work of cowboys because he has worked alongside them. He is also a college-trained veterinarian. He has therefore seen more phases of the livestock industry than an average working cowboy could. Raised in New Mexico, he has long been associated with the livestock and agricultural industries. A nonpracticing veterinarian, Black writes a weekly newspaper column called "On the Edge of Common Sense," in which he often humorously depicts cowboy life, especially its conflict with more conventional facets of modern urban life. He has written eight collections of his poems and stories including his latest *Coyote Cowboy Poetry* (1986), *Croutons on a Cow Pie* (1988) and *The Buckskin Mare* (1989), all available through his Coyote Cowboy Company, Brighton, Colorado.

Black's books are amply illustrated by Don Gill, Bob Black, Dave Holl and other friends including Ace Reid.

 ## The Vanishing Breed?

They call 'em a vanishing breed.
They write books and take pictures and talk like
    they're all dyin' out
Like dinosaurs goin' to seed.
But that's my friends yer talkin' about.

Like Tex from Juniper Mountain.

COW POKES

By Ace Reid

"You got in there, you dang old coyote bait, now come on out.

He carved out a way of life where only the toughest
    prevail.
He's fifty-seven an' countin',
His sons now follow his trail.

And Mike who still ain't got married.
At home in the seat of a saddle, a sagebrush
    aristocrat.
I reckon that's how he'll be buried;
A'horseback, still wearin' his hat.

There's Bryan, Albert, and Floyd,
Cowmen as good as the legends to whom their
    livelihood's linked,
Who'd be just a little annoyed
To know they're considered extinct.

Some say they're endangered species
Destined to fade into footnotes like ropes that never
    get throwed.

To that I reply, "Bull Feces!"
They're just hard to see from the road.

 Crossbred Stew

The steer that topped the show this year was partly
    Chianina.
The bull that threw the biggest calf was partly
    Simmental.
The carcass class was swept away by three-eighths
    Limousiners.
The Gelbvieh cross was judged the best in this year's
    overall.

The feedlot men like Piedmontese to feed as
    crossbred critters
Or any kind of cloven hoof that shows some part
    Charolais.
A Salers cross or Tarentaise that's half or quarter
    blooded
Or maybe half breed Longhorn calves or partly
    Murray Grey.

The Brahma breeders took a bull and made Santa
    Gertrudis
They built a Brangus with a cross and found out
    what to do.
They stirred the pot a couple times and made
    Beefmaster heifers.
Descendants of *Bos Indicus* are now cross Bramer
    stew.

We like exotic crosses in the feedlot and the show
    ring.
What's happened to the Angus and their Hereford
    counterpart?
They may not get top billing though the question
    still remains
If they're only part exotic, then what's the other
    part?

Hello, I'm from the Government . . . I'm Here to Help You

Mr. President, I guess we know you mean well
When you brag about the crops that we all raise
We can hold our heads up high when you talk of
    apple pie
And the prairies where our white face cattle graze.
When our beef cows finally started making money
You applied a price freeze for your next campaign
Then you lent us extra cash to plant wheat and
    succotash
Then slapped the old embargo on our grain.

There are programs to inspect each farmer's business
Be he milking cows or growing pinto beans
Our soil has been conserved and our wildlife is
    preserved
There's civil servants posting quarantines
We're required to fill out forms beyond all reason
From pesticides to predator control
From fertilizer use to the children we produce
The bureaucrats are always on patrol.

You tell us that we need your interference
Without your help you say we'd be a mess
We owe our lives to you, or, at least, you say we do
Not counting OSHA and the I.R.S.
But I think that we could feed us and our neighbors
With less help from your Washington machines
All we need is sun and rain, so I ask you, Don't
    complain
When your mouth is full of good ol' pork and beans.

The government should have three sacred duties
If Constitution guarantees prevail
To help us all survive; stay the hell out of our lives,
Protect our shores, deliver us the mail.
I appreciate the help that you've been giving
I'd even like to thank our Congressman
But please leave me alone, I can make it on my own
I've had all of your help that I can stand.

The Cow Committee

Once upon a time
    At the start of all creation
Angels sat upon a cloud.
    An odd conglomeration
Of buckaroos from near and far
    But not there from the city.
Their job; to build a brand new beast.
    They were the Cow Committee.

"Now me, I'd like some floppy ears,"
    Suggested Texas Jake.
"Floppy ears would freeze plum off
    On the Powder or the Snake!"
"Up north we need some curly hair,"
    Said Colorado Bill,
"Hide that's tight and hair that's thick
    To ward against the chill."
"Hold yer horses, one and all,"
    Said Omaha Eugene,
"Nebraska needs a fleshy cow;
    A real corn machine!"
"She'd waste away!" cried Tucson Bob,
    "What we need's a hump.
One who'll live on tumbleweeds
    And run from clump to clump."

"How 'bout horns?" said Oakdale Pete.
    "Don't need 'em in Des Moines."
"We'll make some with and some without
    And some with tenderloins."
"Some with sheaths that drag the grass
    And some so dadgum tall
To hear her calf down on the ground
    She'd have to place a call!"

"I'd like'm roan," said Shorthorn Mike.
    "No, black," said Angus Tink.
"White or red," said Hereford Hank,
    "I'd even take 'm pink!"

"Whatever suits you tickles me,"
   Said Juan from Mexico.
"I second that," said Crossbred Jack,
   "Just make 'em so they grow."
They made some white. They made some blue.
   They made some orange and spotted.
They never made a green one
   But they made'm tall and squatted.
In every shape and every size
   But no one had decided
How to make the perfect cow;
   On that they were divided.

This went on for days and days,
   In fact, it never ended.
Each time they reached some middle ground
   The project was amended.
They still meet from time to time
   And argue with their leaders.
The Cow Committee carries on . . .
   They're now the purebred breeders.

 **A Rider, A Roper, and a
Hell'uva Windmill Man**

Have you ever been out checkin' cows and makin'
   windmill rounds
   In late November right after a snow?
And up against the fence line and piled in the draws
   Drifts are humped up, clouds are hangin' low.

The wind cuts through your jacket and your seat
   upon the horse
   Is the only part of you that's kinda warm.
You been all through the pasture and you haven't
   seen a cow;
   Then lookin' back up north you see the storm.

You look down in the bottom from your perch upon
   the rise

And hear the cows abawlin' 'fore you see
It don't take long to figger, that damn windmill goin'
    wild
    The pin's sheared off, the blades are spinnin' free.

You fight your way up through the bunch and see
    the water tank.
    It's dry except for half an inch of ice.
You cock your head up skyward whil'st holdin' on
    yer hat
    And what you see makes any man think twice.

The sucker rod has dropped down in the casing all
    the way
    My trouble's just beginnin', I can see.
The pin has broke in two and the gears have slipped
    theirselves
    And the brake has come unhooked, oh, mercy me!

So I start up that ol' ladder with the rungs all slick
    with ice,
    My big ol' clumsy mittens on my hands.
I'm steppin' mighty careful 'cause this windmill's
    real old
    And there ain't no doctor waitin' in the stands.

I'm inchin my way up where I intend to catch the
    brake
    And the sound I hear sends shivers down my
    track:
It's the scream of someone dyin' or a railroad train
    up close
    Or a rabbit when you shoot and break his back.

It's the blades of that ol' windmill just a'singin' in
    the wind;
    It's scary, brother, and I can tell you that!
I poke up through the platform just to take a little
    peek,
    And the vane comes swingin' round and swats
    my hat.

Then I git up there behind it and I'm hangin' on fer
    life
    It's the only time you'll ever hear me pray.

And any windmill ridin' cowboy'll tell ya, it's fer
    sure,
    He'd rather ride a mustang any day!

I start back down to set the brake and on the
    thirteenth rung
    The nails pull theirselves outt'a the pine.
I slip and fall through twelve, and then eleven, come
    on ten!
    And catch myself when I hit number nine.

I'm shakin' when I hit the ground and try the brake
    real slow.
    It works, oh, hallelujah, saved again.
But I got to git down to the shop and bring the
    pulley back
    To pull the rod and git another pin.

I'll git 'er fixed this evening and the cows'll be
    content.
    I'll check the other windmills ridin' in.
And hope they'll all be workin' like Aeromotor says
    they should—
    I don't think I can go through this again.

I've worked a lot of ranches where the windmill
    reigned supreme;
    They might be testy like a pregnant wife
Or good as gold and never give a man a minute's pain.
    But I've never seen a new one in my life!

Nothin' gives me greater pleasure than a windmill
    workin' right,
    An oasis in the middle of an island.
Some may stop and praise its bounty, pumpin' water
    every pull
    But me, why I just ride on by, a'smilin'.

 In Defense of the Chicken

*In a health fad diet conscious culture, to some chicken has
become the most desirable protein source available. This*

intense interest in two-legged fowls has worked to the detri-
ment of the red meat industry, particularly cattle. Black
touches a sensitive nerve here because many cattlemen see the
chicken as a threat to the cattle business. No one doubts the
intelligence level of the chicken, just as most cowboys do not
doubt the intelligence level of bovines. This poem touches that
sensitive nerve that lies between humor and pathos.

Everyone says they love chicken,
  Ambrosia sent from above;
But nobody loves a chicken
  A chicken ain't easy to love.

It's hard to housebreak a chicken,
  They just don't make very good pets;
You might teach one bird imitations,
  But that's 'bout as good as it gets.

Mentally, they're plum light-headed,
  And never confused by the facts.
That's why there's no seeing-eye chickens,
  Guard chickens, or trained-chicken acts.

And everything tastes like chicken,
  From rattlesnake meat to fried bats;
It has anonymous flavor,
  I figger they're all Democrats.

Some say this ignoble creature
  With his intellect unrefined
And lack of civilized manners
  Has little to offer mankind.

But let me suggest, the chicken
  Had two contributions to make:
The first was the peckin' order,
  The second, the chicken fried steak.

 **The Oyster**

Oysters come from the ocean, right? But to many a cowboy
cut off far from the ocean and its products, the only oyster he
knows is called the prairie oyster or Rocky Mountain oyster

*(calf testicles). This poem plays on this confusion, and the
naive young woman who gets the best of the cowboy.*

The sign upon the cafe wall said OYSTERS: fifty cents.
"How quaint," the blue eyed sweetheart said, with
   some bewildermence,
"I didn't know they served such fare out here upon
   the plain?"
"Oh, sure," her cowboy date replied, "We're really
   quite urbane."

"I would guess they're Chesapeake or Blue Point,
   don't you think?"
"No m'am, they're mostly Hereford cross. . . and
   usually they're pink.
But I've been cold, so cold myself, what you say
   could be true
And if a man looked close enough, their points
   could sure be blue!"

She said, "I gather them myself out on the bay
   alone.
I pluck them from the murky depths and smash
   them with a stone!"
The cowboy winced imagining a calf with her
   beneath,
"Me, I use a pocket knife and yank'em with my
   teeth."

"Oh, my," she said, "You animal! How crude and
   unrefined!
Your masculine assertiveness sends shivers up my
   spine!
But I prefer a butcher knife too dull to really cut.
I wedge it in on either side and crack it like a nut.

I pry them out. If they resist, sometimes I use the
   pliers
Or even Granpa's pruning shears if that's what it
   requires!"
The hair stood on the cowboy's neck. His stomach
   did a whirl.
He'd never heard such grisly talk, especially from a
   girl!

"I like them fresh," the sweetheart said and laid her
    menu down
Then ordered oysters for them both when the waiter
    came around.
The cowboy smiled gamely, though her words stuck
    in his craw
But he finally fainted dead away when she said, "I'll
    have mine raw."

 The #2 Hairball

*The livestock business is certainly not an easy one because
cattle are plagued with the same kinds of ailments as humans are. In the following poem, Black comments on the
chronically ill animal that refuses to get well. It is animals
such as this that eat into the profit margin of the rancher
and feed lot operator.*

Ever buy one of those feeders
    That never seems to get well?
Right off the truck to the sick pen
    Straight from receiving to hell.

They're common. Each semi load's got one
    'Specially if they're from a sale.
I call'em a Number 2 Hairball,
    They're fluffy, but thin as a rail.

They look like those two day old cornflakes
    That stick to the side of the bowl.
Pot bellied, wormy and drippin'
    From every unplugable hole.

His muzzle's as wide as a suitcase,
    His tail comes down to his heels,
His hide's as dry as a Baptist bar,
    The last brand still hasn't peeled.

You treat'em for weeks with your potions
    With everything Doc recommends

But sixty days later he still gets his mail
   Addressed to the hospital pen.

Where do these chronics all come from?
   I've had some time to reflect.
There's a purebred herd of'em somewhere,
   At least that's what I suspect.

A place where animal science
   And Doctor Frankenstein meet.
Where the characteristics they breed for
   Are same ones you try to treat.

Like, only one lung ever works right.
   The cough is just part of the deal
And scours is standard equipment
   Plus footrot that never will heal.

No matter which treatment you try out
   You're confused at every attempt.
"Cause one hundred four point seven
   Is really their normal temp!

So you keep pumpin' medicine in'em
   'Til the drug bill is high as the sky
Yet they never completely recover
   But the bloody buggers won't die!

Now, of course, I'm makin' this all up.
   No chronic cow breeder's been caught.
But if I was a medicine maker. . .
   I just might give it some thought.

SAM BROWN

Sam Brown is a fulltime cowboy as well as a genuine cowboy poet. His work on the Quien Sabe Ranch near Adrian in the northern Texas Panhandle and on other ranches across the West has provided much of the inspiration for his poetry, some cheerfully humorous and some ironic. Brown was one of only a handful of Texas poets invited to recite in 1987 and 1988 at the Cowboy Poetry Gathering in Elko, Nevada and at the Texas Cowboy Poetry Gathering in Alpine, Texas.

Born and reared in Amarillo, Brown holds a bachelor's degree in animal science from West Texas State University (1967) and earned a second bachelor's degree, in education, from the same school in 1983. He served in 1969–1970 in Vietnam and has also taught school briefly.

Brown's cowboying goes back to the days of his youth. He was working on the massive Matador Ranch at the time it was split into smaller spreads and recalls that the first wagon he went out on was with the Trujillo Land and Cattle Company in 1956. In addition, he worked on the Masten Ranch as well as other ranches in the Texas Panhandle.

Brown also has considerable experience as a rodeo cowboy. He joined the Professional Rodeo Cowboys Association at age nineteen and spent almost fifteen years on the rodeo circuit, competing mainly in the summers and spending his winters working on ranches.

Brown is also a novelist. His first novel, *The Long Season*, was issued by Walker Books in 1986. He is working on another novel as well as writing poetry.

When Cowboys Sniff a Cork

Other pieces in this collection comment on the cowboys long-standing tendencies to imbibe spirits. When cowboys break the rules and drink on the job, disaster frequently results. Such is the case in the following piece, which Sam Brown based on an actual experience he had with a crew of cowboys working cattle on winter wheat fields south of Hereford. The disaster is predictable and the humorous view not unexpected.

Now, ever'one knows that when cowboys sniff a
    cork they become a rowdy band,
But I hope to show that's nothin' compared to what
    can happen if that cork itself gets out of hand.

This happened down below Hereford on the Masten
    wheatfield farm
That was nestled between two little stores full of
    bottled charm.
I've done a lot of calculatin' as to what exactly was
    the date,
And I'm pretty well convinced that it was in the
    dim, dark year of 1978.

We were shippin' yearlin's to town that day I do
    recall
That had been weaned on the Masten Ranch that
    very preceding fall.
The Masten bunch was there, of course, and some
    neighbors, and a day hand or two
And three or four fellers from Hereford met us there
    and rounded out our crew.

It was around the first of March, and the day was
    terrible cold.
The wind was howlin' from the north and cut right
    through our clothes.
That cussed wind ached our ears and made our
    fingers stiff and numb,
And a heavy scab of clouds withheld any promise of
    the sun.

"Whew, my doctor told me if I didn't quit drinkin' it would kill me, and it nearly did today!"

Now when it comes to size—well, that's one thing
    wheat fields haven't got.
Why, most outfits have more country in their water
    lots.
And so it was that right after first light we had that
    first one rounded up,
And all the cattle the pens could hold were bein'
    loaded on the trucks.

Me and a couple of others were a holdin' up the
    rest,
And I was wonderin' how outta all the things I
    coulda done I ever figured cowboyin' to be the
    best.
Then I saw a pickup blarin' through the morn',
And behind the wheel was Emmett Duke a-smilin'
    up a storm!

Now, Emmett was on a medical mission, and he
    didn't tarry long.
But he left behind some tonsil-tonic, the kind that's
    cheap an' strong.
Now, you may have heard tell of sippin' whiskey,
    where a little gives you bliss;
Well, this stuff was in a gallon jug with a mouth as
    wide as your fist!

Right off, some puncher made a frisby outa that lid
    and sent 'er sailin' south,
And then that jug went like a cowboy lives—that is,
    from hand to mouth.
Why, the neck of that thing was so big any drink
    was a double,
And that's when I began to think that our shippin'
    day was in for trouble.

Now, I aim to keep this record sure 'nough straight
    'n true,
So I'll have to admit I had my own little drink—or
    was it two?
But *only* to get rid of the vile stuff as quickly as
    possible—I hope you understand
That *I* did it for the good of the company, 'cause I
    was a company man.

Well, that bottle made the rounds another time or
    two,
And somewhere along the way about two inches of
    Wm. Penn cigar was added to the brew.
Now to me, that thing looked a big ol' black pickled
    leech,
But them fellers kept a drinkin' and a strainin'
    through their teeth.

Then to one of those little stores on their horses a
    couple of 'em did run,
And I'll swear, I never seen so many freezin'
    cowhands so quickly havin' fun.
The owner of the place didn't hanker much to have a
    horse come through his door,
But they came to buy some whiskey, and he sold 'em
    all they could afford.

That second field was gathered in a least artistic sort
    of way—
I mean, it's not something I'd care to witness
    ever'day.
Oh, part of the crew was sittin' up straight and doin'
    the best they could,
But then part of 'em was a havin' trouble just a
    stayin' in their woods.

But before long we had the cattle bunched right
    where they belonged.
And some of the boys was weakenin', but others
    were goin' strong.
The gate the cattle had to go through was about
    twelve foot wide, an' that's hardly wide enough
To accommodate several hundred head of drunken-
    driven yearlin' stuff.

Those cattle were goin' through that gate like grain
    through a goose,
But them drunks kept a screamin' like Comanches
    on the loose
There was a wreck in the makin', and it didn't take
    long to make; Some cattle started peelin' back an'
    the fence began to break.

Now, I can't repeat exactly just what the bossman
    said,
But I'll tell you his ire was all stirred up and his face
    was awful red.
He didn't need to worry, though, 'cause when the
    spill took place those drunks were on their toes—
They went to shakin' out their loops an' launchin'
    UFOs.

I'm here to state that ropin' was a mess.
Why I've seen buckets of water throwed with more
    finesse.
Some of those cattle were run so far they went to
    cluckin' like a hen,
And some of 'em just gave it up and come turned
    themselves back in.

Yeah, a lot of fence was taken out and a lot of cattle
    shackled down,

But by and by the trucks were loaded and a rollin'
   into town.
About that time the farmer on the place came a
   drivin' up
A-draggin' a rattly wooden trailer behind his pickup
   truck.

"I got one here—where do you want it?" he said just
   as pleased as punch.
Well now, I naturally sorta figured he had a yearlin'
   that had escaped from our little bunch.
"If it's a steer over here, and a heifer over yonder,"
   those were the words I said.
Now, how was I supposed to know he'd picked up a
   zonked-out cowboy from the bottom of a lister
   bed?

The last time I saw that gallon whiskey jug, it was
   cradled in the lovin' arms of one of those
   Hereford men,
And it was down to an inch of slobber and a limber
   Wm. Penn.
They never found that lid, but I think them fellers
   loved it fine.
Which brings me right back to what I was sayin'
   when I began this cock-eyed rhyme—

Oh, cowboys sniffin' a cork might spoil a shippin'
   day,
But just wait till you see what can happen if that
   cork gets throwed away!

 **Dear Mister Hollywood Movie
   Producer**

*The dream of being a silver screen cowboy has appealed to
several generations of youngsters and adults alike. Here is a
piece which shows a cowboy's awareness of that image as
well as a slight reluctance to take on the new job if it does
not pay at least a hundred dollars a month more than the
seven hundred dollars he is presently making as a cowboy.
Measuring Hollywood film stardom against his good ranch
job is a very real consideration for this cowboy.*

I understand you've been lookin' for a new star
Who can make both of you rich and carry you far.
Well, call off the hounds, your search is o'er,
I've found that feller you've been lookin' for.

This comin' attraction of the sliver screen,
So bashful, witty, and mean;
This man so handy with rope, woman, and horse—
This feller is . . . *I*, of course.

I've enclosed a picture of myself so *you* can see
Just why it is I'm so high on me.
Now I guess you saw at very first glance
How I was standin' there in that classic stance
With one hip kinda throwed outa socket,
And a thumb hung three in my old britches pocket.
And I'm sure you didn't miss that glint in my eye
    that made you feel
Like you were seein' the desert sun reflectin' off
    tempered steel.

And no doubt you're thinkin' right now that it's
    strange
How I have the best features of some of the biggest
    names.
Like those slim and sexy Robert Redford hips,
That Thomas Magnum mustache—and those Eddie
    Murphy lips!

Now, there's another picture taken at the wagon in
    '83.
Of those three naked fellers, the one on the right is
    me.
We were takin' a bath in a stock tank, and for those
    nude scenes? I thought you should know
That my tan don't go just *ever'where*, and my legs are
    kinda bowed.
They got like that from punchin' cows since I was a
    kid,
And that ugly tooth right there in front is somethin'
    an old cow once did.

While I'm on it I just as well tell about this arm that
    won't straighten all the way,
And there's a few hairs in my sexy chest that're
    startin' to turn gray.

And, oh yeah—sometimes when I get excited? I
    stutter and get my tongue in a bind,
Just thought for the love scenes you might wanta
    keep that in mind.
Now, as for some possible image buildin' publicity
    scandal regarding women,
I am enclosing a notarized account by a close
    personal acquaintance of us goin' swimmin'.

Well, I reckon that's all.
I'll be waitin' right here for your call.
Now I'll come to Hollywood for eight hundred a
    month but not one dollar less than that
'Cause I'm already drawin' seven right where I'm at.

And I'm takin' it for granted that you'll furnish my
    beef of course.
And it'll be *another* fifty if I have to bring my own
    horse.
By the way, I'm not goin to ride *any* horses that will
    pitch or duck off 'cause I've got a confession—
If I wasn't already tired of them you couldn't drag
    me into this starrin' profession.

In closing, I'll just say: Send cash for fare,
You can thank me out there.
Bet you can't wait to get *me* in town

Yours most humbly, Sam Brown

 A Worthless Old Cow

*There are many stories of outlaw cattle and horses. "The
White Steed of the Prairie" is such a piece about a mustang
that ran wild on the Texas plains, and "That Spotted Sow"
is Texas poet Carlos Ashley's version of the motif applied to
a renegade sow in the Texas hill country. Here is Brown's
version of that tale, skillfully adapted to the Panhandle
ranges that Brown knows well.*

She was born on a cold, black night with the
    mercury hung on six degrees.
The delivery room attendants were decked out in

COW POKES

By Ace Reid

"Naw, we ain't shippin em, we're just practicin loadin em!"

long, prime fur, hopin' for some veal their hunger pangs to ease.

The nursery was a steep cut-bank, frozen sand a bed,
While pellets of sleet from a hard winter sky knitted the cap for her little head.

She was of the Hereford breed and some unnamed seed from which wild things grow,
And the canyons, the rocks, and lonesome would be the only home she'd ever know.
If she wasn't born on the hook, her disposition was surely never mild,
And after being orphaned at a month of age, she grew up like the wayward wind—alone and wild.

With her mother's final breath she was christened an outlaw, and she made one for all she was worth.

The only law she knew and obeyed was the cold,
    hard law of the earth.
But outlaw milk from unguarded teats hones the
    senses keen,
And she grew up dogied and she grew up hard—
    but she grew up lean and mean.

Now, stolen milk is best at growin' out horns, and
    that's about all that grew,
So five-hundred pounds of hide and horns is what
    she was at two.
With a dose of luck and lonesome livin' we missed
    her four gatherin's in a row.
So as a three, she was still as wild and full-eared as a
    mule deer doe.

She didn't take a bull till three nor calve till four,
Though in the next eight years she'd scatter five
    more.
But that kind of calf-raisin' will never do, according
    to what the text books say—
Why, she'd have to have her estrus synchronized, or
    it just wouldn't pay!

But though some people don't know it, there's a few
    places not yet gathered by computer chips and
    charts,
Places where the only thing that matters is the size
    of the will and the heart,
Where wild ones can be born and live, and live and
    die,
And never be seen or tallied by technology's silicon
    eye.

She was one of those kind, I know you've seen 'em,
    with a pair of horns that set real high,
And freckles on her face, and a red neck, and one
    ring eye.
And I never seen her carrying' any flesh, stayed thin
    as an old rail.
Though, you know, usually about all we'd ever see
    would be her disappearin' tail.

We had her gathered one time, the fall she was
    probably five;

She made a circle all the way around the roundup
   and then come out on the fly.
And she wasn't flyin' solo neither, 'cause she
   brought along a passel of friends.
It looked for a while we might spill the whole
   shebang but we finally got everything—but her—
   turned back in.

And then I jumped her one mornin' as she was
   grazin' on a flat.
I built right to her and went to knockin' out her
   tracks.
Boy, ever'thing felt good and I *knew* that old
   worthless thing was mine.
Why, I didn't see any way to keep her outa my
   twine.

I took one more swing and it sure felt good
Just knowin' in a second she'd be anchored to my
   wood.
My old loop shot out like a hawk on the dive,
And when I drew 'er up around those horns, *Man
   Alive!*

That old thang snorted and bawled and pawed at
   her head,
While I was layin' it behind her, fixin' to put her to
   bed.
I screwed way down and got ready for the jerk,
When the next thing I knew I was spurrin' the dirt!

It wasn't nothin' but bad luck and a badger hole that
   brought me an' my old pony down,
But it was her nine-hundred pounds of snort and
   scorn that mashed us in the ground.
She wiped her nose on my behind as I tried to get
   up,
And then my stupid horse was on top of me, just a
   kissin' his butt!

Yeah, it was darn good wreck and probably fun to
   see,
But right then and there it was pretty serious stuff to
   me.
I must've took a hoof behind the ear, 'cause out
   went the lights.

And when the circuit came back on again, there
   wasn't a creature in sight!

Well, I limped and I hunted and I found my horse
   along about dark
With my broken rope a-draggin' and my saddle
   peeled down to the bark.
For two weeks I promised that old worthless cow
   how she was gonna die,
How I'd eat her liver raw and thumb out both her
   eyes.
And I even took it right to the Lord, too, about his
   grievous mistake
Of buildin' a critter like a cow instead of some new
   kind of snake.

I guess the next time I saw her was about two years
   later, and I could tell she was goin' down hill by
   then.
You know, time grinds away at everything, and she
   was always ground pretty thin.
I knew she was runnin' then from something she
   couldn't escape,
'Cause nothin' eludes the slow, sure hand of fate.

No, I don't pretend to know the scheme of things,
   how they come to be or why,
But after all she'd conquered—alone of course—that
   old thing just laid down and died.
Her last rites were held at sundown in a place lonely
   and still.
The sermon was rendered by an old coyote, howlin'
   from a hill.
Then critters gathered 'round and feasted on her
   carcass, 'cause that's the way it's done
Past the end of the pavement when a wild one's final
   race is run.

Looking at her life from this end, a college grad
   might say, "In the modern world, boys, this kind
   of cow won't do."
But us cowboys? . . . Hell, old cow, we take our hats
   off to you.
And if there's some rimrock country in glory where
   things like us go when our livin' on earth is done,

Then we'll be chasin' you again, old worthless cow,
   'cause your spirit and ours are one.

 Dear Larry King . . .

*The following epistolary poem indicates Brown's awareness
of who and what he is, as well as of his literary milieu.
Larry King, a columnist and essay writer, echoed a widely
held belief that the cowboy is dead. Brown responds indig-
nantly but subtly about how his friends react to the notion
that they no longer exist. The reader can plainly see that the
cowboys don't have time to worry about King's observation
because they have to "jingle the horses" or get in their
mount's for the next day, are too busy working cattle to
worry about the opinions of one who would pronounce them
dead and gone.*

Author's Note:
*This poem is in answer to an article Larry King had in an
issue of T V Guide in which he said there were no more
cowboys in Texas. I centered the poem around a specific day
during the fall works in 1986. Everything in it is true,
except for the dialogue.*

You must be as smart and sharp as the cold north
   wind that blows.
Why, magazines pay to print what you write, so I've
   got to figure you know.
Now, Larry, most things you write about I don't
   know from Jack,
But one thing I read you said . . . well, it sort of took
   me back.
You said there weren't any cowboys in Texas, they'd
   all become extinct.
Now if that's the way it is, it is; but it made me stop
   and think.
It hit me all of a sudden while I was forkin' my kack
That things were plenty haywire, a great deal out of
   whack.
This was in the fall of the year, after the frost had
   nipped the sage,

And we were in the saddle before sunup and had
    been for days and days.
Had been, it seemed, in fact, the whole danged year
For no sooner is the spring work finished that the
    fall work is here.
No sooner than we get three thousand calves roped
    and drug to the fire
Than we gotta turn around and start gatherin 'em
    again—deliver 'em to some buyer.

Now this one is the Quien Sabe, cattle scattered over
    two-hundred-and-forty river-breaks sections;
Not any big deal I'll grant ya and probably not
    enough to impress ya,
But it's plenty to keep a man busy, what with that
    and startin' colts an' fixin' windmills and fence—
And, Larry, right there's where things get clabbered
    in my mind and start not makin' any sense.
We were oozin' along that mornin' listenin' to the
    coyotes howl when, like I said, it hit me all a
    sudden
That what I was thinkin' we were—well, you said
    we wasn't.
But I sure think we looked the part, and I guess I
    was fooled a lot
By sixteen pair of jinglin' spurs callin' cadence to our
    trot.
Sixteen horses and sixteen riders lookin' like runoffs
    from a Russell print,
Screwed way down in hand-made woods
    and . . . well, dang Larry, you shoulda seen it!

Then the drive leader dropped us off like drive
    leaders for a hundred years have done,
And after awhile we had five hundred pairs
    gathered, had 'em strung out towards the pens
    and was ridin' up some
When the fellers up in front had a little spill—some
    wild ones started duckin' behind 'em—
But, shoot, they knew what to do—they shook out
    their loops and went and twined 'em.
Jesse had an old fighter on his line when his bronc
    kissed his butt.
Jesse was planted deep enough to sprout, but he
    caught that bronc and climbed back up.

Then everything was penned, includin' them that
    had to be led,
And by late noon all the calves was stripped and
    separated, heifers culled and punchers fed.
Then them five hundred cows had to be culled and
    worked in dust you couldn't believe,
And after that the sun was slippin' its grip on the
    sky, and it was time to leave.

Us on the south side of the river had trailered to it
    and rode across in the mornin' black.
Then we'd gathered a lot of cows, worked 'em good
    and worked 'em right, and now we was crossin'
    back.
I'd been thinkin' on your words of wisdom, Larry,
    and it had made my day some glum,
And now I figured was as good a time as any to
    spring it on my chums.

But then I reconsidered, I wouldn't say nothin' yet,
I'd wait till it was safer, I mean, till after M. L. had
    loaded and left.
He's the feller that lives at George Tank Camp, and
    you can tell 'im if you want
That he ain't no cowboy . . . but, uh, I sure think I
    won't!

After M. L. was gone, I thought I'd tell ol' Frog and
    the Torrey Peak man.
"Hey, you all," I says, "I got something to tell you,
    so listen if you can."
I didn't see any reason to spare 'em, figured they
    weren't no better 'n me.
I says, "Larry King says we ain't cowboys, says
    there's none in Texas, don't you see."

Now Larry . . . I'm sure it wasn't nothin' other than
    the way *I* said it,
But Frog just grinned and said, "Whatever"; and
    Willie just grinned and spit!
Then Frog took off his leggin's, said, "See ya in the
    mornin'"; and he was gone,
And Willie said, "I gotta go, too. Gotta jingle the
    horses when I get home."

For, you see, the next day was just another—we'd
    be up way before the sun,
'Cause we still had a lot of cows to work before we'd
    be done.

So, you see, you've got a real problem, Larry—you,
    and not me.
You're words are in the cities and suburbs, but
    they're not out where they need to be.
Oh, but enough is enough, anyway I guess you
    know I'm playin' a game.
The truth is, Larry, I think all you know about
    cowboys is how to spell the name.
But maybe just spellin's enough for a writer, and you
    make your livin' at that.
If you really want to know about cowboys, though—
    you'd better go where they're at.
You gotta get off the farms and outta the cities; you
    gotta leave the pavement behind;
You gotta go to the breaks and canyons where the
    coyotes still howl at the stars that shine;
You gotta get away from people and the places they
    love to build and plow;
You gotta look on the rimrocked mesas and places
    that'll hide a wild cow.

For it's the wild and lonely places that call the men I
    know,
And you're not apt to see a one at Billy Bob's or a
    big-time rodeo.
You'll find 'em makin their livin' as best they know
    how
On way-out camps tendin' their country, startin'
    broncs and punchin' cows.

No, Mister King, you are wrong, and I don't hesitate
    to say
That the true story of the cowboy's passin' must wait
    some other day.
Oh, it may well be that some day the Texas cowboy
    will give his final yell,
But for now, thank God, the cowboy in Texas is alive
    and well!

The Wages of Sin

Cowboys are long on building reputation and holding it. In the following poem a cowboy has a dream of his severe punishment for breaking one of the rules of cowboying—turning away from a confrontation with an angry cow. The cowboy's pangs of conscience are quite real and only humorous to the outside observer, not to the man himself.

I was troubled by recent sin, and my heart was
    plenty sore,
And when I stepped inside my tepee at dusk to
    sleep, heavy was the burden that I bore.
Sometime later in restless sleep, I dreamed of
    headin' a cow from the brush
When my horse stepped into a gopher hole and sent
    me to hell in a rush.

I mean I dreamed I died! and hell is where I went
Though in my dream I tried and tried my grievous
    sin to repent.
But some sins just can't be erased, and the keeper of
    hell ain't blind
When he sees a feller transgress one of the rules of
    cowboy kind.

Now hell ain't one big holdin' pasture where *all* cull
    men go;
Why, how could it be when one man's sweet bread
    is another's sourdough.
And I guess you might be thinkin' that cowboy hell
    is full of horses too bad to ride,
And long, cold nights in a wet tepee while the wind
    howls outside.

But that's not what I dreamed as I dreamed of
    cowboy hell,
'Cause the hell boss met me at the headquarters gate
    and said, "Here forever and ever you shall dwell.
Now shuck off them chaps and spurs and don these
    shorts and sandals.

Gimme that rope and hoggin' string and take this
here shovel handle!"

Well, I did as I was bid, 'cause I knew my fate was
sealed.
I bowed my head and shed a tear as off came the
spurs from my heels.
"*Oh, please!*" I to the devil did plea. "It was the first
time I done it since I was a kid—"
"Enough! Enough!" the devil cried. "When a
puncher does this he's mine forever, and *you* did!
You likened yourself a cowboy but couldn't live up
to the name;
You broke the biggest rule of all, and now you're *out*
of the game.

From this moment on you're a cowboy no more and
are condemned to live forever by the sweat of
your brow.
Never again will you ever fork a horse and never
ever see cow.
From now throughout all eternity," the devil roared
and hid not his joy,
"You're a *Farmhand in Hell!* . . . so get to work, boy!

Dig me a furrow a million miles long, and it better
be straight and true;
And after that, I've about a million years of
machinery greasin' you can do!"
And then the devil tossed me the grease of hell,
But nothin' scares the hell out of a cowboy like
grease, and that's when I woke up with a yell!

Peekin' out my tepee flap I saw the bright stars o'er
head,
And then I heard the hoodlum rattlin' pots for the
cowboys to be fed.
I dressed and went to the wagon and waited for the
coffee to brew;
I sat there by myself, spinnin' a spur rowel, sure
'nough happy that dreams ain't true.
But when I went to roll a smoke, my joy it came to a
cease,
For there on my hand, dark as hell, was a spot
of . . . grease!!

I dashed to the water wagon, but to my horror and
    shame,
I found that nothin' would wash away that grease,
    and I'd wear it forever like a scarlet letter or mark
    of Cain!
Now it's there forever, but I'll keep it hid somehow,
And you would too, if this brand of shame from hell
    was on you . . .
For turnin' your horse's butt to a cow!

 What Would You Say?

*Salty language has long been one of the attributes of cowboy
life. To the question whether he had ever heard cowboys sing
songs in the 1920s and 1930s when he was cooking, Wor-
tham Key, a long-time west Texas ranch hand, responded,
"No, I never heard 'em sing. All I ever heard 'em do was
cuss." The following piece indicates that the cowboy may be
able to rationalize his speech as appropriate to the situation.*

What's that? You think cowboys are a vulgar lot and
    the way they talk is a shame?
Well, it's not their fault they cuss—*they're* not to
    blame.
It's not that they *want* to cuss and raise the ire of the
    gentle breed.
It's something they *have* to do—it's a habit born of
    need.
Okay, I'll show you . . .
Say you were on this camp alone and had a little old
    bunch of cows you needed to pen,
And by handlin' 'em easy, you was able to ooze 'em in.
And then say you're leanin' over to fasten the gate—
    without gettin' off your horse of course—
When *wham!* one of them cows you've been oozin'
    and easin' hauls off and rams your horse!
You scratch and claw and get upright when your
    horse breaks in two.
You waller him out a couple of jumps before he parts
    company with you.

Your flight's real nice, but your landin' gear's stuck.
You come in on your nose but you end belly up.
You lay there achin' and wonderin' what went
     wrong
When the cows crash the gate and head for parts
     unknown.
No, wait! Wait! *Then* you see your stupid horse has
     took off with the cattle,
And startin' to slip under his belly is your *brand new*
     saddle!
Oh, did I forget! Your pickup's on the other side of
     the trap two miles away!
Now, good fellow, just what would *you* say?
I guess it would be, as you stand up and pat the
     blood from your brow,
"My goodness! What a discerning chain of events
     started by that obstreperous old cow!"

★ 2 ★
Collectors' Items

LAWRENCE CLAYTON

Lawrence Clayton has been researching and writing about cowboy songs, cowboy life, literature, and history of the American West for the past fifteen years. He is author of several books including *Benjamin Capps and the South Plains: A Literary Relationship, Watkins Reynolds Matthews: A Biography*, and *Elmer Kelton* and is editor of a collection of Kelton's short stories. He also wrote *Clear Fork Cowboys* and *Ranch Rodeos in West Texas*, both about the lives and work of some of the men featured in the following stories. He began collecting these stories in 1983.

A native Texan, he has taught English in the public schools and has been at Hardin-Simmons University since 1968. He has taught folklore and literature of the American West and Southwest, as well as linguistics, language history, and medieval English literature. He has degrees from Stephen F. Austin State University, the University of North Texas, and a Ph.D. from Texas Tech University. A former president of the Texas Folklore Society, he has served as a member of the board of directors of the West Texas Historical Association, and in 1990, president of the Western Literature Association. He is a member of Western Writers of America. He is presently professor of English and Dean of the College of Arts and Sciences at Hardin-Simmons University.

 The Bull and the Motorboat

During the drought of 1984, Goat Island, offering several acres of grazing, was accessible by dry land, and cattle frequented the area. When rains began falling in the spring

128

COW POKES
By Ace Reid

"When I git ahold of that jet pilot he's gonna think a **herd**
of Brahma cattle run over him too!"

*of 1985, the cowboy in charge had to remove the cattle before
the water levels got up. But one particularly strong-minded
Brangus bull was determined to stay.*

The cowboy and a friend decided the time had come to get the bull
off the island. The water was, (in their own words) "saddle-
blanket-deep on a tall horse" as the two cowboys made their way
to the rugged island to get the outlaw back on the main part of the
ranch. Two hours later they had succeeded, but the interval proved
challenging to the temperament of the dedicated cowboys.

With a natural aversion to water, the bull was very reluctant
to undertake swimming the two-hundred-yard stretch of water.
After much hard riding, the two men finally had the bull going into
the water. At this point, however, modernity reared its ugly head—
a motorboat pulling a water skier headed through that section of the
lake, either oblivious of the men's efforts with the bull or just
to thwart the cowboys. The men suspected the latter. At any rate,
the motorboat convinced the bull to return to Goat Island, despite
the yells of the cowboys to the bull and not a few comments to
the aquatic travelers. The two men were about ready to give up, but
they decided to make one more effort before admitting defeat and
seeking help. After all, their pride was at stake, motorboat or no

motorboat. Each man gathered as many rocks as he could carry, and the two once more drove the bull down to the approach to the water and began to rock him heavily. This time the bull decided he had had enough, plunged into the water, and headed for the other shore to join the waiting cows.

 ## A Night Out in Austin

Not all of a cowboy's modern problems occur in the county. Here is what can happen when a couple of "innocent" cowboys want a look at the bright lights of town.

Two Central Texas cowboys were sent by the boss to a ranch just outside Austin to pick up a racehorse he had bought. Just before they left for the trip, the rancher said, "By the way, I traded a grain drill for a show heifer down in that same area. You boys pick that calf up as you come back." Well, the cowboys didn't think there would be anything to that—two cowboys versus one calf—and they easily agreed.

They drove from the ranch near Lampasas through Austin and loaded up the horse. Then they loaded the calf. Both of the animals were halter-broke, of course, and loaded easily, so there was no problem. They were so much ahead of schedule that the two cowboys decided they would like to stop off and try a little of that Austin night life. They knew that horse and show calf shouldn't stand in the trailer that long, but the older cowboy came up with a solution to the problem. He said, "My daughter lives in Austin and has a big backyard. We can just take these animals over there, unload them, and leave them in the backyard. They're both gentle, and that won't be a problem."

That part of the plan worked out fine. The difficulty was yet to come, and the two men were so unaware of it that they went out into the Austin night life and kicked up their heels until well past midnight. When they pulled up to the daughter's house to load the stock, they just didn't realize what was ahead of them. They loaded the horse first and experienced no difficulty at all in doing that. He must have been accustomed to night life. One of the cowboys simply led the horse into the trailer and tied it in the front. On the way out, he closed the gate in the middle of the trailer behind him. Then they started on the calf, and that is where the wreck occurred. Something had changed that animal's nature.

They didn't know whether it was the traffic or being left out of the night life, but when the first cowboy pulled on the lead rope, the calf responded with a vigorous butt of her head that broke three of the cowboy's ribs. The second grabbed the rope; and that startled the calf, causing it to lunge ahead and jerk the rope through the cowboy's hands, burning through his gloves in several places and warming his hands up to the point where he surely was uncomfortable. Feeling the pressure on the rope ease, the calf headed for the chain link fence around the yard and cleared that easily and headed for that downtown Austin night life, an idea taking on a new meaning to the two not-so-drunk cowboys.

Even though the men knew this racehorse was broken to ride, they doubted it was trained as a roping horse. And besides that, they had no saddle or rope with them, a pitiful condition for a cowboy. They were also afraid they might injure the horse. So here were two cowboys afoot in downtown Austin trying to corral a runaway heifer, which had an unerring sense of direction for night life—she headed for Sixth Street with the cowboys in hot pursuit. Flower beds and shrubs were not obstacles. Before long the local police became involved in the race, and eventually the runaway was cornered in downtown Austin and once again suddenly became gentle. The police looked suspiciously at the pair. The men quickly loaded her into the trailer and left. It was middle of the morning before they finally got back to the home ranch. The cowboys were a little bit uneasy about how the boss would respond to that, but the boss saw the humor in the situation and let it pass. After all, it was two cowboys out on the town; they had precedent for getting into trouble. The modern complications were not their fault.

 ## The Bulldozed Tree and the Bronc

Landowners today often have bulldozers come in and doze the brush down on their land to keep the plants from sapping the water away from the grass, which leaves a lot of tree roots sticking up. One cowboy learned the hard way about working around dozed-over trees.

This cowboy was riding a young horse that was pretty skittish anyway, and as he rode by the turned-up stump of one tree, that young horse switched his tail and happened to entwine it with a root sticking up out of the ground. Then the horse switched his tail back and put tension on that root, which was not stuck deep in the ground. It jerked loose and slapped the horse right in the rump. Well, the cowboy, unsuspecting that anything was going on, wasn't ready for the wreck. The first thing he knew, that horse had bucked out from under him and left him sittin' in the dirt, his pride and his posterior considerably wounded. The modern cowboy may have it easier in some ways, but there are hazards associated with modern life that make cowboying harder than it used to be.

 Wintertime Wrecks

Cold weather makes the cowboy's life harder, but he still has to get the work done. He takes his chances, which often turn sour on him, as these examples show.

A pair of cowboys calving heifers got into a bad situation directly related to bad weather during a February ice storm. A cold wind was blowing over a sheet of ice and snow that covered the ground. The two decided they would be better off in a four-wheel-drive pickup than on horseback, and things were going pretty well until they saw a heifer in trouble. They knew they had to rope her because she was too far from the pens to drive her in. One of them had a bright idea. He said to his friend, "You drive this pickup alongside her, and I'll rope her." It sounded like a good deal, so they decided to try it. The plan worked, but only to a point. One of the cowboys got into the back and tied his rope to the trailer hitch on the center of the bed of the truck, one of those used to pull gooseneck trailers. He got the rope on the heifer; but instead of just sulling at the end of the rope the way they thought she would, this heifer took off in a big circle in front of the truck. The first real clue they had that they were about to have a wreck came when the heifer ran in front of the truck from the right to left. Just then, the rope came up underneath that big California mirror on the right-hand side. Glass and pieces of metal went everywhere. When the rope came across the top of the cab, it snapped off the CB antenna without even slowing down and came on down the driver's side, taking the other mirror with it. When the heifer came on around the back of the truck, the cowboy had to do a dance to keep the rope from clearing him out. The bed of the truck was covered with ice; and the cowboy slipped and fell as the rope passed over him.

COW POKES By Ace Reid

"All right clumsy, now you're gonna have to re-set this
post and re-stretch the wire!"

All that wear and tear wasn't doing the cowboy or the truck a bit of
good, and it was even harder on the cowboy's lariat, which by this
time was frazzled in several places. The laughter of the cowboy in
the cab wasn't helping any either. The rope did hold, however, and
the two men finally got the heifer down and took care of the
problem. They had a lot of fun telling that one after they knew the
boss wasn't going to be mad for the damage to that pickup.

> *Regardless of the weather, cowboys are dedicated to their
> work, even if it means riding on the ice. Often, however, the
> bronc is not his only problem.*

An older cowboy was breaking out some horses on a ranch, a chore
assigned to one or more of the men, who usually takes pride in it.
This cowboy got up one morning to find a winter storm in
progress—sleet, snow, and freezing rain falling. His wife always
did the milking, but this particular morning she was not feeling
well. Seeking sympathy, she asked her husband if he would milk
the cow. Offended, the cowboy responded, "I'm a bronc rider,
Maw. I don't milk cows." The wife dragged herself out of bed, got
dressed, and went out to milk. The bronc rider went out and

COW POKES

By Ace Reid

"There ain't nothin' as invigeratin' on a frosty mornin' as a ride on a bronc hoss!"

proudly began taking care of his chores by saddling one of the horses he had to ride that day. He eased up on top of that horse, rode around the corral a little bit, and then decided he would take that green-broke broomtail into the pasture for a workout. Just as he came out of the corral gate, his wife came around the corner of the shed with a bucket of milk steaming in the frigid air. The horse shied a little bit at the sight of her and that steam. The old cowboy knew he was in trouble when he saw a gleam come into the wife's eye. She whisked that milk bucket beneath the horse, which was looking for some reason to explode anyway, and said, "Now if you're a bronc rider, let's see you do your thing." That old horse laid him right in the yard gate. She just stepped over him when she saw he wasn't hurt and went on into the house. Even he agreed that she had made her point.

Another wreck on a bucking horse happened at the saddle house on the Nail Ranch one cold morning.

A cowboy topped out a fresh mount, which felt particularly inspired and pitched its way inside the small, wooden-framed saddle house, where two other cowboys were trying to get out the single door to saddle up for the day's work. Amid the crash of saddle stands, tack, horseshoeing supplies, and other incidentals, the cowboy stayed astride the wall-eyed animal. One of the cowboys screamed at the rider to "Git that bag of bones out of here," to which the rider, in characteristic calm, replied, "I wasn't tryin' to ride 'im in here; I'll leave when he's ready."

 ## An Aborted Cowboy Courtship

The opportunity for expression of his love interest is often limited, and a young cowboy may go to extremes in his efforts to find love and understanding. This young cowboy instead found a mother who understood cowboys-and young horses-all too well.

A young cowboy new on a ranch was prowling, looking for cattle in trouble, and decided to check out a story he heard about the daughter of an older cowboy who lived in a camp on the back side of the ranch. The part that interested him most was what he had heard of her beauty. Sure enough, as he rode up to the house, he saw the girl standing out in the yard. She was pretty, all right, and he felt pretty good about everything up to that point. He rode up to the yard gate, and then things began to turn sour on him—he saw the girl's mother hoeing in the garden. She was leery of cowboys, since she was married to one and knew to be leery of them, so she came to the front gate to check out this newcomer. She kept her daughter back and said, "Cowboy, what do you want?" All this man could think to ask for was a drink of water. He always prided himself in thinking fast on his feet, especially in a crisis. He'd had a lot of practice, since a crisis state seemed to be where he stayed most of his life. The mother said, "We don't have any water. The pump is broke." The young man doubted she was telling him the exact truth, but what could he do? He tried to start a conversation by saying, "How much rain did you folks git last week?" Well, this woman ignored his question because she was wearing a big straw hat and, being familiar with livestock, she had noticed the cowboy was riding a young horse just looking for a reason to bust loose. The wind was blowing a good bit, as it does in West Texas, and that hat was flopping. The horse pranced and rolled his eyes at that flopping hat. The woman noticed that reaction, and she just reached up on her head and whipped that hat off and sent it under that horse's feet and said, "Let's see what kind of a bronc rider you are!" Well, that's all that horse was waiting for. He came unglued. He commenced bucking, and the cowboy thought the old lady was going to have a heart attack laughing right there. He kept trying to get that horses's head up to stop the bucking, but when he did the horse went into a dead run. The cowboy decided it was time to end that courting visit anyway, since he wasn't getting anywhere. He just let that horse run, since it was headed back in the right direction and started looking for sick cattle again.

 ## It Was a Big Bunch of Bull

Like their older counterparts, today's cowboys like to prac-
tice their roping skills. They will practice on any cow or bull
that will run from a horse-or sometimes on one that won't.

One rancher had a big-horned Hereford bull that made the unfortunate discovery that if he ran at cowboys, they tended to run from him. That kind of confrontation was hard for a cowboy to win. Since a bull like that is just an accident waiting for a place to happen, the rancher decided he would get rid of this outlaw. None of the cowboys on his ranch had any interest in roping a bull like that, but a bunch of cowboys were talking about the bull in town on Saturday. This one cowboy from another spread looked the rancher right in the eye and said, "Do you want me to come out there and rope that bull for you?" The rancher said, "Sure, come on out." This cowboy saw it as a Sunday afternoon treat. He loaded up his favorite roping horse and went out to the ranch and joined up with the rancher and two more cowboys. All that clattering and banging while they unloaded the horses alerted the bull that somebody was there, and he showed up to check it out. The roping cowboy mounted, shook a loop in his rope, and headed for the bull. He was just pleased that the old bull had made himself easy to find; that way he didn't have to spend his time in the brush looking for the bull. The cowboy headed right for the bull, but true to form, this one headed right toward the cowboy. That didn't phase this man any, though. He spurred that big ol' sorrel horse into a dead run and headed right at that bull. At about fifty yards the bull decided he had made a mistake and started trying to put the brakes and whirl around, which he did, barely managing to go into some brush before the cowboy got his loop thrown. The cowboy stayed right in behind him, though, with that big sorrel horse crashing brush and breaking limbs and the bull plowing down through the creek bed and up on the other side. When the bull cleared, the cowboy tossed his loop and settled it around the old rascal's horns. Well, that horse knew what to do. He set his hind feet and began to pull the bull to a halt. Now two thousand pounds of bull won't come to a stop immediately, but the roper finally got the bull stopped; but then the bull changed his mind again. He decided to see if he could run his tormentor off and headed back at the cowboy. The cowboy had figured on that. As the bull turned toward him, he just turned the horse and spurred in the direction that the bull wanted to go until he managed to get a tree between the two of them and set the brakes on that ol' sorrel. When the bull took the slack out of that rope, it snugged everything up real tight. At that time, the old bull thought he had the man and that horse right where he wanted them. But the man had a little more rope on his side of the tree than the bull did. The bull began to pull and rage, however, and since the rope was around his horns, not his neck, he didn't have to fight for air to breathe. The potential for hazard was high! Even though the horse was big and strong, the bull was gaining ground as he pulled the horse along. The skid marks behind the horseshoes were getting longer! The cowboy began to get a little nervous because those other two cowboys weren't having much luck getting another loop on the bull. That bull would lunge and pull, and that sorrel would be dragged a little closer. The distance between them was getting shorter and shorter. Finally one of the cowboys got a loop on the bull, and the two of them strung the bull out and got the cowboy out of the bind.

The men decided that rather than loading the bull into a trailer, they would take him back to the corral with the ropes. Well, things went pretty well for a time. They had a few small wrecks, but nothing serious. The pasture did look a little like it had been cleared by a pair of bulldozers dragging a chain between them by the time the entourage got to the lot. As they approached the lot, one of the cowboys went ahead and opened the gate. Then they got the bull lined up and started through the gate. As the bull was going through, the roping cowboy thought he had just about had this one made. But he hadn't noticed that the fence along there was barbed wire and that the tops of the posts stuck up about six inches above that top wire. As the bull went through the gate, the rope (as luck would have it) got over one of those posts; and the next thing the cowboy knew, he could see that bull dragging him and the horse toward the fence with the post acting like a pulley. That cowboy was in another bind.

Now most cowboys have a lot of courage, but they are not stupid. This one saw a wreck coming, so he got his foot off the left-hand side of that horse just before the bull snugged that horse and saddle up against the fence. Some cowboys might have cut the rope by then, but not this one. He didn't want to lose a good lariat rope and also lose face. The cowboys finally got the old bull dragged back a little bit and got some slack so the roper could get his rope and the big sorrel horse loose; and they got the bull in the pen and loaded without any further difficulties. Those men enjoyed re-telling that one for some time.

 ## "If You Can Catch It, I'll Ride It"

In addition to believing that they can rope anything, cowboys also have the feeling that they can ride anything that comes along, and they have not always been known as careful people.

Two cowboys were determined to take a ride in one of those two-wing, open-cockpit biplanes that came out to a small airport. The two went up to the pilot; and the first one inquired about the ride, made his deal, and took off. The pilot was careful to look back occasionally to be sure he wasn't making the cowboy sick. This cowboy didn't need any loops, rolls, or dives. They made it back to the ground, and he was glad to have gotten off as light as he did.

His friend, however, had a more daring nature. He walked up to the pilot and said, "I want to go for a ride. But if you can't do any better than you did for my friend, I'm not going to pay you." Well, the first cowboy figured his friend had made a bad mistake. The pilot sank down in his seat a little bit, tightened his seat belt a little tighter, and made sure the second cowboy was strapped in before they took off. From the time he got the wheels off the ground, that pilot kept that plane in a barrel roll or a loop or just flying upside down for the fun of it. He even extended the time of the ride a little bit just to be sure that the plane ride would get the best of the upstart. The first cowboy stood on the ground and watched the flight, groaning for his friend that he knew would be airsick when the plane touched down. Finally the pilot figured the passenger had had enough and eased that plane back to the

BELCHO BEER

THE BEER MADE FROM 1100 COW TRACKS

© ACE REID

"Ain't it sumpin—when I came in here I was loaded down with problems. Now after 4 hours of beer drinking, I'm jist loaded!"

ground. The first cowboy ran out to help the second but to his relief saw his friend undo his belt, climb out, and hand the pilot the fee for the flight, saying "When you learn how to fly that SOB, come back. I'd like to go for a real ride." It's hard to get the best of a spirit like that!

 ## Some Still Drink

Some cowboys have always been prone to drink more than a little when the opportunity presents itself.

There is the story about the old cowboy who had a little more than he could handle one night and was riding his horse home from one of the camps on the ranch. He came to a gate, got off, opened the gate, and led his horse through. In his "fumy" condition, however, he failed to notice that he stepped back on the other side of the fence in order to close the gate. He closed it but found himself looking his horse right in the eye with the fence between the two of them. The cowboy threw the reins away in disgust and said, "Any horse that'll jump the fence while you're closing the gate is too crazy for me to handle." Then he walked off, going the wrong way, of course. That ol' horse held his head out to one side to keep the reins out from under his feet and trotted on to the barn. That cowboy sure felt foolish when he woke up the next morning.

Another cowboy in much the same condition drove his pickup up to a gate late one night. He got out and opened the gate, came back, and drove the pickup through. When he got ready to close the gate, he made the mistake of stepping through to the other side. He closed the gate, locked it, and started looking for his pickup. When he couldn't find it, he just knew somebody had stolen it. He found it the next morning right where he left it. It was days before he told anybody about that experience.

 ## Some Cowboy Revenge

Some of the modern cowboy's humor reflects clever thinking that backfires on him, despite his dead level best effort to do his job well. And one clever deed or remark deserves another. That is the way accidents begin.

When the wrangler brings the horse herd in early in the morning, it is pitch dark. There just isn't much way to count how many are in the herd. On one ranch, a cowboy asked the wrangler how he knew all the horses were coming in. The wrangler told him it was purely a matter of mathematics: "Just count the number of hoof-beats and divide by four. That way I know how many horses I have." That cowboy just turned around, shook his head, and said, "I should have known better than to ask you something like that."

That cowboy began to plot ways to repay that smart remark. He knew that the wrangler had to drive those horses into the corral, so he decided to thwart his opponent at that point. He got some bailing wire and wired the corral gate shut real tight. Then he twisted the ends of that wire with pliers and cut the ends off so close there wasn't any leverage for the wrangler to use to undo that wire in the morning. When the wrangler got down there between three and four o'clock, in the dark, he couldn't open the gate. Finally, the wrangler did get the gate open, gathered the scattering remuda, and penned the mounts. He said nothing but started carrying a pair of wire cutters with him. He never even gave the cowboy the satisfaction of hearing him mention it.

The ranch kept a patch of hay grazer in the horse pasture, not too far from the bunkhouse. Late in the afternoons the wrangler would go down and run the horses into that patch and close the gate. That way he knew where the horses were and had them close to the house the next morning. If the wrangler shaded himself any by cutting his time close, he would be in trouble; because just as regularly as he put those horses in the patch, the boys in the bunkhouse, including the cowboy he was feuding with, would wait until they knew the wrangler was in bed, then go down and open the gate and let the herd out. The horses knew the game as well as the men did, and they always headed for the back side of an eight-hundred-acre pasture and made it as hard as possible for the wrangler to find them the next morning.

The wrangler didn't take all of that lying down, of course. He planned his revenge carefully. One morning when the cowboys were obviously going to run a little late, the wrangler went down to the saddle house and used some small finishing nails to fasten the skirts of the saddles to the wooden saddle stands. The men came in and grabbed the saddles to throw on the horses and were surprised that the stands tried to go with them. They backed off and looked, and tried again, but with the same result, then looked to see if the saddles were girted to the stand, which, of course, they weren't. Then the cowboy he was feuding with started cussin' the wrangler and hunting some wire cutters or nail pullers to get the saddles loose so he could get ready to go before the foreman arrived. Of course, the wrangler had made it a point to hide everything that could be used to pull a nail. He felt revenged, and the battle ended in a draw, with a good laugh on all sides.

 The Dynamited Dog

Cowboys hold strongly to their principles, and sometimes they suffer for it. Here is a disastrous event in the life of a West Texas cowboy, whose desire for revenge becomes costly for him.

An old cowboy on the Matador Ranch set a string of coyote traps that he ran after he had finished up on his feed runs in the winter. One morning he went by one of the traps and saw that he had caught somebody's dog. It made him mad that the dog had gotten in his coyote trap, and he decided to fix the dog up good. The ranch had been dynamiting some post holes in rock, so the cowboy had a stick or two of that dynamite in his truck. He decided to really fix that dog up right, so he got a stick of dynamite and tied it on the dog's tail. He put a fairly short fuse on it, lit it, and then sprung a trap to let the dog out.

Unfortunately, this cowboy was more familiar with coyotes than he was with dogs. A coyote would have taken off for the brush to blow himself up and a hole in the ground. But a dog is different. This dog ran to the only shelter that looked like home—the cowboy's pickup truck parked nearby. With horror the cowboy watched the dog disappear under the tailgate of his faithful old truck. After abbreviated efforts to run the dog off, the cowboy decided he had better take cover—he knew the fuse was getting short. The explosion was significant! The cowboy destroyed the dog, all right, but the explosion destroyed his pickup as well. This cowboy learned the hard way that dynamiting a dog out of existence is not the best way to get rid of him. It was a true case of overkill.

 ## Milk-Pen Humor

Because cowboys still regularly milk cows, the milking pen continues to be a fruitful setting for tricks and pranks. A conducive element is that most of the milking is done in the dark, either early in the morning or at night after the men come in from work. The dark makes a man feel uneasy about things that in the daylight might not bother him at all, and the possibilities for excitement are promising.

One cowboy, who held the job of wrangler, had to get up around 3:30 each morning in order to bring the horse herd in and feed the horses to be ridden that day before the men showed up to saddle just before daylight. Therefore, he was accustomed to working in the dark and had idle time on his hands while the horses were eating. More than once, this prankster slipped in the side door of the feed shed down at the milking pen. He knew that there were several five-gallon metal feed buckets in the shed, and he stacked these up and leaned them against the door he knew the cowboys would use. He'd seen them just walk up and jerk that door open, still half asleep. He also knew they had been out late at a honky-tonk at the county line. Sure enough, one came stumbling along with his milk bucket. He jerked the door open to get some feed for the cow while he milked her, and down those buckets came. Now this ol' boy was a little-light footed anyway, and the shock of being pelted by rattling buckets in the dark in his hungover condition didn't help any. He dropped the milk bucket with a loud shout and not a few blistering curses and ran back to the cookhouse, the only light he could see from the milk pens. The prankster felt he was a success. Rather than stop there, however, he felt inspired. He looked for new material, new frontiers to conquer. And he found one.

Since there was a supply of milk, there was usually a supply of cats hanging around, too. One was an old black tomcat whose temperament wasn't to be tested. The stories of his "attacks" on unsuspecting cowboys over the years were legend, and an especially new and fruitful source of these stories was the wrangler himself. The cowboys were a little suspicious of those stories but couldn't really be sure the cat was not a menace, especially when they were walking up to that milk pen in the dark. One cowboy in particular had a phobia about cats. A few mornings later, this cowboy had finished milking and had a bucket about half full of good fresh milk, with foam on top of it. The prankster planned his actions well and hunkered down in a bush on the trail back to the cookhouse. Just as the victim got close, the wrangler squalled like a mad cat and sailed his big, black felt hat at the cowboy and hit him right in the chest. Well, that cowboy just knew that mean black cat had him. He threw the milk bucket as far as he could and took off running toward the cookhouse. The laughter from the bushes didn't help his feelings at all. He took a lot of ribbing about that during that day and the days that followed, and he also caught the fury of the cook, who lost his supply of milk that day.

Well, the cowboy responded as best he could and enlisted some of his friends to get back at the prankster one morning. The wrangler had some inkling about what was going to happen, though, so he got out into the brush around the feed house. He eased a little bit further out in the brush than he figured they would dare to, and sure enough, here came three or four of them sneaking out. He could hear them saying, "We'd better hurry. He'll be here before long and we wanna be sure to be hid before he comes." So the prankster let one of them get real close and then jumped out and scared him. The men just weren't ready for that. Apparently, they were all a little light-footed anyway, because they took off running. One just couldn't help it and ran into a big tank of water, right on in waist deep early on that frosty morning. That ended the milk pen humor saga on that ranch, at least for a time.

On another ranch, a cowboy was down at the lot milking. The day before, some of the boys had penned up an ol' bad cow that had turned so mean they couldn't do anything with her, and they had put her in the milking lot on purpose. Well, in one corner of this milking pen were several horse stalls with slatted board walls. Sometime earlier one had been a granary. That space was walled up all the way around; even the ceiling was walled in. But the ranch didn't need it for grain storage, so the men used it as a horse stall. This fellow didn't know that the bad cow was in there or he wouldn't have been in there milking his cow. It was before daylight, and this ol' mean cow was irritated by the fact that the fellow was in the pen bothering her. About the time the unsuspecting cowboy got through milking, this bad cow had had about all of him she wanted. When he started for the gate, she started for him. Well, he wasn't paying too much attention, but he saw her out of the corner of his eye and figured the best way to get away from her was to run into one of those stalls and climb over the fence.

That all worked fine, except he made the mistake of darting into that ol' granary instead of into one of those stalls with the slatted plank walls. The cowboys were down there getting ready to saddle up, and they saw the whole thing. They heard the milk bucket crash, and then they heard that ol' boy clawing those walls, trying to climb out with that ol' cow bawling and working on him in there. Finally, he managed to make it to the door and beat her out of there, climbed the fence, and got away. But he was careful about going into that milking pen after that. He always checked to see what else was there.

Not long after that incident, two cowboys played a trick on that same ol' boy while he was milking one morning. The two had killed a rattlesnake the day before. They got that snake, tied a piece of haywire to its neck, and managed to hook the other end of that wire on the ol' boy's pants leg. Then they backed out and waited for the action to start. Well, when the cowboy started to move away from the cow, he detected movement and looked back, saw that snake, and felt a tug on his pants. He looked no further; he knew it was time to move, and move he did. Milk was flying, and he was hollering. Needless to say, the boys didn't have any fresh milk that day, but doing without fresh milk seemed a price well worth paying for the laughs.

A Cowboy Joke

Here's a joke involving an aggie and a too-talkative cowboy on a big ranch in West Texas.

The boss of a ranch went down to Venezuela and bought a big, fine bull, which he brought back and turned loose in the pasture with some of the best cows. Well, there was something funny about this bull, because he didn't have much interest in cows. Even when the bull did seem to have an interest, he wasn't able to do anything about it. The foreman called the boss and told him the problem. The boss became furious. He said, "You call Houston or Austin or somewhere and get the best veterinarian you can find and get him up there to look at that bull." Well, the foreman finally found an aggie (a veterinarian from Texas A&M) to come look at the bull. The vet examined the patient thoroughly and said, "I think I can fix that." He gave the cowboy two bottles of medicine and told him to give the bull one bottle this week and one bottle the next week. The cowboy gave the bull that bottle, and it made all the difference in the world. That bull took care of his business better than any other bull the man had ever seen.

The boss phoned him up before long and asked him how everything was going. The boss was overjoyed with the report. He said, "What kind of medicine was it that you gave that bull?" The cowboy responded, "I don't know what it is called, but it tastes like it has peppermint in it."

Cowboy Tall Tales

Modern cowboys know traditional tall tales, but many of their favorite stories recount activities they either experienced personally or heard about from close friends or co-workers.

A tornado ripped through the country around Woodson in Throckmorton County, and afterward many stories circulated concerning strange occurrences that resulted from the high wind. One involved an old cowboy who kept a flock of Banty chickens, of which he was particularly proud. Well, the storm blew through, and he worried about them, but the rain was so intense that he didn't go out to check. As daylight neared the next morning, he heard his faithful rooster crowing but noticed that the sound made by the bird was strange indeed. He figured that the rooster had caught cold as a result of the rain. When he went out to check, he found that the wind was so strong that it had blown his Banty rooster into a gallon jug with an opening no bigger than a fifty-cent piece. The cowboy didn't convince too many people of his story, but he regularly argued the truth of it.

One other cowboy had a high-wind story that he liked to tell. When one of his cowboy friends asked if the man had suffered any damage during the recent storm, the first cowboy responded in classic style: "Yes, that wind came through there and blew like the devil. Why it blew so hard it turned that big black cast iron washpot in front of my house wrong side out." "The heck it did," the friend responded. "Not only that, but you know I had those legs sitting on those bricks." "Yea," the friend answered. "That storm hit so fast and the wind blew so hard that when that pot turned wrong side out, the bricks are still stuck on the legs of that pot." The friend's amazement turned to a sheepish grin, and as he turned and walked away muttering something about liars and other kinds of people he couldn't trust.

One particularly windy cowboy proved that fishing stories are not unknown in West Texas. Once while he was swimming in the Clear Fork of the Brazos River on the Hendrick Ranch north of Abilene, a cowboy began exploring the washed out places underneath the riverbank and ran head on into the biggest catfish he had ever seen. He decided he would try to get that fish out but was unable to because of the fish's enormous size. When the cowboy came back up for air, one of the other cowboys had ridden up on the bank above his head. The swimming cowboy began to brag about the size of that fish. No doubt being a little bit suspicious of such stories, the cowboy mounted on horseback offered to throw down the end of his lariat so that the swimming cowboy could put it on that fish. The cowboy in the water took the end of that rope and swam back up under that bank and used that rope to fashion a halter on the fish by passing that rope behind the fins and through the mouth. Confident, he swam back out and told his friend to set the spurs to his horse and drag that fish out. Well, the cowboy on horseback tried, but that horse wasn't able to move that fish at all. Too big! The cowboy in the water, undaunted, got out on the bank and got him a pointed stick and dove back into the water. He swam in behind that fish and jabbed him with that pointed stick. With a surge of power, the fish lunged out from under that bank toward deep water at the other end of that deep hole. The cowboy on the bank was expecting that lunge and had his pony set, but rather than snugging that fish up, the next thing he knew, man and horse were jerked off into that river. In order to keep from drowning, the cowboy had to let go of his rope, and the fish got away. He was just lucky he had dallied and didn't tie off. To this day, neither one of them can say for sure how big that fish was. He was a Texas-size catfish, no doubt about that.

One cowboy who had been listening to that story leaned back a little bit and said, "You know, that is a big fish story. But big fish are not the only thing big we have in Texas. We have big ranches, too. I remember one time I worked on a ranch that was so big it had five hundred stud horses on it." The fisherman, despite the enormity of his own tale, realized that he was about to be outdone because if a ranch needed five hundred stud horses, there was no telling how many thousand mares it had and, along with that, how many million cattle it had to have in order to justify that size horse herd. The cowboy-fisherman simply pulled his hat down low over his eyes and said something about needing to get back to the ranch to break a few bad ones and left.

KENNETH W. DAVIS

Kenneth W. Davis is a 1954 graduate of Texas Tech University where he is now professor of English. He received the master of arts degree from Vanderbilt University, where he was a Woodrow Wilson Fellow, 1954–55. He has been a faculty member at Texas Tech since 1955. He earned a Ph.D. from Vanderbilt University in 1963. He is a member of Western Writers of America.

His academic specializations are nineteenth-century British literature and British Renaissance literature. He is also interested in British and American folklore. In addition to his other teaching duties, he offers graduate and undergraduate courses in folklore. He is coauthor of *Blackcats, Hoot Owls, and Water Witches*, (1989). He has published in *Library* (transactions of the British Bibliographical Society), *Western Folklore, Victorian Newsletter, Conradiana, Arlington Quarterly, Papers on Language and Literature, English Language Notes, Notes and Queries, Year Book of the West Texas Historical Association, Proceedings of the Texas/Southwest Popular Culture Associations, Concho River Review, Cross Timbers Review, Lamar Journal of the Humanities, McNeese Review, Conradian* (journal of the Joseph Conrad Society of Great Britain), *New Mexico Humanities Review, Southwestern American Literature, Texas Books in Review,* the *Southwestern Quarterly, Bulletin of the Texas Association of Creative Writing Teachers,* and *Roundup Quarterly* (journal of the Western Writers of America Association). He was president of the Texas Popular Culture Association (1987–89), secretary-treasurer of the American Studies Association of Texas (1988–), councilor to the Texas Folklore Society (1987–88), vice president and program chairman of the Texas Folklore Society (1990), and president of the Texas Folklore Society (1991). In recent years, he has presented thirty-two papers about Southwestern folklore and literature.

A Rose by Any Other Name—
Some Cowboy Nicknames

Cowboy nicknames frequently contain elements of friendly humor and spirited, even harsh satire. The names cowboys call each other may stem from physical or personality traits— or from combinations of the two. The use of nicknames indicates a high level of verbal sophistication. Cowboys who work together closely tend to form bonds of friendship as well as those which derive from rivalries. Generally, however, nicknames stem from camaraderie.

The nearly ubiquitous custom of cowboy nicknames is featured in the writings of Owen Wister, B. M. Bower (a lesser-known contemporary who wrote more than sixty western novels), and in a staple of the Street-and-Smith pulp empire like *Ranch Romances.* Like their literary ancestors or counterparts, present-day cowboys are often better known by their nicknames than they are by their legal names. Who knows the real name of Wister's "Virginian"? And what was the real name of Trampas? Only the most devoted fan of Bower's novels about the mythical Flying U Ranch knows the full name of its cowboy-artist hero, Chip. Some years ago when an elderly cowboy who had worked for years on the Swenson Ranch at Spur died, few of his friends who read the obituary in the newspaper recognized his name. Some friends even missed attending the funeral because they did not know the deceased by his legal name.

Less morose are anecdotes about other modern cowboys whose sometimes bizarre sobriquets reveal much about humor in the ranching country of the Southwest. Near Lampasas a few years ago was a cowboy widely known as "W. T." because of his youthful fondness for drinking W. T. Raleigh Lemon Extract straight from the bottle for its alcohol content. The tag stayed with him despite his eventually finding religion and giving up the use of any form of alcohol.

Bittersweet, however, is the story of a young boy who became the only hired hand on a small ranch near San Saba. He was a mysterious runaway who would not use his legal name until he was forced to do so. When he was in his early teens, half-starved, he came to the small ranch a childless couple operated. The compassionate woman gave the boy a full meal and later told her

COW POKES

By Ace Reid

"Womans Lib er no Womens Lib—I'm a cowboy
—not a cowperson!!"

husband that he all but lapped up the food like a hungry "pooch dog." The man immediately began calling the boy "Pooch." That name stayed with him until about halfway through the Vietnam War. Then he took the advice of his boss and by-now-surrogate father. He registered for the draft, got a social security number, and opened a checking account in his real name. But he steadfastly insisted that he be called Pooch. Like all too many of his generation, he now lies buried somewhere in a military graveyard under his real name. The couple who took him in when he was a waif died three years after Pooch. According to local gossip, they were ultimately brokenhearted when for some reason, they couldn't get the body of their beloved Pooch returned for burial on their ranch.

A story about a cowboy who later became a rodeo clown reveals something about streaks of near cruelty that can be found in the world of cowboying. This man came to the Pitchfork Ranch when he was in his early teens and worked at whatever job he could handle until he was mature enough to be a working cowboy. One day, he threw a rock at a wild turkey gobbler. By accident more than by design, the rock found the turkey's head and killed the bird. The Pitchfork Ranch was a game preserve in which wild turkeys were protected. The boy worried about what he had done. Soon, jeering older cowboys began to call him "Gobbler." One of these older men enjoyed recounting a possibly apocryphal incident in which Cecil Fox, well-known game warden from nearby Spur, Texas, stopped in at the Pitchfork's chuck house for lunch. The young rock thrower who had killed the turkey was so concerned about this game warden's visit that he hurried to his room in the bunkhouse and began packing his belongings in hope of making a getaway. If Cecil Fox ever knew of the unfortunate accident which led to the death of the wild turkey, he didn't mention it to Gobbler, who continued to work for the Pitchfork for several years. In time, he outgrew the uneasiness he felt whenever his nickname reminded him of killing the turkey.

Nicknames of cowboys sometimes stem from meaningful—even if minor—experiences, and they can be attached to a man for no specific reason. One cowboy who worked for all of his adult life on a large ranch in northern New Mexico was known as "Pick." The explanation given for this name was that when he first came to work, he often begged the chuck house cook for pickles to chew on after every meal. As is often the case with people who have nicknames, he grew so accustomed to being called by his nickname that he did not immediately respond to his real given name. On a neighboring ranch was a man also so frequently identified with his nickname that he didn't use his full legal name even for signing checks. His nickname was "Toad." If he knew how he got the name, he wouldn't tell. When he was asked about the name, he smiled a bit and responded "Damn' if I know." No one else in the area knew the reason for this nickname. The barber in a nearby town said simply, "He's jest allus been called 'Toad.'"

Nicknames referring to physical characteristics of cowboys are still heard today. Clutches of Baldys, Skinnys, Fats, and Slims congregate at cowboy reunions such as the yearly ones at Stamford, Texas. A two-hundred-fifty-pound cowboy may be known affectionately or derisively by his peers in reverse truth as Slats, or Bones, or Skinny. One cowboy, supposedly covered all over his body with thick hair, was known for years all over the upper Panhandle as "Ape."

Bawdiness—perhaps of a somewhat innocent sort—now and then plays a part in the granting of memorable nicknames to cowboys. A north Texas cowboy whose success with women was almost as great as his love or need for them answered to "Puss." A

youthful cowboy from far west Texas who boasted drunkenly in a
Juarez saloon of the length his erect male organ was taunted to
prove his assertion by his equally intoxicated companions. When
the braggart responded with a self-assured shout, "Jest git me a
ruler," he was to be known ever thereafter as "Rule." A cowboy
from near Cowles, New Mexico had chronic gastritis with accompanying flatulence. So, he was known, of course, among his fellow
cowboys as "Gassy." Once at a Saturday night dance, his girlfriend
heard his friends call him that crude nickname and asked its origins. The ailing man was so embarrassed that he left the dance and
wasn't seen in town on Saturday nights for several months. "Stud"
is a somewhat common nickname in the Southwest. For most
cowboys who answer to this label, the term is supposed to be a
macho compliment; but it may be given to taunt a man whose
sexual prowess is assumed to be limited. Another nickname with
possible sexual overtones is "Dink," a shortened form of "Dinky."
A south Texas cowboy whose peers called him "Dink" was
rumored to have a short male organ, but because his temper was
supposedly even shorter, no one dared discuss the nickname with
him. This Dink fathered at least half a dozen children with his wife
and was often accused of having perhaps that many more out of
wedlock. His fecundity led one of his older companions to remark
drolly, "It ain't the instrument itself; it's in how it's played." And
there was an animal husbandry student at a major state university
whose fellow dormitory residents gave him the nickname "Hose"
because of his heroic endowment of maleness. This young cowboy
aggie was flattered by the name and gladly accepted it, but was
once sorely embarrassed when his father, an elder in a hard-shell
church in a conservative ranching community, called him at the
dorm. The student who answered the call did not know the real
name of the rancher's son and hesitated a bit before he asked if the
rancher wished to talk with Hose. The father repeated his son's full
name. The student then shouted, "Is Hose here? Telephone!" How
the young man explained his nickname to his pious father is a story
now unfortunately lost.

In 1985 at a truck stop near the Texas-Oklahoma border, I
heard a rugged Marlboro-man cowboy called "Sophie" by several
companions who urged him to hurry about finishing his meal of
chicken fried steak, gravy-drowned mashed potatoes, and hot rolls
dripping butter. Feminine sounding nicknames are not rare in contemporary southwestern cowboy country, but they aren't common,
either. When this powerfully built man called Sophie left, I asked
the cashier about the unusual name. He grinned and replied that

he had answered that question many times. "That man," the cashier began, "works for a big ranching outfit about fifteen miles from here. Some rich folks in New York own it and come out only a couple of times a year to visit a spell and play at being ranchers. While they are gone, they have their foreman put a man in charge of keeping up the fancy owner's quarters—a great big old house with all kinds of high-toned furniture in it. About twenty years ago, the man we're talking about got the job of keeping the dust out of the house, checking the pipes and the hot water heater, and all such mess as that. He'd go over to the house lots of times at around noon and would grab hisself a nap on one of them over-stuffed sofas in the main parlor—a big old room that they used to have dances in when the first owners of the ranch lived on it. Usually, he'd just take a catnap, but one day, so I heard it, he went dead asleep and didn't show up for the afternoon's branding. That evening, when the work was all done, the foreman went looking for him and found him still sound asleep on the sofa. That foreman got hisself a granite wash pan and dropped it on the tile hearth close to the sofa. That old boy on the sofa jumped up screaming and hollering at the top of his lungs, 'God forgive us, don't shoot! God forgive us, don't shoot!' Well, the foreman laughed so hard at the man's hysterical yelling that he didn't even bawl him out for missing work. But he told all the boys at the bunk-house about catching him asleep on the sofa and about how he took on when that granite pan hit them tiles. From then on, ever'body I know of has called him Sophie. And that there's the facts on the matter."

 ## Singing the Bare Body Electric in Texas Ranching Country

These two anecdotes from the oral tradition reveal much about the modern cowboy's delight in situational humor, the humor of incongruity. The incident of bashful cowboy who thinks he is safe behind a wash tub and the plight of the two hapless cowboys surprised by their boss and his young wife are examples of the kinds of predicaments about which cowboys laugh with and at each other.

Despite modern cowboys' frequent uses of bawdy language and colorful swear words, they are still shy around womenfolk and are quite modest about their bodies. Few real cowboys go around with their upper torsos bare; most working cowboys wear long-sleeved shirts for protection from the sun as well as from tree branches and various briars and cacti. Carelessly dressed cowboys around the few surviving chuckwagons will hurry to tidy up their appearances to make themselves presentable and decent if women come to have an outdoor meal or merely to observe the living myth of modern cowboy life. While women are around, cowboys struggle to expunge any scatological or sexual allusions from their speech. The ordinary conversations of cowboys with older women or with the wives of foreman or ranchers have liberal saltings of polite phrases such as "Yes, ma'am," "No, ma'am (often compressed into a 'Nome')," "Beg yore pardon," and "'Scuse me, please."

In the presence of women (and sometimes in the presence of other men) modern cowboys are as diffident and modest about their bodies as they are with their uses of language. This traditional modesty about their bodies sometimes prompts humorous situations. Life on a present-day ranch isn't so harsh and demanding as to make showering regularly at a bunkhouse impossible, so cowboys don't need to bathe in the creeks and rivers of the north central Texas ranching country. Yet no shower or tub bath in a bunkhouse—or in one's own home—can match the perfect delight of skinny-dipping along toward dusk after a hot day's work on a sweaty horse. The cowboy who works on a ranch with a clear-running creek is fortunate if he can arrange his activities so that he can have refreshing open air baths at day's end. But, as one cowboy learned, having such a treat can be embarrassing.

A cowboy on a ranch near Wichita Falls was mildly notorious for his shyness around other humans—females as well as males. He couldn't speak easily in the presence of his fellow cowboys and when women were around, he was tongue-tied. Like some other buckeroos, he opted to follow the cowboying life because of the solitude it offered generally. He slept in the bunkhouse only on the coldest nights of winter; otherwise, he slept out of doors in an L. L. Bean sleeping bag. If he had to bathe during the severely cold weather that made him a prisoner in the bunkhouse, he waited until all the other cowboys had left the communal shower before he took his hurried bath. In warm weather, he rode his horse or drove a pickup to the creek that bordered the ranch on the south side. Here, he could relax in solitary contentment away from human eyes.

One hot August evening, an hour or so after supper at the chuck house, the shy recluse made the usual trip on horseback to his isolated spot at the creek. He enjoyed the coolness in the middle of the creek for a time before he walked back to the bank where he had left his bar of soap. Then he stepped into the shallow waters and stood blissfully alone—he thought—applying soap to his body. But just as he was ready to return to the deeper waters to rinse away the soap, a young woman, daughter of the foreman on a neighboring ranch, stepped from behind the willow trees that line parts of the creek's banks. She giggled nervously as she observed the shy cowboy's embarrassed terror.

He quickly covered his face with both hands. Then, with that dreadful insight that extreme stress can provoke, he realized that his face was not the part of his body he longed desperately to conceal. He wanted to hurry back to the deep waters in the middle of the creek, but his feet and legs perversely refused to obey his anguished commands to them. In desperation, he reached for a rusting three gallon tub some fisherman or beer guzzler had left at the water's edge. He held the tub just below his belly button. Anxiety caused his voice to become a croaking whisper:

"Ma'am," he began, "I beg yore pardon. I don't know what you're thinking . . . "

Before he could finish his sentence, the woman laughed, then said, "I know what you are thinking. *You're thinking* that old rusty tub still has a *bottom* in it!"

At this information, the cowboy made an heroic effort to flee to the security of the deep waters, but as he turned, he twisted his right ankle and fell, landing belly side up in shallow water that didn't begin to cover him. The injury to his ankle was so painful that he couldn't stand up. Nearly dead—not from physical pain but from embarrassment—he had to accept help from the woman who had seen his nakedness. She managed to get him dressed and on his horse.

As painful to the man as having been seen utterly naked by a woman was the necessity to explain his bootless and much swollen right ankle when he returned to the ranch's headquarters where the foreman ordered him to sleep in the bunkhouse. When his companions there forced the story from him, he blushed furiously as he spoke:

"There I was, all lathered up and bare-assed naked when this woman come up and saw me. Thought I'd die and wish I had of."

Whoops and yells greeted the account of a man's embarrassment. The victim stopped bathing in the creek and began to sleep in the bunkhouse. His shyness persisted about allowing his friends at the bunkhouse to see his naked body, however. Just before Christmas that year, he left the ranch and never returned.

Another story about nakedness reveals the delight some cowboys take in humorous but potentially dangerous practical jokes. On a ranch near Marfa, such a practical joke had nearly disastrous consequences. No cooling creeks or rivers regularly enhance this remote spread. Gully-washing rains only occasionally make creek and river beds in the area run with water deep enough for bathing. So cowboys on the ranch sometimes bathe surreptitiously in large, galvanized steel-stock watering tanks kept filled by slow-turning windmills.

One late autumn afternoon when temperatures in the Big Bend country remained brutally high, two cowboys stopped their pickup a short distance from one of the ranch's many watering tanks. They debated about taking a cooling dip. Both the ranch's owner and its stern foreman had ordered all the hands to stop bathing in the stock tanks. The owner didn't mind drinking water into which cattle and horses had put their mouths, but he was not willing to drink water in which sweaty cowboys had soaked the dirt from their bodies. The cowboys in their pickup—whose air-conditioner had long ago ceased to work—could all but feel the coolness of the water so tantalizingly near. At last, temptation won out over reasoned good sense. They assured each other than by the time the owner again visited this remote corner of the ranch, he couldn't detect evidence that humans had bathed in the tank. As quickly as they could get to the tank and take off their clothing, they were splashing about as happily as children taking a forbidden dip in a creek.

The two never thought about what their fellow cowboys would do when they drove by the tank on their way to the ranch's headquarters that late evening. When a second pickup stopped near the tank, the bathers assumed their friends would join them in the tub. The friends had other ideas. Instead of sharing the pleasures of a cool bath, they grabbed the bathers' clothes—boots and all—and drove away in a heavy cloud of dust and exhaust fumes. The bathers hurled epic curses at them for taking the clothing; but when they saw that their boots were gone, too, their rage turned to chagrin. Their pickup was parked only twenty or so yards from the tank, but these few yards contained enough grass burrs and goatheads to intimidate any barefooted cowboy in the world.

The bathers sat in the tank wondering what mad gods had provoked so swift a retribution for the sin of skinny dipping in a stock tank. Then they noticed low on the northern horizon a bank of deep blue and gray clouds that warned of a coming norther, the first of the season. One cowboy turned to the other one and observed somberly, "I don't know about you, but I reckon getting stickers in my feet ain't quite as rotten as being froze to death naked as a jaybird in a stock tank."

His fellow sinner agreed, so they walked cursing all the while to the pickup, where they were overjoyed to find that the keys were still in the ignition. They sat on the tail end of the pickup and picked what seemed to be thousands of grass burrs and some goatheads from their feet. They were so occupied with ridding their feet of these that they didn't notice that the norther was coming closer and closer. Just when they had removed enough of the burrs and goatheads to be comfortable, the norther hit. With it came heavy dust that reduced visibility to a few yards.

The naked cowboys hurried into the pickup, rolled up the windows, and started slowly toward the ranch headquarters about eight miles away. Even with the pickup's headlights on, the two men could hardly see the dirt road. The man driving now and then veered into the ditches along either side of the road. One such departure from the straight and narrow path caused yet another agony for the hapless bathers. As the driver of the pickup gunned the motor to get back on the road, the right rear tire ran into a surveyor's wooden stob. It neatly penetrated and ruined the tire. The driver lamented the situation:

"Godamighty diggity damn!" he began, "Here we are without no clothes in a damn' dust storm of a blue norther and we got a damn' flat tire. There ain't no justice for us working cowboys, and we was just trying to keep from smellin' bad, too."

"Yeah," his companion chimed in, "we're damned if we do and damned if we don't. If we don't put that spare on, we'll ruin a wheel and have to pay for it, or we can sit here 'til our butts freeze off. And if we get out in that damn' cold wind, we'll catch pneumonia or our balls will freeze up or both. It just couldn't be no worse."

The two sat in silence as the skies grew darker and the temperature dropped. At last, the driver got out and began hunting in the truck's tool box for a jack. His companion got out to help. Together they struggled to get the pickup's right rear wheel jacked up enough so that they could put the spare on.

While they labored and shivered in the near-freezing winds, they cursed the General Motors Corporation for the jack that came with the pickup, the Michelin Corporation for making tires a little old two-inch wide stob could penetrate, the National Weather Service for not predicting two days in advance the arrival of the season's first blue norther, their friends for stealing their clothing, the ranch's owner for being so picky about his drinking water, and every grassburr and goathead between Laredo and El Paso. And they worked frantically to get the flat tire off and the spare in place. They were so busy they didn't hear the rancher's quiet Mark IV slip up behind them. The rancher and his young second wife (the first had died after forty years on the ranch), had been to Marfa for some shopping and were creeping slowly toward home without headlights when they came upon the two naked cowboys frantically changing a tire during a blue norther's windy presentation of a west Texas dust storm.

Almost at the same time, the two naked men realized that something or someone was watching them. They turned about to look and saw through the dust the outline of the silver gray Mark IV. By reflex action, they turned their backs to the occupants of the car and waited to hear the fractious voice of the old rancher telling them they were fired. What they heard was more painful than that—laughter. The rancher and his wife continued to laugh as they drove by the two embarrassed men. When the car was a hundred yards or more away, one of the cowboys turned to the other and asked "What do you think them two saw, really? It being so dusty and all, surely they couldn't see too much, now could they?"

His friend answered, "Hell, it ain't what they seen that worries me so much; it's what they heard. Was we cussing him or them damned foreign tires when they drove up like that on us so sneaky and all? If that old skinflint heard what we said about him and how he don't want us splashing around in them stock tanks, we are dead soldiers so fur as this ranch goes."

"Damn' if I can remember what we was saying when that big old car of theirs drove up," the cowboy who was tightening up lug nuts said. He added, "And at this stage, I don't give rip of a damn what I said. I just about got this tire on and we're hauling on towards home. If that old coot aims to fire us, they ain't nothing we can do about it, anyhow. What we got to do is get to that bunkhouse before we freeze solid or whatever."

Later, while they drove slowly toward the ranch headquarters, they tried again to remember what they had said about the rancher when they were changing the fire.

"Hellfire and damnation!" the driver of the pickup shouted. "If that old devil can't take a little bad-mouthing, he ain't worth workin' for anyhow."

His companion agreed.

"But how can we ever look that pretty wife of his straight in the face again? I guess all we can do is move on. I'd just as soon work to the south of here for the winter. This norther has made a true believing sun worshipper out of me."

"Yeah, I guess we done wore out our welcome here. But, damn! We got to stick around long enough to get even with them bowlegged bastids that swiped our boots and stuff. I don't mind the clothes so much, but I am damn' sure not goin' to fergit havin' to go without footwear." He amplified on his doubts as to the legitimacy of the birth of the two pranksters.

At the bunkhouse, they found their stolen clothing and boots neatly stacked on the porch. The men hurried to dress and put their boots on. Then they walked slowly to the ranch's black-smithing shop, where some oak barrel staves had rested for years. Each man got one stout stave and began walking with grim deter-mination toward the bunkhouse.

Several cowboys saw them coming and warned the two who had taken the clothing and boots from near the stock tank. The tricksters hurried out the back door and weren't seen again for two working days. When they returned, the two whose love of cool baths in stock tanks led to all the difficulties had calmed. Some weeks later, these skinny dippers left to take winter jobs near Brownsville. The rancher whose tanks they had polluted tried to keep them from moving on, but once a cowboy makes up his mind to leave, little can be done make him stay. One of the victims of the stock tank joke told a lady friend about the incident before he left for far south Texas. He concluded his account with a plaintive observation:

"I was allus told that cleanliness is next to godliness, but that bath me and my buddy took in the stock tank must have been the work of the devil. And we never did find out if that old man who owned the ranch heard what we said about him when we was freezin' half to death nakeder than one of them little old Mexican hairless dogs as we was changing that tire."

 ## A Texas Cusser in the Twentieth Century

This story is a conflation of brief anecdotes that may still be circulating in small ranching and farming towns in central and north central Texas. The central figure's ability to use

COW POKES
By Ace Reid

"Thank gosh, ole hoss, we ain't got another foot of
rope—maybe now we'll get 'em."

*strong language—the language of the branding pen and the
auction arena—made him an original, a kind of folk hero.
Although the man's favorite term,* son of a bitch, *remains
offensive to some, it has worked its way into the mainstream
of contemporary society. The Texas Cusser's use of it tran-
scended the offensive to become creative, poetic, and highly
comic.*

A twentieth-century practitioner of the ancient art of cursing
was a modestly successful cattle trader in central Texas whose colorful language fascinated ranchers as well as his fellow townsmen
from about 1920 until his death in the late 1950s. His ability to curse
inventively, colorfully, and earnestly was the subject of many ser-
mons in the area's several churches. Perhaps ministers of the gos-
pel were right to chastise this cattle trader whose use of forbidden
words became an art, but if these pious men had dared to come
within earshot of him, they would have learned that in his cursing,
he imposed some strict limits. Although he did not formally es-

pouse religion until shortly before his death, he would not "take the name of the Lord in vain." He forbade his employees to invoke the names of Jesus or of Mary in any irreverent ways. He did not use lewd or salacious sexual references or imagery in his swearing, and he never called any living creature a "bastard"—a term common then as it is now. Not until after his death did the spit-and-whittle crew who sat under the sheet iron awnings on hot summer afternoons learn his reason for refraining from using this word.

The cattle trader relied heavily on a term that is a fixed element in the Texas folk tradition of cursing: *son of a bitch*. He knew hundreds of ways to dress up the term. Before his health began to fail, he picked adjectival modifiers from his profession. The sons of bitches in his epithets in those days were "brindled," "dehorned," "castrated," "bobtailed," "springing" (soon to calve, especially if it's first time), "blinky" (that is, "blue john," an all-but-butterfat-free milk given by cows that are undernourished or about to "go dry"), "one-eyed," "leather-assed," "spavin-kneed," "split-hoofed", and so on.

Although his major trading was in cattle, he sometimes bought and sold horses, especially during off seasons. When he was concentrating on the horse business, his modifiers changed so that they would be appropriate. He dressed up his favorite swear word with *pie bald, sway backed, spotted, pinto, roan,* and *Indian pony*. When Roy Rogers' splendid palomino Trigger became so popular, the trader came up with a phrase that kept the whittlers under the awnings chuckling for several weeks. The trader had been trying to get a reluctant mare into his new horse trailer to take her to a neighbor's ranch to be bred to a registered stallion. The mare stepped on the trader's foot. This perhaps unpremeditated act of violence prompted what the spit-and-whittle crew swore was the best oath they had ever heard of. He called the mare a "stumblebum, six-shootered, gas-bagged son of a bitching bitch of a damned fool palomino horse." The retired notary admired this glorious string of derogatory terms so much that he mused aloud about sending a transcription on a postal card to his grandson in the army in the South Pacific. A good friend, the postmaster, advised him, however, that to write such "filth" on a postal card was against "the federal laws of Washington" and added that if such terms were put in a V-mail letter, the Yankee censors would suspect some kind of spy code and would surely ink out the passage. The former notary sighed and said that this made him hope all the more that his grandson wasn't killed by "the little squinty-eyed sons-a-bitchin' Japs." This aged worthy seldom swore or used strong language of any sort, but when there was a mention of the Japanese or the Germans, he borrowed the trader's better phrases to blast them verbally. He never used such language about the Italians for, as he said, "all of them bastardly foreigners, 'cept for the British and some of the Frenchies, is the same as the Germans and Japs, so there ain't no use wasting breath on 'em." His distrust of the Russians was vast, and he fumed about "President Franklin Delano Roosevelt givin' them Ruskies all them Balkan countries without charging a cent, just like a hick town slut."

Not long after the recalcitrant mare stepped on the trader's foot, his health began to fail. The spit-and-whittle boys argued for years that the mare that didn't want to get "serviced" by the neighbor's stud was the cause of their friend's decline and eventual death. His various illnesses after the mare mangled his foot did cause a dramatic change in the kinds of adjectives he used to modify his standard swear term. Various diseases—diabetes, arthritis, and a "mysterious swelling of the neck glands"—as the ex-notary observed—made him a frequenter of waiting rooms at Temple's Scott and White Hospital and later in hospitals in Houston where the doctors found that the most serious disease he had was lymph cancer. Ever a man to improve his mind and his vocabulary, he read all the medical journals the doctors now and then left in their waiting rooms for the mystification of their patients. He also went to a large bookstore near a major hospital in Houston and bought a medical dictionary.

For almost two years after the trips to Houston for treatments, his health improved, and his cursing changed. Instead of using adjectives from the cattle business, he seasoned his favorite phrase with arcane medical terms. He lashed out daily at "metastasized," "strangulated," "debrided," "herniated," "occluded," "infarcted," "hyperventilating," "suppurating," and "eclamptic'" sons of bitches. The town's doctor, himself formerly an olympian among cursers, would shake his head in amazement when the spit-and-whittle crew relayed to him their more-often-than-not mispronounced imitations of their ailing friend's swearing.

As is too often the case with victims of advanced diabetes and cancer, the trader's health deteriorated after the short remission. He then had to spend most of his time resting in bed or stretched out in a glider on the side gallery to his house. During the long hours in the glider, the region's many native birds—as well as birds of passage—drew his attention. One of his two college-trained sons bought him an illustrated bird book. He set about memorizing it and soon won local respect as an ornithologist. With the coming of cool weather in late autumn, he began attending a cattle auction now and then mostly to observe. His cronies at the Taylor auction and his spit-and-whittle friends soon noticed another change in his use of adjectival modifiers. He now fulminated at "sap-sucking," "yellow-breasted," "pileated," "migratory," "nocturnal song-singing," "ruffly plumiated" (surely his own coinage), and "roseate-spoonbilled" sons of bitches.

His patient wife, who by her own admission had worn callouses on her knees praying that her husband would join the church and give up bad language, despaired when she heard some of his ornithological swearing. But her many prayers were finally answered. A few months before his death, the trader joined the church. Much to the wistful sadness of his longtime friends, he gave up the colorful cursing they had enjoyed for nearly forty years. The ex-notary missed the swearing so much that he became morose. His peers under the sheet iron awnings or at the south side of the brick drugstore building all but stopped talking to him. Then, a story the trader's wife shared with the Loyal Women's Bible Study Group percolated its way through town. When the ex-notary heard it, he rejoiced.

One sultry May afternoon, so the story went, the neighbor boy across the street slipped around to the back of trader's house and quietly entered the henhouse where a dozen or more fat Leghorn hens sought refuge from the mid-afternoon heat and humidity. This boy was called by the gentler souls in town "feeble." Those who were more plainspoken called him a "flat-out idiot." In the 1980s, some would describe him as having "an information processing deficit." (For this example of obfuscation, I am indebted to a clerk in the guidance center at a major state university.) Regardless of the way he was described, he was much given to mischief. He soon had two of the drowsy hens inside the cab of the trader's GMC pickup with its windows rolled just an inch short of the tops of the doors.

The trader awakened from a fitful nap half an hour after the boy imprisoned the hens in the pickup's cab. Leghorns are normally placid enough, but even the gentlest chickens closed up in a pickup on a day when the temperature and the humidity level are both in the upper nineties will succumb to frantic claustrophobia. When the trader stumbled from the gallery to the pickup, he didn't see the desperate hens. Diabetes had taken a severe toll on his vision and his pain medications made him far less alert than he once was. As he opened the door, the hysterical hens flew by him screaming indignation. One dug her claws into his right leg so fiercely that she tore two plugs out of his trousers and took with her some of his disease-weakened skin. After several attempts to fly up and peck his hands and arms, she fled to the clump of mesquites at the back of the lot. She didn't lay an egg for two months.

The raging hens so unnerved the man that he gave up any hopes of being able to drive the three blocks to have coffee with his friends. He walked unsteadily back to the glider where an hour later his wife found him in a state of collapse. She quickly brought him a restorative glass of iced-tea laced with mint leaves fresh from the front flower bed near the hydrant.

When he had recovered enough to tell her what happened, she mused for a few moments, then afraid the incident might have provoked foul language, asked, "Honey, what did you *say*?"

He responded wearily, "I didn't say a damned word, but I never in my life thought of so many different kinds of sons of bitches so fast."

Some four months later, cattle buyers, ranchers, farmers, their wives, and nearly everyone who knew the trader congregated in an open tabernacle on a bitterly hot early September afternoon to hear an ancient Jeremiah explain away the deceased's almost life-long indulgence in strong language and his avoidance of formal religion until the "eleventh hour."

After mercifully brief graveside remarks at a chalk hill cemetery, one of the spit-and-whittle crew gave a better eulogy by far; the ex-notary standing at the back of the mourners with his daily companions whispered huskily to them, "He was the best son-of-a-bitcher I ever hope to know of."

Later on that autumn, when the trader's will was probated, the reason he never used the word *bastard* in his epic cursing became known. In a curious codicil, the trader forgave the Civil War veteran from Virginia who in his late fifties fathered him out of wedlock. The youthful mother defied all efforts of her parents to force a shotgun wedding. She reared the boy at her parents' small ranch where he had complete freedom to roam about listening to the cowboys and to the hands who farmed the land to raise hay for cattle and horses. In this setting, he heard the sorts of inventive, even poetic cursing that gave him patterns to build on for most of the remainder of his life.

 Persuaded to Piety

In the oral tradition in central Texas this account of a nineteenth-century Methodist circuit rider survives. The

version recorded here is from the late Grady Ferguson of near Salado, Texas. He heard the basic elements of the story from his grandfather, who was the preacher in it. Like most good folktales, this one has accepted many additions and variations over the years. Its structure reveals its indebtedness to traditional oral narrative.

In the middle 1850s in the cattle-raising country in Texas west and north of Austin toward Stephenville, a cowboy-turned-Methodist-circuit-rider tried to bring true religion to various isolated settlements and to individual homes scattered amongst the hills and valleys of what has come to be called the Texas hill country. At that time, the country was still being fought over by white settlers and some remaining Comanches, as well as some renegades. The life of an itinerant minister required physical stamina as well as a certain intellectual toughness. The circuit rider who made the rounds from Austin to Stephenville carried in the same saddlebag a King James Bible and a ball-and-cap pistol. He had a Tennessee bear rifle strapped to the right side of his saddle. He thought of himself as having on the full armor of the Lord. He rode about his district fearlessly. Once, in self-defense, he had killed three Indians and two drunken renegades who were so covered with dirt and grime that their ethnic origins couldn't be determined. His parishioners respected and feared this imposing presence who sought to make God's dominion known throughout a sometimes savage land. Word spread of his quick draw. He had a reputation for being a man not to be messed around with.

Late one June afternoon when the heat and high humidity had turned the river bottoms along the Salado Creek into outdoor steam rooms, this rider came upon a small cabin all but hidden in an acre or two of thick mesquite bushes and trees. He called out, "Hello, the house! I'm Brother Andrew come to hold a service."

From within the small cabin a woman's voice responded, "Quote John 3:16 if you air a preacher. If you can't say them blessed words, I'll shoot you straight off that fancy saddle horse of yourn."

Brother Andrew made haste to recite the comforting message of God's great love for the world and waited. The door to the cabin opened. A blonde woman, harried and old beyond her years, stepped out with a long-barreled rifle in her hands.

"You just set on that horse 'till I can git my man in from the corn patch. Him and the boys are pullin' weeds and grass whilst the ground's still muddy." She motioned for the preacher to guide his horse toward the scant shade of a mesquite tree. Then she took an axe and began to beat on a rusty sweep that was hanging from the extended ridge pole of the cabin. The bell-like sounds soon brought a sweat-stained, heavily tanned rancher and farmer running frantically toward the house. Trailing him closely were three boys, about seven, nine, and eleven years old, and the family's large dog. Indians were still a threat in those days. The man and the boys feared that the pale woman had seen or heard, or—as some would say—smelled Comanches or marauding outlaws.

When the man learned that the cause for the clanging sweep was only a circuit rider, he was so overwhelmed with relief and with joy at having company that he begged the man's forgiveness for such a cold reception. He told the boys that the day's work was over—a full two hours before the usual quitting time. The boys began to run and whoop as if they had never been tired.

The man and his wife sat out in the yard chatting with their guest. When the boys were out of earshot, the preacher asked if the couple needed to have a wedding ceremony. In those days, couples often lived together for years without having been formally married. They didn't necessarily believe in free love; instead, they lived together until some peripatetic preacher happened by to perform a ceremony.

The woman thanked the man and said that she and her husband were married in old Kentucky before they headed out for Texas. She assured him they had a license. After a time, she went in the house to bring out some parched-corn coffee. With the bitter coffee substitute, she had a piece of paper she proudly offered the minister as proof of the legitimacy of her marriage to the sweat-stained man she obviously loved. The minister looked at the paper and smiled. The paper was a bill of sale for two oxen the couple had bought in San Antonio when they got together enough belongings to make the trek to Bell County. The minister then understood that the couple could not read or write—even if the woman claimed to recognize passages of scripture such as John 3:16. The couple took his quiet smile to be approval of the legality of their marriage.

After a suitably long visit, the minister asked if he could hold a brief service of worship before he rode on toward Salado where he was to spend the night before he resumed his usual somewhat more westerly ride toward Stephenville. The man and woman were pleased to have a service at their home. They called to the boys who were engaged in a fierce wrestling match with each other and with the watchdog, Old Tige. The four came hurrying to the house. The boys, like their parents, were pleased to have the merciless routines of an isolated existence changed. The service—whatever that was to be—would be something new for them. Not one of the boys had ever been to Sunday preaching. Like their parents, they could neither read nor write.

The man suggested that everyone go into the small parlor room of the cabin to escape the intense late afternoon sun. For a few minutes while the minister spoke earnestly of God's eternal love and mercy, the boys were interested. But then, their attention was distracted by Old Tige, who was rested up a bit and eager to continue the wrestling match. (Like his devoted playmates, the dog was in great need of a bath. Soap was a scarce commodity. The only soap the family had had for several months was some home-made lye bars—a lethal combination of hog fat and beef tallow with lye concocted from ashes of post oak wood. The soap was strong enough to remove paint, but, of course, the cabin didn't have any paint. The boys flatly refused to use this potent soap. The youngest boy, then about seven years old, insisted that it "itched" him and caused him to "peel all over.")

When the three boys saw Old Tige come in the overcrowded parlor, they rejoiced. They fell on the eager dog. Soon three boys and one dog became a writhing knot of smelly bodies. The stench was more potent than the noises—human and canine. The circuit rider, long accustomed to the roughness of the frontier, ignored the disruption and continued with vespers.

When the service ended, the man and woman begged the preacher to return whenever he could. He promised them he would be back.

Late in the fall just before time for first frost, the preacher found his way again to the mesquite-surrounded cabin. His welcome this time was hearty. No one threatened to shoot him off his fancy horse. The family was working to build a lean-to barn to store the corn crop and some prairie hay for the winter. The circuit rider rolled up his sleeves and helped with the work for several hours. When the time came for the worship service, the group retired to the parlor where the three boys immediately knelt down. They assumed attitudes of piety that would grace altar boys at any fancy European cathedral. The service was about half over when Old Tige came sauntering into the room in hopes of a good wrestling match. The oldest of the three boys turned to him and in a desperate stage whisper admonished, "Kneel down, Tige, or pa will beat hell out of you!"

In his benediction, the circuit rider thanked God for the mysterious ways in which His will is made known even to the little

children. And he asked God's mercy and forgiveness for all wrong-
ful deeds done by man or beast.

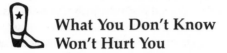 ## What You Don't Know
Won't Hurt You

*This Texas variant of a folktale occasionally heard in Ten-
nessee and Arkansas is one kind of humorous yarn told
around campfires or on bunkhouse front porches in the contemporary American west. The story shows the influence of
formal literary traditions on modern cowboy humor. The
story's high-toned lady, wife of a ranch owner, is outwitted
by a person of a lower economic class just as the upper
classes are often enough outwitted by servants in the plays
of Plautus and Terence or in Shakespeare's comedies. The
version recorded here came from a former merchant who
said the incident really happened in his general
merchandise–grocery store during the Great Depression.*

Wednesday morning, bright and early, P. L. Bigham's wife came
driving up to the side entrance to my store. You all know old P. L.
He was the one who had the fastest running-iron in three counties
until he got out of debt and bought into the bank. Well, anyhow, he
was well off, but he stayed tight with his money. Even his foreman
said old P. L. was so tight he'd skin a flea for his hide and tallow.
He married into money. That blonde-headed wife of his was from
that rich feedstore family out in San Angelo. I can't recall her
maiden name. But it doesn't matter all that much. She and old P. L.
were quite a match. She had always had money and aimed to hang
on to it, and P. L. was of a mind to get as much money as possible.
The two of them teamed up made for something that was sure to
prosper. When she moved out to P. L.'s ranch, the first thing she
did was to make him build her a dairy barn and get in from up
north—somewhere in Wisconsin, I think it was—a bunch of fancy
milch cows. Even though she was rich in her own right, she wasn't
work-brittle when it came to making extra money. Of course, the
cowboys working there hooted at those Yankee cows, but Mrs. P.
L. shut them up when she said that they wouldn't be laughing
when the time came that they got paid with money those cows
brought in. And that's the way it turned out, too. But I am getting
ahead of myself.

That Wednesday morning I am talking about, when she drove that big Buick Roadmaster—you know the kind, it had those spare tires up on the front fenders (one on either side, as a matter of fact)—up to the side door, I knew something was fishy. In those days, only the coloreds used the side entrance. I had told them they could come into my store right through the front like everybody else, but you know how long it takes to change things like that. So I knew Mrs. P. L. was up to something when she drove up to the side; and, too, she was way early in the day. She brought her butter in for me to sell every Monday, Wednesday, and Friday, but usually about noon. Anyway, there she was. And she looked all upset. She came near to dropping a paper sack she had, and she motioned for me to come to the back of the grocery section near the cooler where she couldn't be seen.

I asked what I could do for her, and she up and told me. She wanted to exchange a pound of her butter for a pound someone else had churned. Of course, I was puzzled. I knew that almost all of her cows had gone dry at about the same time; so she didn't have much butter to use at home, much less any to sell just then. I also knew that she made the best butter in the county. She made old P. L. buy good cottonseed to feed those Yankee dairy cows of hers and she tended to them herself. Worked just like a man, she did.

I probably shouldn't have done what I did then; but I did it, and it worked out all right. I asked her why she wanted to trade a pound of her perfectly good butter, the best in the country, for a pound that surely wouldn't be nearly as good as hers was. Well, sir, she looked all around, sort of walling her eyes to make sure there wasn't anybody else in hearing distance, and then she told me.

"Bob," she said, "it's like this. I was sitting out on the porch yesterday evening in the cool and got to thinking that it was just sinful of me to sit there in that wonderful cool doing nothing at all. Times being so hard, you know. So I got out my churn and did my churning. And when I lifted the lid on that churn to see if the butter had come, a little old field mouse jumped down off the bannister right into that churn of buttermilk and good, fresh butter. I snatched that mouse right out of there and stripped all that buttermilk and what little butter stuck to him right off and pitched him clear across the front yard. Then I didn't know what to do with all that good butter. I could feed the buttermilk to the chickens and the hogs; they wouldn't know a mouse had been in it. And I got to thinking, what you don't know won't hurt you. So I finished what little churning needed to be done, molded that pound of butter, and put my wrapper on it. I knew all along I couldn't eat a bite of that butter, but what could a little old, clean field mouse do to hurt it? Somebody who didn't know about that mouse could enjoy that butter just the way my chickens and hogs lapped up that buttermilk. What I want you to do is just trade my pound for a pound someone else churned. They won't know, so they can get the benefit of my good butter; and I can have a pound that will do to cook with, anyhow."

Now, I ask you, what was I do do? Mrs. P. L. was one of my few cash-paying customers. Sure, she traded butter for a few groceries now and then, but whenever she or old P. L. bought goods from me, they always had the cash money to pay. Times were hard and I couldn't lose a good customer. And I couldn't in good conscience sell some customer that pound of butter a mouse had been so close to. In a flash, the solution came to me.

"Mrs. Bigham," I said, "I understand your feelings on this matter and I'll be glad to accommodate you. I got some fairly good butter in just yesterday; and while it isn't as good as yours, it will even do to eat on biscuits." Then I up and went into the cooler by myself and shut the door. And I took her pound of butter and peeled her wrapper off of it and replaced it with a wrapper the widow Nelson used on her butter. Then I stepped right out of that cooler, shaking like I was cold. I wish you could have seen the look of relief on Mrs. P. L.'s face when she got that butter. She left happy and kept on trading with me. I guess I ought to be ashamed of myself, but after all, she said it herself, "What you don't know, won't hurt you."

Mrs. P. L. lived on until just a few years ago, just before I retired. She left instructions that she was to be driven to the cemetery in that old V-12 hearse. I guess it was a good thing I kept it after the war when I got one of those fancy fish-finned Cadillacs. Anyway, I had the devil's own time keeping a straight face as I drove that waxed old Cadillac to the burial. Every time I remembered what the preacher had said about her life of honest hard work, I almost laughed out loud. And, I still to this day don't know if that mouse died from jumping into Mrs. P. L.'s churn.

JOHN R. ERICKSON

John Erickson has worked as a cowboy and can write about that kind of life from a first-hand perspective, as he does in the material in Part 1, where he is also included. In addition to being a good hand with a rope and a horse, however, he is a talented observer and creator of personalities of cowboy life. The two represented here have at least one thread in common—they are "characters" in the richest sense of the word. They have one major difference— Ace Reid is a genuine raconteur of the finest sort, and the other is a creation of Erickson's fertile imagination.

Reid, whose perceptive cartoons enrich this volume, told Erickson these stories during the interviews from which Erickson gleaned the information for his biography of Reid. Geared for the oral presentation Ace often does across the United States at conventions and gatherings of various kinds, the stories are rich in outrageous exaggeration and metaphor. His colorful style and flair come through in these stories.

The antics of Erickson's most significant creation, Hank the Cowdog, are a must for this collection. Now in well over a dozen book-length adventure tales, Hank embodies the many worthless ranch dogs of the sort Erickson says he has found on ranches across the West. Hank may be a problem for his owners, but to readers he is a delightful persona through which to enjoy life on today's ranches. On cassette tapes accompanying each volume, Erickson himself does the more than thirty individual and distinctly different voices which he ascribes to the various people and animals in the tales and sings songs he wrote and set to music in collaboration with Trev Tevis, his business associate. One of Hank's adventures was a segment of CBS *Story Break* in 1985.

Here are some fine examples of humor from the point of view of a gifted observer, not a firsthand participant, who is one of the best talents in the field.

 **Thoroughbreds**

In his delightful biography of cowboy cartoonist Ace Reid, Erickson includes several stories told by the talented humorist and artist.

Here's a story that Ace told about horses:

I had me a racehorse, me and my dad, bought him up at Tucumcari, bought three of 'em. They was about half Thoroughbred. That was about when the Quarter Horse thing was just getting started. I'm a Thoroughbred man, I like Thoroughbred blood in my horses. Dad liked the bulldog type. But these horses had a neck on 'em and they had legs.

This old horse, I fell in love with him. He was easy broke, I had no problem, he never pitched, but when that son of a gun got hot, there ain't no telling where you was gonna go, cause there wasn't any way of stopping him.

One day I took him out and I had figure-eighted him out there in an old wheat field and I had him hot. We knew he could run, we had timed him. I said, "You crazy outfit, I'll just see if you'll run into that telephone pole."

We headed for that telephone pole and I plow-reined him. He went into it, face-first, and my face was the next one to hit the pole. Knocked both of us plumb crazy.

He'd eaten loco weed in New Mexico. We didn't know, couldn't figger it out, but it didn't take us long. We run him for a quarter one day, down one of those old lanes. Dad had a stopwatch, throwed his hat down. That's when I weighed about 150 pounds, and I come down that road flying, that wind was coming by my ears.

I passed old Dad and I pulled up. There was no pull. I kept a pulling. Finally I reached down and I got the bits. There was no stopping there. The highway was getting just a little closer and closer. We got to the highway and that dumb son of a buck turned and went right on to the ranch house and he pulled up at the gate.

Reprinted from *Ace Reid: Cowpoke* (Perryton: Maverick Books, 1984), pp. 96–97.

I fell off, I was exhausted, I was wore to a nubbing. And Dad, here he's coming in the car, he says, "You just wind-broke my horse!" And I said, "By god, I'm wind broke too!" Dad was hotter than a pistol.

 ## The Mad Hatter

It was sometimes hard to tell if Ace's promotional schemes were intended as jokes or serious money-making ventures, but he was always coming up with a new idea. Stanley Frank and Charlie Schreiner III once offered to put up five hundred dollars apiece if Reid would quit thinking.

At various times, Ace was in business with goats, Quarter Horses, Hereford cattle, Longhorn cattle, and his beer joint. He bought willow root hats out of Mexico and sold them at auction barns. He promoted the mule race in Ruidoso and the Longhorn trail drive to Dodge City. He dabbled in radio work, television, and movies.

One of his most imaginative promotions surfaced in 1976. In working around the set of the "Pony Express" movie, he noticed that all the actors wore hats that were dirty and sweat-stained, and he knew that most actors didn't sweat enough in a whole lifetime to cure and culture a good cowboy hat.

Well, one day he happened to be in Austin at a hat store. This was back when dressing cowboy was coming into style, and he saw several hippie-looking fellows come in and buy new hats. The first thing they did was stomp on the hats and drag them through the dirt to make them look authentic.

The wheels began to turn. Here was a whole new and undiscovered market for western hats! These kids may have looked poor, but they all had a Visa card in their pocket and they could buy what they wanted. They would buy a pre-sweated cowboy hat.

Ace went to some of his friends on the movie set and asked them how they made a hat look old and beat up. They revealed their secret: rub mineral oil around the crown and sprinkle potter's earth on the oil. It made a perfect sweat stain.

Ace was in business. He bought up a supply of hats and had them treated with the formula. He ran into a newspaper reporter in

Reprinted from *Ace Reid: Cowpoke* (Perryton: Maverick Books, 1984), pp. 101–102.

a bar and told his story. It came out in the Austin *American-Statesman* and was then picked up by UPI and ran all over the country. *Playboy* picked it up from UPI and ran a photograph of a naked woman wearing an Ace Reid sweat-stained hat.

Orders poured in and Ace sold out at twenty-five dollars a hat. He might have made himself a million, but when he went back to reorder, there were no more hats to be bought. The cowboy fad had struck, and every hat company in the country was sold out. Ace had to give up, but then he began thinking about promoting a line of T-shirts with prestained armpits.

 ## Republican to the Death

The following tale is one Ace Reid enjoys telling. It shows the "grit" of an old-timer.

Old man Raymond Schnell was lieutenant governor in North Dakota. He was a good friend of mine, owned three auction barns. Old man Ray was the *he* of the bunch and a tough old son of a buck, and the old man died of cancer. They called me and told me this story about when he died, what went on. It's a humdinger.

The old man was a wild-eyed Republican and he thought if you voted any other way you were a terrible man. The old man got cancer and he knew he was gonna die. So in Dickenson, North Dakota, they pushed him in his wheel chair and he addressed a big group of people there.

And old man Ray sat there with his microphone. He said, "I have worked for my state. I have worked for my country. I have tried hard. And I know why you're having this party for me tonight. I'm to die soon, but before I die, I'm gonna do one more thing for my country and my state. I'm resigning from the Republican Party."

They said it got so quiet there, you could drop a pin and hear it.

"I am joining the Democratic Party."

You heard a few gasps. Then it got quiet again.

"Because when I die, there'll be one less of them sons of bitches."

Reprinted from *Ace Reid: Cowpoke* (Perryton: Maverick Books, 1984), pp. 102–103.

COW POKES   By Ace Reid

"Now from here on, this part of the county
voted Republican!"

 LBJ Was Here

*No one was safe from Reid's humor, not even the President
of the United States.*

While Lyndon Johnson was President of the United States, Ace
discovered that he could reproduce LBJ's signature so well that
even people who worked for Johnson couldn't tell that it was a
forgery.

As you might imagine, he had great fun with this. When he
was performing at the Smithsonian Institution in 1968, he forged
LBJ's signature on the guest book and caused a great stir when
visitors began whispering, "The President is here!"

When Beverly King, banker and prankster from Graham, Texas, discovered Ace's talent, he had him sign a stack of blank checks

Reprinted from *Ace Reid: Cowpoke* (Perryton: Maverick Books, 1984), pp. 106–107.

with LBJ's signature and had a merry time giving them to his friends.

Well, one night Ace and Madge and Joe Burkett III and his wife drove to Comfort to have supper at Grandpa Damon Holmes's popular Hill Country restaurant. As they were going in, they met a phalanx of Secret Service agents who were clearing a path for President Lyndon B. Johnson.

The Cypress Creek Inn happened to be one of LBJ's favorite spots, and when he was in the Hill Country, he liked to stop in for supper.

President Johnson emerged from the men's room and walked out the door. He and Ace knew each other and they exchanged howdies. Johnson climbed into his car and drove away. Ace went straight to the men's room. Directly above the toilet, he wrote, "Lyndon B. Johnson was here," signed it with Johnson's famous signature, and dated it.

Everybody in Comfort knew that LBJ had been in the restaurant on that very night, and while it might have seemed a little strange that the President of the United States would sign his name on a bathroom wall, there was the evidence.

No one but the Reids and the Burketts knew about the prank, and they didn't talk. Grandpa Holmes was completely taken in. He was so proud of the graffiti above his toilet that he built a frame around it and covered it with glass.

There is no record of what LBJ thought about it.

 ## Confessions of a Cowdog

Erickson has had his greatest success with Hank the Cowdog, a worthless but likable composite of the dogs Erickson has known on ranches where he worked and visited. Hank is the head of ranch security and is as unappreciated as an extra inch of snow in February in the Texas Panhandle. His determination to carry on the family tradition of excellence is not swayed by his unappreciative audience. He knows who he is; he just wishes others could see it his way, especially his spineless companion, Drover, who looks for a dark corner of the tool shed when Hank's wild

Reprinted from *The Devil in Texas and Other Cowboy Tales* (Perryton: Maverick Books, 19810, pp. 41–46.

*schemes go bad, as they always do. Slim and High Loper,
the two cowboys on the ranch, are usually the ones who fail
to appreciate Hank. Hank showed them, however, when he
appeared in a television segment of CBS* Story Break *in the
spring of 1985.*

August 15: My name's Hank. I'm a cowdog on a ranch in Texas. I
never heard of a cowdog keeping a diary, but I'm going to give it a
try.

My ma came from good stock. They were Australians, back
to who laid the chunk, and they were all good with cattle. Ma used
to say that Uncle Beanie was the best cowdog in South Texas.

But she fell in with a bad crowd when she was young, and
that's where she met my old man. She used to tell me about him:
"He was a good bloke, but just a wee bit south of worthless."

I asked her what it was that attracted her to him. She got a
far-off look in her eyes and sighed. "We were both young and
foolish. He was a dashing rogue. Hank, that daddy of yours could
pee on more tires than any dog in Texas." That always stuck with
me, kind of gave me a standard to aim for.

August 25: It was terrible hot today. This long hair makes me
awfully uncomfortable. Me and Drover spent most of the morning
shaded up beneath the gas tanks. I didn't think I had enough
energy to move—until Pete came along.

Pete's the barn cat around here. I don't like him. I don't like
his looks. I don't like his attitude. I don't like cats in general. I
whipped him and ran him up a tree.

That got me all hot and worked up, so I went up to the septic
tank. It overflows and there's always a nice cool puddle of water
there. I plopped down in it. Oh, it felt good. I rolled around and
kicked all four legs in the air. When I got out, I felt like a million.

I trotted down to the house, just as Slim and High Loper
were coming out the yard gate. I trotted up to say howdy. I rubbed
up against Loper's leg and gave myself a good shake. I guess I hit
him with some mud and water. Made him mad.

"Git outa here, Dammit!" He's a funny guy, gets mad at little
things. When he's in a good humor, he calls me Hank. When he's
mad, he calls me Dammit. When he's really mad, he calls me
Dammittohell, whatever that means. I answer to all three.

September 1: It was cloudy and cool today. Me and Drover
were sleeping down at the corrals. Drover's my running buddy, a
small, short-haired white dog. He's got no cow sense at all, just
doesn't understand the business. I think he's scared of cattle.

Well, I was sleeping, don't you see, and Drover woke me up. "Hank, get up, boy, there's cattle coming this way, a whole herd of them, coming in like elephants!"

I'm in charge of ranch security. I don't allow cattle up around the place. I came out of a dead sleep and jumped to my feet.

We went ripping out of the corral, me in the lead and Drover bringing up the rear. He was right about the cattle. It was a by-gosh invasion, fifty, sixty head of stock.

As I went on the attack, my ma's words came back to me:

Bite 'em on the heels
Bite 'em on the nose
Take a hunk of hair out
Make 'em shake their toes.

I went straight to the lead cow. She was a horned wench, and had an evil temper to boot. She dropped her head and started throwing hooks at me. Out in the pasture, maybe I would have backed away. But not this time. I was protecting the ranch (did I mention that I'm in charge of ranch security?), and I was prepared to give my life if necessary.

She rolled me once with them big horns, which kind of inflamed me, don't you see, and I put the old Australian fang-lock on her nose. Ma would have been proud of me. In seconds, I had that north-bound herd going south. Drover was right behind me, cheering me on. "Git 'em, Hankie, sic 'em, boy!"

I sicced 'em, all right, but come to find out, Slim and High Loper were trying to pen them in the corral. How was I supposed to know? Next thing I knew, High Loper was coming at me, swinging his rope and calling my name. "Damnittohell, git outa here!"

I got chased up to the yard. I don't know what happened to Drover. He just sort of disappeared when things went sour. He does that a lot.

September 15: Had a wild time last night. Me and Drover was sleeping by the yard gate. Along about midnight, he woke me up.

"Hear that?" he whispered. I listened and heard it. Coyotes, and they were close. "Let's run 'em off."

"You think we should?" I was still half-asleep.

"Heck, yes. This is our ranch, ain't it?"

"Good point. But I don't want any rough stuff. Those guys are thugs."

We loped up the hill until we could see a coyote standing in the road, a skinny, scruffy-looking little villain. I barked at him and told him to scram, we didn't allow no coyote trash around our ranch. He told me to drop dead.

I was ready to leave it at that, but Drover thought we had a responsibility to the ranch. "Let's give him a whipping. There's two of us and only one of him."

I counted, and sure enough, we had him outnumbered two to one. "Well, all right, if you think we should."

He thought we should. So I swaggered out and jumped the coyote. I throwed him to the ground while Drover nipped at his tail.

I sure was surprised when that little coyote's uncles and cousins and big brothers showed up. All at once I was in the midst of a coyote family reunion. Man alive, they was biting me in places I'd never been bit before.

"Come on, Drover!" I yelled. "Don't save anything back, boy, this is the real thing!"

Drover had disappeared. I managed to escape with everything but two pounds of hair and part of my left ear. An hour later, I found Drover, huddled up in the darkest, blackest corner of the machine shed.

I was all set to whip the tar out of him, but he cried and begged and told me that, down deep, he was opposed to violence. How can you whip a dog that says that?

November 1: Got into trouble today. High Loper and Slim were doctoring sick cattle this morning, running them through the squeeze chute and giving them shots and pills and stuff.

Me and Drover were hanging around, watching. The cowboys went to dinner and left all the medicine beside the chute.

Drover went over and sniffed at a cardboard box full of big white pills. "You know what these are? Amino acid boluses. They're supposed to give energy to sick cattle. They're good for cowdogs too."

I walked over to the box and sniffed. "Smells good. But wouldn't the cowboys be mad if we ate 'em?"

"Oh, heck no. It says right there on the box that cowdogs are supposed to eat them."

I squinted at the box. "So it does."

I pulled one out and chewed on it. Say, that stuff was good. I went back for another one, and another one, and then I went back for seconds. It beat the heck out of that cheap co-op dog food.

Before long, the box was empty. When the cowboys came back from lunch, I was sunning myself beside the chute, full and happy and feeling good. I gave the boys a grin and wagged my tail.

High Loper stared at the empty box. "Where did those . . . " He looked at me. I must have had a few crumbs on my chops. "Why you worthless cur, that box cost twenty-one dollars!"

Huh? I looked around for Drover. He had disappeared. About then the rocks and sticks started flying, and I ran for my life.

I found Drover in the machine shed and I jumped right in the middle of him. He cried and begged but I didn't listen this time. My momma didn't raise no fool.

"Wait!" he cried. "If you won't whip me, I'll tell you a deep, dark, awful secret."

"Huh? An awful secret?"

"Yeah. Listen. It was all Pete's idea. He wanted to get us into trouble."

"Naw. No foolin'?"

He raised his right paw. "It's God's truth, Hankie."

"Why that sorry, no good for nuthin' cat! Come on, Drover, it's time to clean house."

I marched down to the saddle shed, caught Pete plumb by surprise, whupped him, re-whupped him, and ran him up a tree. Drover was behind me all the way, cheering me on.

"Git 'im, Hankie, git 'im!"

That was that. We went up for a roll in the sewer, and I said to Drover, "Boy, I can't believe Pete would try to pull a deal like that on us cowdogs. How dumb does he think we are?"

He shook his head. "Pretty dumb, Hank, pretty dumb."

★ **3** ★

Belles Lettres

ELMER KELTON

Elmer Kelton has been a writer of livestock news, history, and fiction for all of his career, but he started out a cowboy. He protests that he was not cut out to follow that line of work despite the fact that most of his family followed cowboying, but he has remained close to the West and cowboy life. From the post of farm and ranch editor for the San Angelo *Standard-Times*, which he took on graduating from the University of Texas in 1948, he moved to the *Sheep and Goat Raiser Magazine* and then to the prestigious *Livestock Weekly*. Along the way he has produced nearly thirty novels, a host of short stories, most of them for pulp magazines in the 1940s and 1950s, and some excellent historical writing about the settlement and development of Texas. Kelton's chief love has been the writing of fiction and he has won numerous awards from Western Writers of America and the National Cowboy Hall of Fame. From his first novel, *Hot Iron*, in 1955, to, *The Man Who Rode Midnight*, in 1987, Kelton has interpreted the efforts of men and women who face the challenges of living on the frontier in a constant state of flux as new developments force change on the people who are to survive. An excellent literary craftsman, he has concentrated on depicting the qualities of the wide variety of characters he has created in his fiction—not trail dust and gun powder!

 The Coyote Hunt

Kelton uses humor subtly and sparingly. His characters joke and pull pranks, but an element of danger is present in some

of their "humorous" antics. The passage that follows comes from The Time It Never Rained, *Kelton's excellent novel of the contemporary West. When two coyotes begin to plague the flock of sheep that aging rancher Charlie Flagg is trying to run on his San Angelo-area ranch during the big drought of the 1950s, Flagg does the only thing he can— asks his neighbors to help rid the range of the menace. But he hasn't counted on the new difficulties cars and a plane can bring.*

When the hunters returned to headquarters at noon they found that women had brought cakes, pies, and fruit salad. Charlie swore a little at sight of two washtubs filled with iced-down beer. He started to call Mary and demand to know who in the hell had ordered that. Then he saw Suds O'Barr, and he knew. No telling what a few cans of beer might do to somebody's nervous trigger finger. But this was supposed to be a party, after a fashion. He didn't want to throw a wet blanket over it.

He had invited a minister out to say grace before the meal. Charlie seldom went in to hear his sermon; always too busy, seemed like. But Mary usually went, hoping to pick up enough religion that some would rub off on her reluctant spouse. Failing that, maybe she would develop enough influence Up Yonder to get him into Heaven anyway. Charlie saw the minister staring disapprovingly at him over the tubs of beer. Charlie shrugged in innocence and retreated.

He noted that the minister in his blessing said nothing about the reason for this gathering today, to kill coyotes. He suspected the minister's sympathies were more with the coyotes than with the men; they weren't raiding his flock. But no matter, Charlie fed him anyway.

The meal done, the live-oak motte looked as if a tornado had swept it. The men sat around rubbing their bellies, smoking, drinking up the last of the beer. They talked about dry weather, horses, sheep, cattle, and women, more or less in that order, though Charlie observed that Tom and the younger set tended to put women first, even ahead of horses.

"Yes, Mr. Writer, we still have cattle stampedes . . .
nearly everytime we head 'em toward a feed
trough!"

Weather warmed considerably after dinner. The afternoon
sun caused most horsemen to peel their coats and tie them behind
their cantles. The pickup riders rolled their windows down. They
found nothing in the first pasture. They worked the second, and
still no luck.

Late in the afternoon Charlie worriedly let down a wire gate
and motioned the hunters into the final pasture. By now he had
lost a large percentage of the crowd. As the remaining men gathered around him he said, "We've cleaned this place like a fine-tooth
comb. If they're not in this pasture they've drifted plumb out of the
country."

The flying hunter had had to go to town to land for a tank of
gasoline. Now he had returned to finish the drive. Leisurely he
worked back and forth, the rough roar of the motor causing Charlie's
roan to shy every time the plane passed over. Charlie glanced up
and thought how low that contraption would have to dip for the
flyer to shoot a coyote on the ground, low enough to get mesquite

thorns in the gas tank. Charlie wouldn't ride with him in that kite for all the wool in Boston.

The line ragged out. Charlie felt the same disappointment that slumped the shoulders of the other riders. The pair of coyotes must have drifted away. Looking for fresher game, perhaps. But that probably wouldn't be the end of it. Chances were they would come back. When a coyote developed a liking for your place, he was loyal to it. You never counted yourself rid of him until you saw him dead.

The racket started abruptly. To Charlie's right a horn honked. Someone shouted. A shotgun blasted and the race was on. He could see horses running, pickups and jeeps pulling in. He caught a blurred glimpse of tannish color.

Coyote!

It had jumped up ahead of the hunters and had tried to hit the fence. The wing men headed it off and turned it back toward the center. Now it was running like a deer, dodging in and out of the brush. The warwhoops came to Charlie as the riders pressed in. There was a gunshot, another and another.

Motors roared. From all over the pasture, drivers floorboarded their pickups and jeeps to be in on the kill. Autumnhardened mesquite splintered under the impact of speeding vehicles, branches flying like chaff from wheat. Charlie heard a windshield smashed by a heavy limb, but the pickup never slowed. He heard a loud bump and saw a pickup leap into the air, then plump down hard. It was Rounder Pike's. His brother Yancy gripped the door and seat and looked pale enough to die. Rounder was grinning like a monkey eating bananas, never missing a stroke on his cud of chewing tobacco.

The horsemen had the coyote hemmed in—or thought they had. Some were swinging ropes, trying to get a throw. But they were casting their loops too quickly and spoiling their chances. The coyote doubled back between a horse's legs, and the horse set in to pitching. The rider dropped a shotgun. The horse stepped on it, snapping the stock.

The flyer circled once for a look. He couldn't get a shot because of the riders.

Tom Flagg and his rodeo friends Shorty and Chuck went spurring by Charlie as if he were standing still. Tom and Shorty were shaking down their ropes, building loops. Chuck carried a shotgun. Tom let out a jubilant yell and cast a quick throw as the coyote barreled past him. The loop missed and caught instead around a mesquite stump. Riding full tilt, Tom hit the end of the rope before he could pull up. The impact set the mount back on its haunches. The rope snapped. Tom slid over the gray's shoulders and rolled in the dry grass. He jumped up, grabbed his hat, then caught the reins before the horse could break away. Tom was back in the saddle before the dust cleared.

Now two pickups were in full chase. One was an old model with a running board. A cowboy stood on it, his right arm hooked over the rear-view mirror for a hold while he kept a two-handed death grip on a shotgun. He trained the barrel on the coyote just as the pickup lurched and a thorny mesquite limb raked him, taking half his shirt. The buckshot blasted through the front fender and blew the tire.

The other pickup was almost upon the coyote, the driver trying to run the animal down. The coyote swerved abruptly and changed direction. The driver wheeled about in a vain effort to keep up. His front wheels dropped into a hole and stopped him dead in the path of the other pickup, which was still rolling. Brakes squealed. Men shouted. The pickups bumped with a crunch of metal and glass. The cowboy on the running board slid belly down in the dirt, the rest of his shirt strung out behind him.

Charlie reined up and let the chase go. In disgust he slapped his felt hat against his leather chaps. He shouted, "Hell's bells and damnation!"

Tom Flagg made a quick splice. He and Shorty were still in the chase, swinging their ropes. Shorty missed. Tom's loop went around the coyote, but the animal was through it and gone before Tom could jerk up the slack.

Shotgun in hand, Chuck Dunn shouted excitedly, "He's comin' at me. I got him, boys!"

He raised the gun and squeezed the trigger just as his horse made a jump. The muzzle flew up. Out of killing range but close enough for a burn, Shorty Magee's mount caught the force of the pellets across the rump. The horse bawled and went straight up. Shorty squalled once, grabbed at the saddlehorn and missed it. The horse came down without him.

Page Mauldin, old as he was, had caught the fever. He spurred after the coyote, rope in his hands.

Charlie shouted after him, "Page, you watch yourself!" He had as well have been talking to his own roan horse. Page had reverted, for the moment at least, to his wild old cowboy days. Charlie could hear him yelling in delight, closing in on the coyote. Manuel Flores spurred after him, close behind.

Charlie didn't see what Page ran over, but he saw the horse

spill, saw Page's hat go sailing as if the old ranchman had thrown it. In a swirl of dust he saw the horse staggering to its feet, Page hung to the stirrup. Frightened, the horse began to run.

Charlie swallowed, his heart almost stopping. "Oh, my God!"

But Manuel Flores was there in seconds, grabbing the loose reins, wrapping them quickly around his saddlehorn, bringing Page's horse to a stop. Before Charlie could get there, Page had kicked his foot free of the stirrup. He lay on his right hip, propped upon his elbow. Page shook his head, looking around wildly for a moment, afraid of being kicked by the horse. But Manuel had led the animal off twelve or fifteen feet, out of the danger range.

Charlie swung heavily to the ground and found Diego Escamillo had beaten him there. Diego bent down over his employer, his black eyes wide with concern. "I'm all right," Page said. He was feeling foolish and showed it. "Dammit, Charlie, did I do that?"

"You sure as hell did. I thought for a minute you was one of them kids."

"I reckon I got carried away. But I like to've caught him."

"And like to've killed yourself. If it hadn't of been for Manuel, you'd of had your tail in a crack."

Page turned his eyes to Diego. "Get me up from here. Let's see if there's anything broke."

Diego carefully helped him to his feet. Page took two or three short, cautious steps. He was shaken but otherwise all right.

Charlie said, "Hell of a note, the richest man in Rio Seco brought down by a coyote."

Page Mauldin jerked his chin at Manuel, and Manuel brought him his horse. Diego tried to help Page back into the saddle, but Page impatiently waved him away. He mounted stiffly and slow, reaching down to pat the nervous animal on the shoulder. "Be gentle now," he said quietly to the horse. "Wasn't your fault, it was mine." Page turned then to young Manuel.

"Boy, I owe you."

Manuel shrugged, self-conscious at the attention. "It was easy."

"Not from where I was. I'll pay you, boy."

"You don't owe me nothin', Mister Mauldin."

"You got a horse of your own, muchacho?"

Manuel glanced at Charlie. He had the exclusive use of a couple, but they really belonged to Charlie; everything on the ranch did. "No, sir."

"You'll have one. I'll give you a colt to raise and break for yourself."

Manuel glanced again at Charlie, his eyes asking if it was all right. Charlie said, "Page, I'll hold you to that. He could use a good horse."

In the dust and confusion the coyote would have been lost had it not been for the flyer. He got the animal lined out, swooped down like an eagle after a baby lamb and sent it rolling with a single shot.

Charlie rode up to the red-faced Chuck Dunn and pointed with his chin. "You better take that gun and go finish the coyote off." But Chuck had lost interest in shooting. Charlie went ahead and gave the animal a coup de grace with his own .12-gauge.

Charlie sat at the supper table with Mary, munching leftover kid from the noon barbecue, eagerly looking at the variety of pies and cakes brought by the women who had spent the day here. He knew he had better eat his fill tonight, for Mary would give them all to the Flores family to prevent his having the pleasure of them. Tomorrow there would be nothing for him but turnip greens.

He had used some salty language in the heat of frustration this afternoon, but now he chuckled as the memories came back to him in the comfort and quiet of the kitchen. Mary demanded, "You going to tell me, Charlie Flagg, or are you going to sit there and laugh to yourself all night?"

Charlie shook his head. He doubted it would be funny to her, but he told the whole story the best he could. Only a time or two did he catch the flicker of humor in her eyes. He said, "It was worse than the wreck of the old 97. Most of them took it in good humor, though, except Shorty Magee. He was lookin' for somebody to fight. Tom had to leave the bunch and take him to town."

"You never did see anything of the second coyote?"

"Not a hair. The one we got was the bitch. I reckon the old dog-wolf has strayed out of the country."

"Without his mate? That doesn't sound natural to me. Anytime you find a female, there's usually a male nearby."

Charlie took that to cover more than just the coyotes; he took it for pride in her sex. He shrugged. "Comes a time a man just has to get away to himself."

Mary was not impressed. "I'll bet you just missed him."

"Not hardly. The way we screened them pastures, not even a jackrabbit could've got by without us seein' him."

She said indulgently, "Maybe you're overrating yourselves."

"No-siree. I tell you, we didn't miss a thing."

The telephone rang. Charlie set down his coffee cup and walked stiffly over to answer it. It was still the same old crank-up wall set August Schmidt had turned over to him years ago. "Hello!" He always shouted as if he were afraid the phone wouldn't work and he wanted them to hear him anyway. "Who is this? . . . Oh, hello, Tom . . . What's that? Doctor's just got through workin' on Shorty? I didn't know Shorty caught any of that buckshot . . . Oh, I see."

He cupped his hand over the mouthpiece and explained to Mary, "Wasn't buckshot, it was prickly pear thorns. When Shorty fell off, he landed square in the pear."

He turned back to the telephone. "What's that you say? You just saw Rounder Pike?" Charlie's eyes widened a bit. "No! That old liar is just hoorawin' you . . . What? He really did? . . . They really did?"

BENJAMIN CAPPS

Born in ranching country in Archer County, Texas, Benjamin Capps has written eight outstanding novels dealing with the American West. Perhaps best known are *Sam Chance*, *The White Man's Road*, *A Woman of the People*, and *The Trail to Ogallala*. He has won Spur awards from the Western Writers of America and the Levi Straus Golden Saddleman Award, and he is a member of the Texas Institute of Letters. Although he worked at several jobs during his life, even as a college professor for a two-year period, he spent a decade as a tool and die maker in Grand Prairie, Texas. He left this trade in 1961 to become a full-time writer.

He earned his master of arts in English at the University of Texas. His thesis is a still-unpublished novel called *Mesquite Country*, done under the direction of folklorist Mody C. Boatright. Part of that novel is printed here. A private person, Capps has kept pretty much to himself, but he used his time wisely to produce a body of literature that ranks him among the best authors ever to produce interpretive fiction about the American West.

 Slim Wilkinson

Ranch country people like their dogs, and here is a poignant but funny story about some good old boys and a pack of hounds on a wolf hunt that shows how it was done before airplanes and helicopters. Several characteristics of ranch life are noticeable in the following story, published here for the first time. Confidence in tried and proven animals and

190

COW POKES

By Ace Reid

"Jerk the backstrap, cut the hams into steaks, the rest into chili, and have the head mounted!"

distrust of younger ones are evident. Most significantly, the nostalgic view that the best times and the best dogs are in the past is replaced by a positive attitude that good things still lie ahead.

Buck Holmes stomped back and forth on his back porch, shaking the loose flooring with his cowboy boots and causing the tin patches on the roof to rattle. Every time he looked at the big black-and-tan hound that lay on the edge of the porch, he cursed. He said with fervor, "I ought to kill that fool Perkins! I'll horsewhip him; that's what I'll do! I'll cowhide him!"

Buck was not a handsome man. He had one top front tooth missing where a yearling steer, which he had been trying to bull-dog, had stepped in his face at a rodeo fifteen years ago.

When he had calmed down, he stood with hands on skinny hips, looking at the hound. The dog looked back with big serious eyes, his jaws drooping, his forelegs before him on the porch; one paw was twisted outward unnaturally and was matted with dried blood. Buck rubbed his red beard stubble, slowly shook his head, then yelled in through the screen door, "Myrtle! you got anything for Old Rip to eat?"

His wife came to the door. She was a big woman with a broad kind face and straw-colored hair. "Why, it's Old Rip, isn't it, Buck! Old Rip's come home."

"Yeah, but I'd just as lief he hadn't. Look at his leg."

"I'll swan!" Myrtle said. She opened the screen to peer at the old dog. "What could have done it, Buck? Is he been in a fight someplace?"

"He's been in one of that Perkins's wolf traps. Confound that old man! I'll get even with him if it's the last thing I do!"

"Well, he never meant to catch him," Myrtle said in a soothing voice. "He's just trying to trap and make a living."

"Make a living! Look at my dog, Myrtle! The best dog I got! Ruint! And you tell me old Perkins is got to make a living. Trapping all the wolves and putting them up in a cage! How's a sporting man going to get in a decent wolf hunt?"

Old man Perkins lived in a tent over on Webb Creek and trapped skunk, opossum, coon, and badger in the winter and coyotes the year around. In the summer the skins were no good, but Baxter County paid a bounty of two dollars for a pair of coyote ears. The coyotes Perkins caught in the autumn he sometimes caged up and saved until cold weather when their fur would become thick and salable.

"Fightin'est dog I ever had," Buck went on. "I knew he was getting old, but I didn't expect him to end like this." Suddenly a pleading note came into his voice. "Look at him, Myrtle!" He turned and smashed his bare fist against the gray weatherboarding. "Look at my best dog!"

"Good lands!" Myrtle said. "Don't do that, Buck. You'll hurt your hand. I'll get something for him to eat."

She went into the kitchen and brought back a slab of yellow cornbread. Buck broke it into chunks on the porch. The big dog hobbled over eagerly. "Look at him walk! And him the fightin'est dog I ever had!" He shook his head slowly as he watched the dog gulp down the cornbread. "I aim to get even with that Perkins. I'll cut him down like a broom weed. I'll take me a bear trap over there and set it in the door of his tent and see how he likes to get caught."

Buck stood over the hound, without the swagger he usually had in his bearing. His bony hips weren't pushed out in front as usual. "I haven't got the wolfhounds I once had, Myrtle. There was Old Rosy. I've never had another dog like her. She was the trailin'est dog I ever had and the smartest. And there was Old Tip; he was the runnin'est dog I ever had and a good all-around dog, too. Now here's Old Rip, the fightin'est dog I ever had, and he's as good as done for. It's like a sign, that's what it is. The sporting in this country is about over."

Myrtle wished to pacify him. She said hopefully, "Well, there's the pups, Buck. Maybe one of the pups will turn out good." "The pups! Myrtle, you oughtn't to even mention the pups when I'm talking about dogs like Old Rip. The pups! Slim Wilkinson, for instance. He will do good to get his full growth without bothering to turn out good. He'll fall in the cistern and drown or else break his back from jumping around like a fool."

"He might turn out to have a good nose," Myrtle suggested. "He's always smelling of something, seems like."

"Yeah, he's always smelling of tobacco spit or where you throw out dishwater. You look at my dogs a minute, Myrtle. Right now I got Ike and Bob and Wing and Fan and Trailer and Rome and Pete and Jip and Ringer. Ringer would be a top dog outside of running rabbits. And then I got the four pups, four if you count Slim Wilkinson. I got enough dogs, Myrtle. They make a good pack if Old Rip is with them. But look at him. I guess the sporting in this country is about over."

Old Rip sopped up the last cornbread crumb, as well as some dust out of the cracks, then hobbled down under the porch to lie down. Watching his pitiful attempt to walk, Buck moaned, "Why couldn't it have been one of the pups, instead of Old Rip."

Buck's "pups" were over a year old. The largest, Slim Wilkinson, was almost as big as Old Rip and still growing. He was white with a scattering of large and small black patches. About the young hound, Buck would say "That Slim Wilkinson is the clumsiest fool dog I ever had. All I got for him is hopes he might change. If he was to tighten up in the joints some and stop that crawling up to you on his belly with his legs flopping out at the sides and him grinning and slapping his tail on the ground, then he might be a passable dog."

But Buck Holmes's four boys, none of them the connoisseur of hounds that Buck was, loved the pups, which they had helped raise. Elmer, an unlikely youngster of nine years, even went so far as to think of the loose-jointed Slim Wilkinson as his favorite.

The boys mourned Old Rip's crippling almost as much as Buck did, for they knew the old dog was a great one. They knew it because Buck said it. They did not think of their father as an irresponsible tenant farmer or an unsuccessful rancher—both of which he was—but as a man who could not be judged by any ordinary standards at all. Indeed, their pa had done everything worth doing, such as riding the meanest horses in the world when he used to follow the rodeos, and he knew everything worth knowing, such as how to break a dog from chasing rabbits. Their pa could still do anything worth doing; he had built a dog trailer as good as a factory-made job and had covered it with the chicken wire from the garden fence; it didn't matter if the chickens got into the garden because the grass burrs and ragweeds always choked out the vegetables anyway.

For several days Buck did nothing but feed Old Rip and mope around the house, occasionally muttering some vile threat against the trapper Perkins. Then one day just after noon, he walked out, followed by the four boys, to the windmill a hundred yards from the house. They turned and faced the house. Then Buck began to yell, "Old Rip! Hyah, hyah! Hey, Rip! Hyah, Rip!"

The boys took up the call. Dogs poked their heads around the corner of the cane stack and from under the barn and smoke-house. Old Rip scrambled out from under the back porch and ran toward them eagerly, but he was favoring his right front leg. When the old dog had covered a third of the distance to the windmill, the pups bellied out from under the smokehouse, led by Slim Wilkin-son, and came pounding down the same trail. They got to Buck and the boys as soon as the old dog.

Buck squatted on his boot heels, patting the old dog and wallowing the loose skin on the dog's neck; but he was shaking his head. "He can still run, kids, but not like he used to. And he'll get to where he knows it, and it'll kill his sporting blood. He'll be just another old pot-licker hound."

Slim Wilkinson was bounding around gaily, like some kind of jubilee was in progress. He finally settled down on Elmer, the only one of the boys who would let the young dog lick him in the face. "Pa," Elmer said, "did you see the way Old Slim Wilkinson came scooting down here?"

"Good night, Elmer!" said Wayne, who was next older than Elmer. "This sure isn't the time to say anything like that."

Buck's hand was still over the old dog's shoulder. "Kids, I sure would like to have one last good wolf chase while Old Rip's still got some sporting in him."

"Boy!" Elmer said, "Old Slim Wilkinson is the runnin'est dog of all the pups, isn't he, Pa?"

"Good night, Elmer!" Bert said. "You haven't got a lick of sense. You oughtn't to say 'runnin'est.' The runnin'est dog Pa ever had was Old Tip and a long time before you were born. You ought to know better than to say some fool pup is the best at something, without Pa says it first. Good night! Pa, I ought to kick Elmer a little and try to learn him something about dogs."

"Naw, don't be kicking." A crafty look had come into Buck's face, along with the dejection. "Kids, isn't this Saturday? And doesn't Perkins always walk in to Baxter City on Saturdays?"

"Yeah," Red said.

"And doesn't it take him all day to buy grub and pack it back out to his camp?"

"Yeah, he never gets in till dark."

"Kids, I'm going over to Perkins's camp to see if he'll pay me for catching Old Rip. Red, you go up in the barn loft and get me a tow sack and throw it in the car. I been promising you all I'd take you wolf hunting some day. Well, we might go tonight."

He refused to answer any of the boy's questions. Five minutes later he had fired up the old car and headed out the wagon road toward the highway.

"Pa's going to take that tow sack," Elmer said, "and throw it over old Perkins' head, and beat him up."

"Good night, Elmer! Perkins isn't even at his camp now," Red reminded him.

"He said he'd like to set a bear trap for that Perkins," Myrtle said. "I hope Buck don't go over to his camp while he's gone and make some kind of trouble."

An hour later Buck came back. He swung open the car door and stepped out with some of the swagger he used to have. The back of his hand was marked with a long red scratch. He stood at one of the back car windows, the glass of which was missing, while the boys gathered around. In the back of the car on the floor lay the tow sack, full, a heap of something that didn't move, but seemed to tremble slightly.

"Pa's got old Perkins in there," Elmer said, awestruck.

"I got me a growling, spitting cyclone in there," Buck said. He sucked at the scratch on his hand. Then he said, with a drama in his voice which sent goose bumps up the spines of the four boys, "Namely, a wolf! Catch up the dogs, kids. Get your chores done. We're going wolf hunting tonight."

They hurriedly cut the cookstove wood, slopped the hogs, gathered the eggs, milked old Bessie, and began to put the hounds into the trailer so they would have them all in before dark. The old hounds saw what was going on and came running up to get into the trailer. Sensing that something important was afoot, Slim Wilkinson scrambled into the front seat of the car.

"Slim Wilkinson, doggone your hide," Buck said. "I reckon you can go, but you dern sure can't drive."

Elmer, who had never been on a hunt before and who was as excited as the pup, had preceded Slim Wilkinson into the car. "Pa, could Old Slim Wilkinson ride in here with us if I'll hold him in my lap?"

"Hold him in your lap, nothing! He's twice as big as you are. Stop hugging that clumsy pup, Elmer, and come out of that car. We're not leaving till sundown."

At supper Buck was thoughtful. He had eaten half of his first helping of red beans when he lay down his fork and cleared his throat. "Kids, I better talk to you a little bit. I better tell you some things about tonight, so you'll know."

"Stop smacking, Bert," Myrtle said. "All you kids stop eating, so's you can hear your pa better."

"Kids, it's something about sporting I want to say. I want to start with your grandpa. He wasn't a good looking man. He had big red ears, like Elmer here has got; or come to think of it, all you kids has got sort of red ears. But that isn't the point. Your grandpa had something real unusual about him; he was a sporting man. It was a kind of magic he had. But, kids, you know he had a dog—Old Tiger." Buck screwed up his face and fingered one of his big red ears, finding it hard to say what he was trying to. "Well, kids, I've had lots of dogs myself, and I've had three kind of like Old Tiger. But that thing is passing away. It's going. And the last of it is out yonder in the dog trailer with a busted foot—Old Rip. He's the last." Down Myrtle's broad, simple face two fat tears ran and dropped from her chin down to her heavy bosom.

Buck went on. "It's hard to talk about that sporting thing, but you could tell it plain when you saw it. If it was in a dog, that dog would do things you wouldn't think any dog could do. You take Old Rosy. Red, you remember Old Rosy; she was still alive when you was little. Well, say we had Old Rosy here, and there was only one wolf in Baxter County, and we take Old Rosy out hunting; I tell you she would pick up that wolf's trail. That's how good she was.

"Well, kids, so that's why we're going on this hunt. We've got a wolf, and we'll have a good hot trail. Old Rip will get him, with the others helping. You see, Old Rip won't hunt much more; after a while he'll get sad about his foot. And the other dogs will get to understand about his foot, and they won't respect him any more. The sporting in this country is about over. So that's why I want you kids to go with me and know what we're doing; we're just going to take Old Rip out and turn him loose and see that magic work one last time."

They all ate in silence for several minutes. Then the four boys began to talk again. The solemnity of the occasion, as explained by Buck, could not alter their thrill at the thought of the night ahead of them.

After supper, Buck and the four boys went out to the car, Buck with his dog-calling horn slung over his shoulder on a leather thong. The mesquite brush in the west made a ragged silhouette against the setting sun as they started out.

"Whereabouts we heading for, Pa?" Red asked.

"I believe we'll go over to Chaparral Ridge. There's a wagon road goes right up there if it hasn't grown up too bad. This wolf will stick to the high ground mostly, and maybe we can follow them quite a ways in the car."

The car was noisy. When they hit a rough place it sounded like a chain-drive grain binder. One of the headlights blinked off and on. A half-moon began to brighten up overhead.

They came out of the north end of Chaparral Ridge. It was a wide, uneven stretch of land, partly clear of brush, which came up out of the rolling hills to the west and sloped more sharply away on the east to flat bottom thickets and Webb Creek a mile away. The ridge extended south three or four miles.

Buck turned off the ignition. "Here she is, kids. Now, Red, you get by the trailer door. When I give the word, swing her open." He took the tow sack from the car and walked out across the clearing, holding the sack away from himself and unwhirling the top as he went. The coyote was a good load. Old Rip began to whine like a baby.

A hundred and fifty feet away, Buck threw the sack down and jumped back. The sack writhed. The coyote came out like a steel spring uncoiling. He became a part of the dim moon shadows on the ridge, and Buck waited an eternity of ten seconds.

"Let 'em go, Red! Hyah, Rip! Hyah, Rip!"

Boys and dogs ran forward together. Old Rip went past Buck in a fast but limping run, wound back and forth across the coyote's trail with his nose to the ground and with a long bay of discovery took off trailing. The other dogs followed. Slim Wilkinson bounded around between the boys, barking, kissed Elmer on the nose, then pounced on the tow sack and shook it savagely. The other dogs were out of sight when he started after them in a long, leaping gait.

The sounds from the dogs became fainter and fainter. Buck and the boys got into the car and headed on south down Chaparral Ridge. They stopped once and heard the chase still ahead of them, then drove on a half mile farther.

"They're down there in the flat, Pa," Bert said.

"Yep. I believe that wolf is taking it into his head to make some circles."

"I can tell which one is Slim Wilkinson, can't you, Pa?" Elmer said. "He sounds so glad."

"Don't talk so much, Elmer," Red said. "Good night! we can't hear the dogs with you talking."

"Kids," Buck said, "I want you to listen to Old Rip. He's that deep one with the mournful sound. Hear him! He don't bark much."

They could hear the bark, like a deep-throated sob, with a musical note in it. It came across the night air at intervals of fifteen seconds, and each time it tapered off and died away slowly.

"Kids, the first time I heard that note, it was up north of Baxter City. Your grandpa was standing by me. I wasn't any bigger than Elmer here. And it wasn't Old Rip barking; it was Old Tiger. Listen! Hear it? Old Rosy had that note, kids, only it was shriller in her. And Old Tip had it too."

He was silent a minute, then said, "They're coming this way."

The trailing bark of the dogs came directly up toward them and then seemed to be turning again. Old Rip missed one of his regular barks.

"Hey, kids!" Buck said.

Old Rip broke into a sharper bark. He was running fast. "Hey! That wolf picked the wrong place to cross his trail. Old Rip's right on him, kids."

Then not two hundred yards ahead of them, the coyote broke against the skyline at the edge of the ridge. Old Rip was ten feet behind. The coyote turned and slashed at him, then ran on. He was more than a match for Old Rip in speed. But the other dogs were coming up now.

"Kids!" Buck yelled above the sudden roar of the car engine. They barely had time to get a handhold before Buck had it in second gear. He'll turn around again, and if Old Rip gets hold of him, he's a goner."

Buck came plowing around a clump of trees and skidded the wheels. He hit the ground running, like a boy instead of like a man with twinges of rheumatism. As they ran up the rise toward the tumbling mass of dogs, one dark form broke away and struck out south.

"There's one of them pups taking out, Pa," Red said.

"If it is, I'll stomp his rump into the ground," Buck said, puffing. He came up to the melee of fighting dogs. "Here! What's going on here? What is this?" He shoved dogs aside roughly with his legs and hands. "Fan, Pete, Ringer! This isn't any wolf you've got; it's Slim Wilkinson!"

As soon as Old Rip was untangled from the snarling mass, he struck out south, trailing in the direction the coyote had gone a minute before. The other dogs took in the situation and followed him. Slim Wilkinson, who had been at the bottom of the heap, scrambled about as if hunting for the fight he had been in. He rared up clumsily on Elmer's chest and licked him in the face, bounced about a moment, barked, and ran after the other dogs.

They got into the car and followed the chase south along the ridge for a mile and a half. The coyote went out into the hills to the west. "If we had some horses we'd go out that way," Buck speculated. "We'll wait and see if he's coming back to the ridge before we try it in the car."

Elmer and Wayne wanted to build up a fire while they waited. Buck agreed, though the night was not cold. They sat around the fire of dry mesquite wood and heard the voices of the dogs echo back from over a mile away.

Buck talked of the ways of coyotes. "When a wolf is fresh, he's bad about circling back and cutting his trail. Or sometimes, he'll backtrack and then cut off his trail in another direction. That's a good trick, because a good trailing dog hates to go backwards on a trail worse than anything, and if backwards and forwards is the same way, they don't know what to do."

Buck was squatting with his hands spread out to the fire. His back was in darkness and the light flickered over the front part of him as he talked into the flames. To the four boys he seemed a magician talking.

"But about the most fouled up you can get a wolfhound pack, if they're not really good, is to get two smart wolves a hold of them. The wolves will tie their trail up in knots like they was knitting a sweater. Your dogs will be backtrailing and going ever' which way. Sometimes, if you got two extra good dogs—I mean real wolfhounds—they'll split up the pack, and they'll take both of them wolves. I've seen Old Rip and Old Tip do it when they was both in their prime. And once Old Tip and Old Rosy did it when Old Rosy was over ten years old."

They sat by the fire for half an hour, and the chase wound around again toward Chaparral Ridge. When the dogs came in near enough that their barks could be heard clearly, they sounded tired. Buck and the boys wet on the fire and kicked dirt over the steaming coals, then stood listening while Old Rip and the pack came slowly over the ridge a quarter mile south of them. "Come on, kids," Buck said. "Let's drive up a ways and see if we can get closer."

They drove up and stopped to listen. The coyote had taken to the thick brush in the flat again, between there and Webb Creek. He was running straight away. "He won't circle any more," Buck said. "He's too tired. We got to get over there some way."

The ancient wagon road over the ridge ran into the highway two miles farther south. They bounced down it, part of the time in the road, part of the time out. The dog trailer swung crazily behind them. They turned out on the highway, came back north two miles, and stopped to listen again. The chase had turned up Webb Creek. "Where in the Sam Hill is that crazy wolf going?" Buck said.

They turned in at the Welty place, drove past the house, and on down to where the Welty's north fence cut across Webb Creek. There they climbed through the fence, then ran up the creek toward the barking of the dogs.

"They got him bayed, haven't they, pa?" Red asked.

"I think so," Buck said, puffing. His boots were making a lot of noise on the uneven ground. "But I don't like it."

"Say, pa," Bert said, "that's right close to where Perkins has got his camp, isn't it?"

Buck grunted in answer. Up ahead they could see the dim flash of a lantern. They scrambled down into the dry creek bed and ran along its gravel-covered bottom. Elmer, panting along behind the others, said, "Pa can whup any man in the country."

They came out of the creek bed and stopped. No more than thirty feet away was an eerie scene, the center of which was Perkins and a kerosene lantern that sat on a rickety cage. The skinny old man was nailing a slat back onto the cage with his right hand and cradling in his left arm a double-barreled twelve-gauge shotgun. Around the edge of the dim circle of light the dogs moved, barking and whining in frustration.

Perkins raised the lantern high, showing his ragged white beard. His voice was a cackle. "My coyote got out. But he come back. Yore dogs ain't much good at catching coyotes, air they?"

On the floor of the rickety cage crouched a dark heaving form. The coyote's small eyes gleamed like points of fire.

Buck stood silent a minute, then blurted out, "You caught my best dog in one of your blasted wolf traps!"

Perkins laughed shrilly. "I ain't got no wolf traps. Just coyote traps. Besides, I turned yore old dog loose. He, he, he! Yore best dog! He, he! I can outrun any dog you got, and me eighty-two year ole." He shifted the shotgun over into the crook of his right arm.

"Pa, I don't see the pups," Elmer said. "Where's old Slim Wilkinson?"

"And Ringer," Red said. "Ringer's not here, Pa." Buck did not answer them. He was watching the old man and the coyote in the cage. Then he said, loud enough for Perkins to hear, "Kids, I sure hope that old man don't ever try to shoot that old rusty gun he's got, because it will probably blow up in his face." With that he turned and started back toward the car. "Bring the dogs, kids." They could hear Perkins's shrill laughter behind them.

They called the dogs and herded them back to the trailer. Bert said, "Boy, I sure wish we had caught that wolf, Pa, don't you?"

Wayne said, "Aw, we don't care anything about catching him, but just chasing him. We don't care, do we, Pa?"

Red said, "Let's don't talk about it."

"Pa," Elmer said, "we got to find Old Slim Wilkinson. Do you reckon he could be after a wolf?"

Buck shook his head. He was limping badly from the rheumatism. "I reckon him and the other pups and Ringer got after a rabbit and got lost. Ringer is bad about rabbits, and I guess they followed him."

"Well, I thought Old Slim Wilkinson was out in the hills, because I can tell when I hear him," Elmer said. "And I didn't hear him come back across the ridge with the rest. Let's go find him, can't we, Pa?"

Buck agreed, half heartedly. They drove down the highway and turned back up the wagon road toward Chaparral Ridge. Buck drove slowly. The blinking headlight had gone out. They pulled up on the south end of the ridge and stopped.

They could barely hear a faint moaning bark away out in the hills and farther north. "It's Slim Wilkinson!" Elmer said. "He don't sound glad now, but I can tell him!"

As they climbed back into the car, he said suddenly, "Pa! Maybe Old Rip and Old Slim Wilkinson split up the pack!"

"Good night, Elmer!" Wayne said. "I'm going to bust you right in the mouth!"

They drove up a couple of miles, and Buck pulled into a clearing at the west edge of the ridge. He shut off the motor. "That's Slim Wilkinson doing most of the barking," he said. "Like Elmer says, you can tell him; and I sure don't like to hear it." He looked up at the clear half-moon. "It's not right. That note! It's like a half-dollar made out of lead. I'd as lief see a man spit in his own grandma's face, as to hear Slim Wilkinson bark like that. Liefer. It's not right."

Old Rip was whining back in the trailer.

Buck climbed out of the car and took the steer horn from his neck. He raised it to his lips, hesitated, then lowered the horn and stood listening. "Kids, I don't understand it at all. He sure puts me in mind of Old Tiger."

Old Rip was whining like a baby.

"Kids, I don't see how a sorry dog can bark like that, especially chasing a rabbit." He stood listening while a tenseness came into his body, and he spoke with a quick wonder in his voice, "Kids, no dog would run a rabbit for two hours like this. And listen to that note!"

Elmer was jumping up and down. He uttered a sound that was half scream and half laugh.

Buck whooped like a rider when he comes out of the chute on a mean bucking bronco. Kids! Turn them dogs loose! Slim Wilkinson can't catch a wolf by hisself."

Red threw open the door of the dog cage, and the hounds came pouring out, tumbling over one another with short, excited yelps. The hounds lined out immediately, running silently, in the direction where Slim Wilkinson had been heard. They were a stream of jumping white spots in the moonlight until they disappeared in the brush.

"Reckon he's in sight of it, Pa?" Bert asked. "Or is he still trailing?"

"I can't tell," Buck said. "He's too tired. But listen to that note, kids. Listen to that fool pup!"

They stood listening to the bark of the persistent young hound, punctuated occasionally by a weak bark from Ringer or another pup. Suddenly, the other dogs broke in with sharp, fast running barks. It was like a band of fiddles and banjos and guitars, all trying to tune up at once.

Buck and the boys piled into the car and headed west for the roughest ride of the night. There was no overgrown, washed-out wagon road this time, for no one had ever been fool enough to take a wagon along the route Buck took. They straddled mesquite bushes five feet high. They went in and out among the trees as a snake goes through a weed patch. A long section of prickly pear leaves was dragging from the trailer. They could hear the dogs just ahead, even above the threshing machine noise of the car. The boys poked their heads out the windows and dodged back in to avoid the limbs.

They came right up to the howling, jumping, happy pack of dogs. There seemed fifty of them, rather than fifteen. Buck and the boys walked into the center of the confusion. There on the ground lay a big, well-chewed coyote. His fur was ruffled and wet. Blood flowed freely out of his throat.

On one side of the coyote sat Old Rip; on the other side, Slim Wilkinson. The big pup's tail twitched back and forth in the dry grass. One long ear dripped blood, slashed by a mesquite thorn or the fangs of the coyote. His red tongue hung out of his mouth six inches. Slim Wilkinson was grinning.

Buck took out his knife and cut the ears off the coyote. "Kids, I believe we'll take these ears by, and wake up old Perkins, and show them to him—just for the heck of it."

When they were putting the dogs back into the trailer, Elmer said, "Pa, do you think Old Rip could ride in the car with us, and maybe Old Slim Wilkinson too? He could set on my lap."

Buck nodded. "You might turn out to be a sporting man, Elmer. I believe you might." When they were in the car, Buck took Slim Wilkinson by the loose skin on top of his neck and shook him slowly back and forth. "Kids, this clumsy fool pup is the grin-nin'est and eagerest dog I ever had."

CAROLYN OSBORN

A ranch manager, short-story writer, college teacher, newspaper reporter, wife, mother—Carolyn Osborn is or has been all of these and more. Presently a resident of Austin, Texas, she nonetheless takes time to run the family ranch near Lampasas on weekends and at other times as necessary. Born in Tennessee but a naturalized Texan, Osborn has two degrees from the University of Texas at Austin. She has published numerous short stories, some of which have been issued in two collections—*Horse of Another Color* and *Fields of Memory*. More and more attention is being directed to Osborn and her work.

Osborn is not a "Texas writer" in the pejorative sense in which critics use the term, for her concerns transcend regionalism. Her subjects include sexually frustrated women, outrageous cousins, kooky college professors, retiring old maids, and a host of others. Her settings range from Jamaica to the deep South to Central Texas. She is an interpretive writer dealing with the problems of people today, without the old clichés and jargon. Her view is keen, and her skill is remarkable.

 My Brother Is a Cowboy

Getting a grip on the contemporary cowboy and his sense of humor—and honor—is not always easy. Mixed with the

Reprinted from Carolyn Osborn, *A Horse of Another Color: Stories by Carolyn Osborn*, Illinois Fiction Series, by permission of Illinois University Press. Copyright © 1977 by University of Illinois Press.

"This thing is too expensive . . . since I put it up, I've missed one brandin' and five hay cuttin's!"

humor in the following story is a sense of the loss of a way of life of one who belongs in the tradition of the old-time cowboy but who was, as these men say, "born a hundred years too late" to be part of it. Kenyon, the cowboy in this story, faces life with the same determination and resilience that his forefathers had—for as Osborn shows, "Kenyon is a cowboy." Here is the modern cowboy, drawn with the precision of a graphic artist but with the keenness, wit, and humor of a poet.

My daddy used to advise my brother and me, "Don't tell everything you know." This was his golden rule. I keep it in mind as I constantly disregard it. I've been busy most of my life telling everything I know. My brother Kenyon took it to heart. He tells nothing, not even the most ordinary answers to questions about his everyday existence. If my mother asks when he'll be home for supper, he says, "I don't know." The nearest he'll come to giving the hour for when he'll come in or go out is "Early" or "Late." His common movements, the smallest events of his day, are secret.

Mother follows these like a female detective. "Kenyon left the bread out this morning and the pimento cheese. I wonder if he had pimento cheese for breakfast, or took sandwiches for lunch, or both?" If, after she counts the remaining bread slices, sandwiches seem a possibility, she wonders where he has to go that's so distant he needs to take lunch with him. The names of surrounding towns come to her mind. "He won't be going anywhere near Lampasas because they have good barbecue there and he wouldn't take pimento cheese if he could get barbecue." She has advantage over Daddy; at least she's observed Kenyon's eating habits through the years and can spend hours happily trying to guess what he's going to do about lunch and whether or not he's going to turn up for supper.

Daddy doesn't care about where Kenyon eats lunch. What he wants to know is how many ranches Kenyon is leasing, how his sheep, goats, and cattle are doing, if he's making money or not.

We all want to know if he's ever going to get married. Does he have a girl? Does he want to marry? He is almost thirty, taller than my father's six feet, though how much we don't know for he won't stand and be measured. He has dark hair that curls when he forgets to get it cut, which is most of the time. The curls come over his forehead and disgust him so much he is forever jamming his hat down low to cover his hair. When we were children he made me cut the front curls off. I was spanked for doing it. His nose is long and straight. There is a small slanting scar just missing his eye running over his left eyebrow. His eyes are brown. His mouth is wide and generally closed.

When we ask if he's ever going to marry, and nothing will stop us from asking, he says, "Find me a girl who'll live out in the country, cook beans, and wash all day." He runs his hands over the creases in his clean blue jeans, sticks the shirttail of his clean shirt in, and laughs. Mother gets angry then. She's responsible for all his clean clothes and feels sometimes this is the only reason he shows up at the house. Often she says, "He doesn't need a wife! He needs a washer-woman!" Not once, however, has she ever said this to him, fearing he'll put on his boots and walk out the door to some unknown cafe one last time.

She isn't curious about where I'm going to eat. Everybody in town knows I eat lunch every day at the Leon High School cafeteria. I'm the singing teacher. Wouldn't you know it! Since I've already told you Kenyon's almost thirty, you might as well know I'm almost twenty-six. At least nobody asks me when I'm going to get married, not to my face anyway. Being related and having practically no heart at all, Kenyon has the gall to wonder out loud if I'm ever going to catch a man. When he does this, I tell him I have as much right to uphold the long tradition of old-maidhood as he has to represent the last of the old west. My brother is a cowboy.

I tell him, "You're the last of a vanishing breed, the tail end of the roundup of the longhorn steers, the last great auk alive, a prairie rooster without a hen!"

All he replies to this is,"Sister, there ain't no substitute for beef on the hoof." He gets out real quick before I can go on about helicopters substituting for horses and feed lots replacing the open range.

Since the wires have been cut between Kenyon and his family, we have to depend on other sources of information, the weekly newspaper for instance. That's where we found out he'd been riding bulls in rodeos the summer after he flunked out of college. He got his picture on the front page for falling off a Brahma bull headfirst. The photographer caught the bull still doubled up and Kenyon in midair, his hands out in front of him right before he hit the dirt. My daddy strictly forbade any more bull-riding on the grounds he wasn't going to have his son associated with a bunch of rodeo bums.

Kenyon said, "These bums are the best friends I got and I'll associate with whoever I want."

"You are going to kill yourself and me too." Daddy put his hand over his heart like he was going to have an attack that minute. "And, furthermore, I'm going to cut you out of my will if you keep up this fool riding." Then he laid down on the bed and made me take his blood pressure. I was home on vacation from nursing school in Galveston.

Kenyon smiled, showing he still had all his teeth, and the next thing we read in the newspaper was he'd gone off and joined the paratroopers, joined of his own free will, mind you, for three years. Daddy, who'd been in the infantry in WW II, was half proud and half wild. "He doesn't have enough sense to keep his feet on the ground! If he isn't being thrown from a bull, he's throwing himself out of airplanes!" He wrote an old army buddy of his who'd retired, like he did, near his last post except the post was up in Tennessee where Kenyon was stationed instead of Texas where we are. This old buddy wrote back saying:

Dear Willie,
    Your boy is doing fine. I talked to his C.O. yesterday.

He told me Pvt. Kenyon K. Lane is making a good
soldier.

Yours truly,
Henry C. Worth, Lt. Col., Ret.

P.S. He told me Kenyon inspires good morale because
he jumps out of planes with a wad of tobacco in his
mouth and spits all the way down.

Your friend,
Lt. Col. Henry C. Worth, Ret.

I think Daddy was happy for a while. He showed the letter
to me before he went downtown to show it to some of his friends at
the drugstore where they all meet for coffee. By the time he came
home, Mother was back from the grocery.

"William, how can you go around showing everybody that
letter when I haven't read it!" She read it and was crying before she
finished. "Who taught him how to chew tobacco? He'll ruin his
teeth. He was such a nice clean boy."

"Ruin his teeth!" Daddy shouted. "You've got to worry
about his teeth when he's falling out of airplanes every day!"

"He's not falling," I said. "He's jumping and he's doing it of
his own free will."

"Free will nothing!" Daddy turned on me. "Don't you be
telling me about free will in the U.S. Army. I know about the army.
I spent twenty years in the army."

I had to take his blood pressure after that. He spent the next
three years writing to his army buddies near whatever post my
brother happened to be on, and getting news of Kenyon from
them. All his letters were signed Col. William K. Lane, Ret.

I spent those years finishing my education, they thought. In
the daytime I was. I wore a white uniform and low white shoes and
went to nursing school in Galveston. Friday and Saturday nights I
put on a red sequined dress and a pair of red high heels and went
to sing at one of the nightclubs. My stage name was Gabriella and I
wore so much makeup nobody from Leon would have known it
was me. I had learned something from Kenyon, not to tell everything I knew and to follow my own free will. It worked too. When I
was home I took Daddy's blood pressure and Mother's temperature; when I was in Galveston I was singing two nights a week.

Don't get any ideas either—singing and wearing a red dress
was all I was doing. The men in the combo I sang with were more
strict with me than they would have been with their own daugh-
ters if they had any. I could drink soda pop only, and I had to sit

with one of them while I was drinking. Except for the sequins I might as well have been in a convent. I sang songs like "I Can't Say No" without ever having a chance to not say it. Still, I was satisfied. Singing was what I wanted. I thought if I could support myself by nursing, I could gradually work my way into show biz and up to New York. So I was down in Galveston nursing and singing while my brother was on some army post jumping out of airplanes, I supposed.

One Friday night I was giving out with "Zip-Pah-De-Doo-Dah" trying to cheer up a few barflies when in walks Kenyon. He knows me right away, red sequins, makeup, and all. He is wearing a tight fitting paratrooper's uniform, his pants tied up in his boots, which laced to the knee practically. Very spiffy and clean. Mother would have been happy to see him.

"My, oh, my, what a wonderful day!" I finish. The barflies applaud. My brother just stands quietly while I slink off the platform. It's time for the break, so Tiny the drummer, who is actually a big fat man, married with a wife and baby he calls every night in Dallas, takes me by the arm to a table. Kenyon comes right over. I can see immediately he has gotten himself all shined up for one reason—to get roaring drunk—to the disgrace of family and country. He's just off the reservation and ready to howl. Obviously, I'm in his way.

I smile at him and say, "Hi. What are you doing down here? Are you AWOL?"

"No," he grins, "I'm on leave. You're the one that's AWOL."

Tiny says, "Scram, soldier boy."

"It's my brother, Tiny. He's in the paratroopers. He jumps out of airplanes."

"Gay Baby, don't pull the brother bit on me."

"But he is," I insist. "Show him your birthmark or something, Kenyon."

"Jump on out of here, flyboy," says Tiny.

"If I go, you go too, Gay Baby," says Kenyon with a merciless smirk.

"I'm not going anywhere till I finish here tonight. You sit down and behave yourself. Have a beer."

"You're leaving right now. My sister isn't going to hang around no honky-tonk." With this he grabs me by the arm and I scream at him, "Let go!" But he doesn't and by this time I'm furious. "You auk! You dodo! You idiot!"

Tiny rises like a giant blimp slowly filling with air. Before he can signal to the other fellows though, Kenyon pulls me to my feet.

The other four members of the combo—Louie, the piano player; Max, the bass; Joe, the sax; and Evans, the trumpet—run to assist us.

Kenyon turns the table on its side. "She's going with me," he says.

I peek between the fingers of my free hand to see if he's got a six-shooter in his free hand. He's got nothing, nothing but swagger. Pretty soon he has a cut over his left eye—Tiny did it with a chair—and I have not one red cent left of all my savings from singing nights. My going–to–New York money has gone to bail Dangerous Dan Kenyon McGrew out of the Galveston jail.

"Listen, Kenyon," I tell him, "this is not Leon and this is not the nineteenth century. It's the second half of the twentieth in case you haven't noticed it from your airplane riding. There is nothing wrong with me singing in a quiet respectable bar."

"No sister of mine—"

"You just pretend I'm not any sister of yours. We're so different one of us must have been left on the doorstep."

"You think I'm a bastard?"

"Well, you're the one calling the cards," I said and flounced out of the jail. I was mad and in a hurry to get home to bed. All I cared about right then was sleep. That particular Saturday I had to work the 7:00 A.M. shift at the hospital. Kenyon being such a zipper-lip type, I certainly wasn't worrying about him telling anybody I was working in a nightclub and him spending some time in jail. I should have let him stay in jail. He got in his car that very same night and drove straight to Leon. And, when he got there early the next morning, he told. He told everything he knew.

They didn't give me any warning, not a phone call-nothing. Daddy appeared in full uniform, the old army pinks and greens with eagles flapping on both shoulders. He had been getting ready to leave for a battalion reunion at Ft. Sam Houston when Kenyon showed up, and he didn't waste time changing clothes. He should have. His stomach had expanded some since WW II so his trousers were lifted an inch too high over his socks.

The first thing I said when I saw him was, "Daddy, what on earth are you doing down here in your uniform? It's non-reg. They don't wear that kind anymore."

"Sister, don't you tell me about the U.S. Army regulations. I gave twenty years of my life to them."

"Well, they are likely to slap you in the loony bin here for walking around dressed up like that."

"If I was you, I wouldn't be talking about how other people are dressed."

"Daddy, there is nothing wrong with my uniform," I said. I'd been wearing it for eight hours and hadn't spilt a thing on it. There was nothing wrong with the way I looked at all except for the circles under my eyes from staying up till 2:00 A.M. getting a certain person out of jail. I was just about dead from exhaustion. "I hear you've got another dress, a red one."

We were talking in the lobby of the hospital and when he said that I wanted to call for a stretcher.

"No daughter of mine is going to hang around with gangsters at nightclubs."

I don't know where he got the gangsters, probably from the last time he was in a nightclub.

"This isn't 1920 and I don't know any gangsters. The fellows Kenyon got in a fight with are musicians. They were trying to protect me." He wasn't listening. He didn't want to hear my side. His mind was already made up.

"You go and get your things," he told me. "No daughter of mine is going to be corrupted by jazz and booze."

What could I do? I'd spent my savings getting Kenyon out of jail. I went with Daddy back to Leon thinking it would all blow over after a while. Mother, at least, would be on my side since she knew what it was to live with a husband who still thought he was in the first half of the twentieth century and a son who hadn't progressed past 1900. When we got to Leon though, I found out different. The very first thing Mother did was to show me my and Kenyon's birth certificates.

"Look here, young lady, neither you nor your brother was left on anybody's doorstep. I hope this is proof enough for you." She shoved, the yellowed pages with their loopy-de-loop handwriting in my face and started crying before I could say I never really meant it.

I stayed home that weekend and the rest of that semester. Good-bye nursing. I wasn't so crazy about it anyway. I guess what happened to me could happen to anybody, but I wonder how many girls end up teaching a bunch of high school kids to sing "Sweet Adeline" after they started out with a great career in show biz. Daddy took me completely out of school. In January he let me enroll in a Baptist church college only forty miles from Leon. I got my teacher's certificate there in music education and that's all I got. They had a short rope on me.

When I finished I was twenty-three, due to the interruption in my education. Daddy had a heart attack that year and I went home to help Mother nurse him and to teach singing in Leon High School.

My brother, when he was through with the paratroopers, came home too. He started working on ranches and slowly saved enough to lease places of his own. He hadn't paid me back the bail money yet. I hadn't paid him back either, but I was planning on how I was going to. Someday, I thought, he is going to find some girl who wants to quit riding the barrel races in rodeos and get married. When he brings this cutie home in her embroidered blouse and her buckskin fringes, I am going to tell everything I know, not about him being in jail. The fact he spent a few hours in the Galveston jail wouldn't bother her. Galveston's a long way from Leon.

I wasn't going to tell this rodeo queen Kenyon was bound to drag home about his past; I was going to predict her future. I was going to let this little girl know she might as well throw away her western breeches and get into a skirt that hit the floor. And, I was going to tell her she'd better wave goodbye forever to the bright lights, the crowd, the band, and the Grand Entry Parade because all that was in store for her was a pot of beans to stir and blue jeans to wash at home on the range. She wasn't to expect any modern appliances to help her out either, because I knew Kenyon. He wouldn't buy her a single machine, not even a radio. If she wanted to hear any music she'd have to invite me out to sit on the front porch and sing "Zip-Pah-De-Doo-Dah" as the sun sank slowly in the west.

I had it all planned out, a feeble sort of revenge, but at least I'd have my say—me, the Cassandra of Leon, prophesying a terrible future for a fun-loving cowboy's sweetheart. Of course, like a lot of too well planned revenges, it didn't turn out that way. I got restless sitting around in the teacher's lounge, going to the movie every Saturday night with a man I'd known since we were both in high school, Alvin Neeley, the band director. We weren't anything to each other but companions in boredom, chained together by what everyone thought was our common interest, music. We were supposed to be a perfect couple because we could both read notes. Everyone imagined we were sitting on the piano bench warbling duets, but we weren't.

Alvin was a marcher. He kept in step even when we were walking a few blocks down the street, and believe me, he wasn't marching to the sound of any distant drum. Alvin had his own drum in his head, and when he puckered his lips, I knew he wasn't puckering up for me; he was puckering up for Sousa. Sometimes, just for diversion, I'd refuse to march in step with him. If he put his left foot forward, I'd start out on my right, but he'd always notice and with a quick little skip in the air, he'd be in step with me. Off we'd go marching to the movie to the tune of "The Stars and Stripes Forever" every Saturday. And all this time Kenyon was stomping in and out of the house bird-free, intent on his own secret purposes.

Mother would come and sit on the foot of my bed after I got home from a date with Alvin. "Did you have a good time?" she'd say.

"All right." I wasn't going to tell her I'd had a bad time. She had enough troubles as it was. Since his heart attack my daddy spent most of his time sitting around the house with his right hand on the left side of his chest the way actors used to indicate great pain in the old silent films.

She'd ask me what movie we saw and I'd tell her, Monsters of the Slimy Green Deep or whatever it was. Nothing but Grade B movies ever made it to Leon, and Alvin and I went regularly no matter what was showing—like taking a pill on schedule.

"Well, how is Alvin getting along?"

She wasn't interested in Alvin's health. What she wanted to know was how Alvin and I were getting along. I'd say all right to that too. I kept on saying the same thing till one night she said, "I sure would like to have some grandchildren."

"Mother, you better get Kenyon to work on that because you're not going to get any grandchildren out of me and Alvin Neeley."

"Why not?"

"I'd have to marry him—that's why, and I'm not going to even if he asks, and he's not going to ask. He can barely hold a conversation anyway. All he can do is whistle—and march." I was sitting across the room from her rubbing my aching legs.

"Why do you keep on going out with him then?"

"I don't see anybody else bashing the door down to ask me to a movie. I go out with Alvin because he takes me. It's one way of getting away from this house, a way of getting out of Leon even if it's to go to the Slimy Green Deep."

"You worry me," said Mother.

"I worry myself," I told her and I did. I was stuck with Alvin Neeley in Leon. I'd done what they all wanted me to do and now they were stuck with me. They had me on their hands.

Mother evidently spoke to Kenyon about my miserable unwed existence and insisted he find somebody for me. I say Mother did it, put the idea in Kenyon's head that he find somebody for me, because, left to himself, Kenyon was not at all bothered by an old-maid sister. He thought he'd saved me from the gutter. From there on I was supposed to be continually thankful and permanently respectable.

When I got home early one Saturday night I was told, before I had time to say anything, that he'd fixed up a date for me the following Saturday.

"Who with?"

"Fellow named Frank Harwell from Lampasas. He ranches out west of town. He's going to take you dancing."

"He's from a big family. I know some of them. Harwells are spread all over Lampasas," Mother said happily.

"He served in Korea, in the infantry," said Daddy as if he'd just pinned the Distinguished Conduct Medal on somebody.

They all knew what they wanted to know about Frank Harwell and I didn't know a thing. "How old is he? Is he short or tall, skinny or fat, intelligent or ignorant, handsome or ugly?" I could have gone on all night throwing questions at them, but I quit. They were all sitting there looking so smug.

"He's the best I could do," said Kenyon. "You'll like him. All the girls do."

"Where are we going dancing?" Since Leon's in a dry county there's not a real nightclub within twenty miles.

"We'll go out to the VFW Club," Kenyon said.

"We? Are you going too? Who do you have a date with?"

"Nobody. I'm just going along for the ride."

"Kenyon, I'm twenty-five years old going on twenty-six, and I'll be damned if you're going anywhere as my chaperone."

"Sister, watch your language," said Daddy. "Is he a good dancer, Kenyon?"

"Daddy, what do you care if he's a good dancer or not? You're not the one who's going to be dancing with him"

"I don't want my daughter marrying some Valentino. Good dancers make bad husbands."

"Daddy! You are hopelessly behind times! If you'd turn on your TV set you'd see people dancing without even touching each other. The Valentinos are all gone. Anyway, I'm not going to my wedding Saturday night. I'm going to the VFW Club!"

They had me. I was trapped into having a date with Frank Harwell just to prove to Daddy he wasn't a Valentino. I didn't mind so much. After all, I'd endured a long dry march in the desert with Alvin Neeley. And, I wanted to know what Kenyon did with himself when he wasn't riding the range.

On Saturday night I pranced into the living room in my best and fullest skirt. You have to have plenty of leg room for country dances. Kenyon was standing talking to Frank Harwell, who looked like a cowboy straight out of a cigarette advertisement, lean, tanned, and terribly sure of himself. He was every young girl's dream, and old girl's too. My knees were shaking a little when he looked me over. For a minute I wished I hadn't worn a sensible dress. I wished I was all togged out in my red sequins and red high heels again.

We all three got in Frank's pickup. He and Kenyon did most of the talking. We hadn't gone two blocks before Kenyon insisted he had to stop and look at some stock at the auction barn on the way to the VFW.

"Fine," said Frank in a grand, easy-going way. He was the most totally relaxed man I'd ever seen. He drove his pickup through town with one hand on the wheel, guiding it to the right and left as if he were reining a horse.

When we got to the auction barn Kenyon shot out of the truck, leaving the door open behind him.

"Always in a hurry," said Frank and leaned over me to pull the door shut. I felt like a huge old cat had fallen in my lap.

"You don't seem to be."

"Naw." He eased himself up, pulled out a package of cigarettes, lit one, then leaned back and blew smoke out. I kept expecting to hear an announcer's voice saying something about how good cigarettes were so I waited a minute before saying anything myself. Finally, I asked him about his ranch. He told me about his spring round-up, how much mohair had been clipped from his goats, how many cows had calved, the number of rattlesnakes he'd killed, how much a good rain would help, and other interesting things like that. We sat there, with Frank worrying about his wells running dry and the miles of fence he needed to repair; I was worrying about whether we'd ever get to the dance. The VFW Club was on top of a hill behind the auction barn. We could have walked up there, but it could have been in the next county as far as Frank was concerned. He got a bottle of bourbon out of the glove compartment and took a long swallow from it. When Kenyon came back he passed the bottle to him. Neither one of them offered me a swallow and I knew I'd have to be seventy and taking whiskey for medicinal purposes before either one of those two would dream of offering a girl a drink.

Kenyon was excited about a bull he'd seen. "He's that same old Brahma that throwed me. I'd know him anywhere. Gentle as he can be outside the ring, but let somebody get on his back and he goes wild. Wonder why they're selling him. He's a good rodeo bull."

"Getting old maybe," Frank drawled. They both laughed as if he'd said the most hilarious thing in the world. Then they both took another drink so they were in a good mood when we got the VFW at 9:30 P.M. The hall was an old WW II army surplus barracks the veterans had bought and painted white. Judging from the noise coming out of the place, the men standing around cars outside talking and sneaking drinks, and the two cops at the doorway, it was wilder than any Galveston club on a Saturday night. The cops nodded at us as we went in. The girl who was selling tickets to the dance warned Frank and Kenyon to hold on to them because nobody was allowed to come back in without one.

Frank swung me out on the dance floor and that was the last I saw of Kenyon for a while except for a glimpse of him out of the corner of my eye. He was dancing with one of my ex-students, a not so bright one, who'd somehow managed to graduate the year before. Every once in a while Frank would excuse himself to go out and take a swig from his bottle. I sat at a table by myself drinking soda pop and thinking about my Galveston days when I at least had the company of some grown men when I was drinking. The musicians at the VFW that night, by the way, hardly deserved the name. They sawed and wheezed through their whole repertory which consisted of about fifteen songs, all sounding alike. It's fashionable now to like what everyone calls "country music," but if you had to sit out in the VFW and listen to it, you'd get pretty tired of the music and the country.

After a while I caught sight of Frank strolling in the front door. He stopped by another table for a minute to pat a girl on the top of her frizzy blonde head, then he ambled on over to me.

"Where's Kenyon?" I was tired of listening to the whining songs, tired of being flung around the dance floor. The new dances I'd told Daddy about hadn't gotten to Leon yet—they probably never will get to Frank Harwell. The more he drank the harder he danced, not on my toes, but stomping hard on the floor taking great wide steps and swinging me around in circles. It was 1:00 A.M., time to go home. Nobody else seemed to think so though. The hall was even more packed than when we first came in.

"Last time I saw him Kenyon was outside arguing with the cops. He's lost his ticket and they won't let him back in."

"Why doesn't he buy another one?"

"He thinks they ought to take his word he already bought one. You know he's got high principles and—"

"I know about his principles all right. He's got high principles and no scruples!!"

"Aw, don't be too hard on your brother."

I was getting ready to tell him that Kenyon had been hard on me when we both turned our heads to see what was causing all the shouting down by the door. It was my brother leading that gentle old Brahma bull by a rope around his neck. The crowd was parting before him. Some of them were jumping out the windows and everybody else was headed for the back door. The blonde Frank had patted on the head was standing on top of a table screaming, "Help! Somebody do something!" Nobody was doing anything but getting out. Kenyon staggered through the hall with a mean grin on his face, drunk as the lord of the wild frontier and cool as a walking ice cube. Behind the bandstand the musicians were crawling out the windows. The bass fiddler tried to throw his fiddle out first, but it got stuck. He left it there, half in, half out, and wriggled through another window. A man following him didn't watch where he was going and caught his foot in the middle of a drum.

Behind Kenyon the bull, uncertain of his footing on the slippery floor, was trying to adjust himself. He slid along, his tail lashing frantically, his hooves skidding in all directions. When Kenyon slowed down a little to get past some tables the Brahma snorted and jumped—like Alvin Neeley doing his little skip in midair to keep in step.

"Come on. We can't stand here gawking. Somebody's going to get hurt if Kenyon lets that old bull go." Frank grabbed my hand and we headed for the back door. By the time we got out Kenyon and the bull had the VFW Club to themselves.

We waited out back. The cops waited too. Kenyon appeared in the doorway. The bull nudged up behind him. He turned and scratched the bull's head.

"I told you," Kenyon hollered at the cops, "I already bought one ticket." Then he walked down the steps carefully leading the bull, talking to him all the way. "Watch your step, old buddy. That's right. Easy now."

The cops let Kenyon put the bull back in the auction pen, and when he was finished, they put him in their car. He was laughing so hard he couldn't fight very well, but he tried.

"Oh, Lord!" Frank sighed lazily from the safety of his pickup. "If he wouldn't fight, they'd let him go. Those boys were ready for that dance to break up anyway."

"Aren't you going to help him?"

"Naw. He took this on hisself. You want us both in jail?"

"In jail?"

"Yeah," Frank drawled and hoisted his big handsome self across the seat toward me.

"Shouldn't we follow them?"

"Look at that moon."

There wasn't a moon in sight, not a sliver of one. Gorgeous Frank Harwell was so sleepy drunk he mistook somebody's headlights for the moon. All the excitement on top of all the dancing we'd done was too much for him I guess, because the next thing I knew he'd passed out. I lifted his head off my shoulder, propped it up against the window, and climbed into the driver's seat.

I got to the jail in time to hear them book Kenyon for being drunk and disorderly and disturbing the peace. He paid his own way out this time, but the only reason they didn't lock him up for the night was I was there to take him home. Of course, I couldn't take him home in this condition. Daddy would have had an attack, and Mother would have probably fainted at the sight of him. Her clean-cut, hard-working, tight-lipped boy was a living mess. He looked like he'd been riding the bull rather than leading him. I managed to brush most of the dust off of him. The cops gave him back his hat. We stopped at Leon's one open-all-night cafe, where I went in and got a quart of black coffee. When he'd finished this he was sober enough to go in the men's room and wash his face. Frank slept through the whole rehabilitation.

Kenyon wanted to park the pickup on the square across from the jail and walk home, leaving Frank there snoring. "Maybe the cops will come out and get him," he said.

"It's not any use to get mad at Frank. It was your idea to bring that animal into the dancehall."

"You are taking up for him?"

"I got you out of jail, didn't I?"

Kenyon nodded. I went in the cafe to get some more coffee for Frank. When I came back out Kenyon started shaking him, but before he got him awake he turned to me and said, "Sister, don't tell everything you know."

"Why not? Mother and Daddy are going to find out anyway. By church time tomorrow everybody in town will be talking—"

"I'd rather they get it second-hand."

By this time I was so mad I jabbed Frank with my elbow, handed him the coffee, and lit into Kenyon. "You'd rather everybody get everything second-hand. Nobody is supposed to do anything but you."

"What are you talking about?"

"Never mind! You wouldn't understand if I kept talking till sunup, but I'll tell you this, Kenyon—I'm not going to devote the rest of my life to keeping you out of jail. From now on you are on your own."

"Sister, I've always been on my own."

How contrary can a person be? Here I'd just saved him from a night in the Leon County jail, not to mention the time I got him out of the Galveston jail. I didn't argue with him though. I knew if I told him he wasn't on his own till he left home, he wouldn't wait a minute before telling me the same thing with Frank Harwell sitting right next to me taking in every word.

"You want me to drive?" Kenyon asked him.

"Naw, you have got in enough trouble tonight, you and that dancing bull. I'll make it."

They both laughed. Frank even tried to slap my knee, but I dodged him.

"I want to go home," I said.

"Gal, that's where we're going."

It was 2:30 A.M. I could imagine Daddy sitting on the front porch wrapped in his overcoat with his M-1 stretched across his knees. For once, we were lucky. Mother and Daddy were both in bed asleep. Kenyon and I tiptoed to our rooms without waking either one of them. When they asked us the next morning where we'd been so late, Kenyon said, "Dancing." Since they were used to short answers from him he didn't have to say anything else. Of course Mother came and sat on the foot of my bed and asked me all about Frank Harwell.

"Mother, Frank is a very handsome man and no doubt all the other girls like him, but he is a cowboy and I think one cowboy is enough in the family."

Then I told her. "In June I'm going down to San Antonio and look for a job in one of the schools there."

"You can't—"

"Yes, I can. If I don't leave home now, I'll be right here the rest of my days."

"She might as well," Kenyon said. He was leaning in the doorway, eavesdropping to see whether I was going to tell on him. "She's too uppity for anybody in Leon." With that he turned around and left. He didn't know it, but it was the best thing he could have said. Daddy blamed himself for giving me too much education and Mother was so anxious to be a grandmother I think she'd have been happy to see me off to New York.

In June I went to San Antonio and found a job at one of the high schools. I found a husband, too, a fine doctor who sings in the chorus during opera season. That's where I met him, in the chorus. We were rehearsing for La Traviata. His name is Edward Greenlee. Dr. Edward Greenlee.

"Can he rope?" Kenyon asked.

"Can you tie a suture?"

"What branch of the army was he in?"

"He was in the navy, Daddy."

"Is he from a large family?"

"Mother, there are Greenlees all over San Antonio."

We had a June wedding in the First Methodist in Leon. Daddy gave me away. Kenyon was an usher. He looked handsome in his white tux jacket, the only one he'd ever worn in his life. I told him so when I got to the church in my bridal finery. He said thanks and grinned his tight-lipped grin. I looked down. The black pants covered all of the stitching decorating the tops, but I could plainly see, and so could everybody else at my wedding, that Kenyon had his boots on. I guess he'll go on being true to the code and die with them on. He's living out on one of his ranches now, fifteen miles from the nearest town and ninety miles from San Antonio. Sometimes on Sunday afternoons Edward and I take the children and drive up to see him. There's no way of letting him know we're coming because he doesn't have a telephone. We don't have to worry about inconveniencing anybody though; Kenyon lives by himself.

The last time we were there we missed him. My five-year-old boy, William, walked around on the bare floors and said, "Doesn't he have any rugs?"

When we were checking the cupboards in the almost bare kitchen Cynthia, our three-year-old, wailed, "Doesn't he have any cookies?"

"No, he doesn't have any rugs and he doesn't have any cookies. But he does have a bathtub, hot and cold running water, a bed, a fire, three cans of chili, a sack of flour, two horses, a sheep dog, and a whole lot of sheep, goats, and cattle."

"Why doesn't he have any cookies?"

"This sure is a lumpy old chair," said William. He should have known. He was sitting in the only one in the room. "Is Uncle Kenyon poor?"

"All of your Uncle Kenyon's money is tied up in stock, the sheep, and goats and cattle," said Edward, who always tries to explain things.

"Uncle Kenyon is a cowboy," I said, which was really the only explanation.

GLOSSARY

Adio mi chaparito (v). Corruption of Spanish for "goodbye, little britches"—term of endearment.

Broomtail (n). Disparaging synonym for horse, particularly an unattractive or mean-spirited horse.

Calf-pulling frame (n). A simple tool composed of a chain, hook, and ratchet attached to a metal frame. It is used to attach to a short chain fastened around the unborn calf's front feet in order to draw the calf through the mother's cervix.

Cantle (n). The back portion of the seat of a saddle.

Caprock (n). In Texas, a geologic formation which marks the beginning of the Llano Estacado or Staked Plains.

Chouse (v). To run cattle back and forth in a pen until they become irritated and difficult to handle.

Clabber (n). Sour milk that has thickened or curdled.

Cold jaw (adj). (Of a horse) which takes the bit in its teeth and runs away.

Combiotic (n). A medication compounded of the drugs tetracycline and penicillin.

Come-along (n). Winch-like device that operates by a hand-actuated handle.

Corriente steer (n). A castrated male bovine from Mexican stock; usually used in the Southwest for team roping.

Cow (v). (Of a horse) to work cattle by countering their moves without being reined.

Cow brute (n). A bovine possessing hard headedness and lacking common sense.

Cross bramer (n). (Of cattle) a cross-bred animal with some Brahma blood; known for wildness.

Croton-oil (n). A thick yellow to brown oil from the Croton plant; acts as a drastic cathartic.

Cull man (n). In feedlots, a man who sees after the cull or rejected and ill cattle.

Dallies (n). A dallied rope is one that is wrapped only around the saddle horn. The cowboy must hold the loose end to keep the rope secured. Dallying is a dangerous practice, for a finger caught under the wraps is neatly amputated when the lunging animal applies tension to the rope. Half hitches may be added on top of the dallies to keep the rope securely attached. The advantage of dallying is that it allows the roper to take up the slack in the rope without having to back the horse away from the snared animal.

Dally (v). To wrap

Dingy (adj). Crazy, insane.

Dogied (adj). (of a calf) orphaned or otherwise forced to rely too early on grass for nourishment. The result is a potbellied conformation and fuzzy hair; hence the term *hairball*.

Fumy (adj). Drunk.

Gatherin's (n). Roundups.

Get into a storm (v). To approach a demanding if not life-threatening situation.

Glider (n). A porch swing.

Gooseneck (n). A type of trailer used for hauling livestock. The hitch is on the base of a long neck connected to a mount in the bed of the pulling vehicle, usually a pickup.

Hairball (n). A dogied or motherless calf which develops an enlarged abdomen and long, frizzy hair, a sure indication of poor nutrition and growth.

Hay grazer (n). A forage crop grown by stockmen to provide grazing for their animals; often cut for hay as well.

Heeling (v). To rope an animal with a loop thrown under the back legs and jerked tight as the animal steps into the loop.

Hold [the] herd (v). When cattle are gathered and held or kept in a location, some cowboys are assigned to keep the cattle from wandering or running off.

Hoodlum wagon (n). In most usage, the wagon carrying bedrolls and other gear on a long drive. Some use the term to indicate the chuckwagon.

Hoof nippers (n). A pincerlike tool used to shape or "nip" a horse's hoof prior to nailing the iron shoe in place.

Hub stumps (n). (Of wagons) the likelihood of hitting a tree stump with the hub of the wheel, a sure path to breaking the wheel.

Igod (int). A slang proununciation of the blasphemous "My God!"

Jingle the horses (v). To gather the horses to select mounts for the next day's working.

Kack (n). Saddle.

Lay the chunk. Figure of speech indicating the beginning of time.

Light footed. (adj). Easily frightened; quick to run in a crisis.

Lister bed (n). The land banked or "bedded" up by a plow when preparing land for planting row crops such as corn.

Manada (n). A herd of horses, particularly a breeding band of wild horses consisting of a stallion, mares, and young horses.

On the prod (adj). Looking for trouble; anxious or agitated.

P.A. (n). Prince Albert, a popular brand of tobacco, mainly for pipe smoking but also rolled into cigarettes.

Pigging string (n). A short piece of (usually small) rope used to tie the legs after the animal is thrown.

Plow rein (n). A long rein or rope used to pull the horse's head in the desired direction.

Rannihan calf (n). Erickson calls this a Beaver County, Oklahoma, term for a "scrawny, snot nosed, wildeyed calf; but its area of currency is more widespread.

Razzoo (n). A quick, aggressive move.

Remuda (n). A herd of saddle horses kept for cowboys to ride.

Rimfire (n). A saddle with front and back girths, the front one of which is rigged below the swell of the fork and the second below the cantle.

Rimrock (n). A shelf or layer of rock on top of a mesa.

Ringy (adj). Strongly averse to orders or even advice from someone else.

Running iron (n). A straight or curved metal rod used to burn or alter brands on livestock.

Sale barn (n). The auction ring where livestock is marketed. The sale also has a strong social function in the community it serves.

Scours (n). The animal equivalent of diarrhea; usually caused by an abundance of fresh green grass or an intestinal infection.

Shade oneself. To give oneself an edge over an adversary.

Snuffy (adj). (Of a bovine) sniffing or snorting through its nose in anger, causing a distinct sound that often precedes a charge.

Spur rowel (n). The usually round, rotating metal disk on the end of a spur shank; used to goad a horse.

Squeeze chute (n). A device made of welded pipe with hinged panels and bars to hold stock for working.

Stob (n). A small stake or post often used by land surveyors to mark boundaries, rights of way, and the like.

Stretch out (v). To stretch an animal's back legs out, causing it to fall. The operation requires two mounted ropers. One ropes the head, and the other the two hind legs (see *Heeling*) with ropes either wrapped around or tied to the saddle horn. Then the two ropers back their horses away from the animal.

Sull (v). To withdraw or refuse to act normally; be sullen or balky.

Sweep (n). A plow with long arms extending from the plow point; used to plow the area between crops planted in rows.

Tack (n). Horse gear-saddles, bridles, girths, etc.

Twine (n). Lariat rope.

V-mail (n). Micro-filmed letters (World War II) shipped overseas then printed out for delivery to members of the armed forces; letters from members of the armed forces to friends and loved ones were also microfilmed to be printed out later.

Wood (n). Saddle, from the wooden tree or form on which the leather of the saddle is attached.

Work-brittle (a). Reluctant to work, lazy shiftless.

Wraps (n). The hitches and wrapped loops of rope used to secure the pigging string.

Wreck (n). A disaster that befalls a cowboy in the line of duty. It may consist of a horse's bucking at the wrong time or a rope's becoming tangled in the brush or passing under a horse's tail when there is a mad cow on one end and a cowboy and feisty horse on the other.

SELECTED BIBLIOGRAPHY

Aarne, Antii. *The Types of the Folktale: A Classification and Bibliography*. 2d rev. ed. Helsinki: Academia Scientiarum Fennica, 1964.

Abrahams, Roger D. "Folklore and Literature as Performance." *Journal of the Folklore Institute* 9(1972): 75–94.

————. "Introductory Remarks to a Rhetorical Theory of Folklore." *Journal of American Folklore* 81(1968): 143–58.

Anderson, John Q., Edwin Gaston, Jr., and James W. Lee, eds. *Southwestern American Literature: A Bibliography*. Chicago: Swallow Press, 1979.

Auden, W. H. "Notes on the Comic." In *Comedy: Meaning and Form*, ed. Robert Corrigan. San Francisco: Chandler Publishing Co., 1965.

Ball, John. "Style in the Folktale" *Folklore* 65(1954): 170–72.

Bascom, William. "The Forms of Folklore: Prose Narratives." *Journal of American Folklore* 78(1965): 3–20.

Bauman, Richard. "Any Man Who Keeps More'n One Hound'll Lie to You: Dog Trading and Storytelling at Canton, Texas." In *And Other Neighborly Names: Social Process and Cultural Image in Texas Folklore*, ed. Richard Bauman and Roger D. Abrahams. Austin: University of Texas Press, 1981.

Ben-Amos, Dan. "Toward a Definition of Folklore in Context." In *Toward New Perspectives in Folklore*, ed. Americo Paredes and Richard Bauman. Austin: American Folklore Society, 1972.

Biebuyck-Goetz, Brunhilde. " 'This is the Dyin' Truth': Mechanisms of Lying." *Journal of the Folklore Institute* 14 (1977): 73–95.

Bier, Jesse. *The Rise and Fall of American Humor*. New York: Holt, Rinehart and Winston, 1968.

Blair, Walter. *Horse Sense in American Humor from Benjamin Franklin to Ogden Nash*. Chicago: University of Chicago Press, 1942.

————, ed. *Native American Humor*. New York: American Book Company, 1937.

————. "The Popularity of Nineteenth-Century American Humorists." *American Literature* 3(1931): 175–94.

_____. *Tall Tale America*. New York: Coward-McCann, Inc. 1944.

Blair, Walter, and Hamlin Hill. *America's Humor: From Poor Richard to Doonesbury*. New York: Oxford University Press, 1978.

Boatright, Mody. *Folk Laughter on the American Frontier*. New York: Macmillan, 1949.

_____. *Gib Morgan, Minstrel of the Oil Fields*. El Paso: Texas Folklore Society, 1949.

_____. "The Tall Tale in Texas." *South Atlantic Quarterly* 30(1931): 271–79.

Brandes, Stanley J. "Family Misfortune Stories in American Folklore." *Journal of the Folklore Institute* 12(1975): 5–17.

Brown, Carolyn. *The Tall Tale in American Folklore and Literature*. Knoxville: University of Tennessee Press, 1982.

Brunvand, Jan Harold. "Len Henry: North Idaho Munchausen." *Northwest Folklore* 1(1965): 11–19.

_____. *The Study of American Folklore*. New York: Norton, 1968.

Cerf, Bennett, ed. *An Encyclopedia of Modern American Humor*, Garden City, NY: Hanover House, 1954.

Clough, Ben C., ed. *The American Imagination at Work: Tall Tales and Folk Tales*. New York: Knopf, 1947.

Cohen, Hennig, and W. B. Dillingham, eds. *Humor of the Old Southwest*. Boston: Houghton Mifflin, 1964.

Degh, Linda. "Folk Narrative." In *Folklore and Folklife: An Introduction*, ed. Richard M. Dorson. Chicago: University of Chicago Press, 1972.

Dobie, J. Frank. *I'll Tell You a Tale*. Boston: Little, Brown, 1960.

Dondore, Dorothy. "Big Talk! The Flying, the Bage, and the Frontier Boast." *American Speech* 6(1930): 45–55.

Dorson, Richard. "The Identification of Folklore in American Literature." *Journal of American Folklore* 70(1957): 1–8.

_____. *Man and Beast in Comic Legend*. Bloomington: University of Indiana Press, 1982.

Dundes, Alan. "The Study of Folklore in Literature and Culture." *Journal of American Folklore* 78(1965): 136–42.

_____. "Texture, Text, and Context." *Southern Folklore Quarterly* 28(1964): 251–65.

Eastman, Max. "Humor and America." *Scribner's* 100(1936): 9–13.

Emrich, Duncan. *Folklore on the American Land*. Boston: Little, Brown, 1972.

Etulain, Richard. *A Bibliographic Guide to the Study of Western American Literature*. Lincoln: University of Nebraska Press, 1982.

Freud, Sigmund. "Jokes and the Comic." In *Comedy: Meaning and Form* ed. Robert W. Corrigan. San Francisco: Chandler Publishing Company, 1965.

Georges, Robert. "Towards an Understanding of Storytelling Events." *Journal of American Folklore* 82(1969): 313–28.

Gorn, Elliot. "'Gouge and Bite, Pull Hair and Scratch': The Social Significance of Fighting in the Southern Backcountry." *American Historical Review* 90(1985): 18–43.

Greig, J. Y. T. *The Psychology of Laughter and Comedy*. 1923. Reprint. New York: Cooper Square Publishers, 1969.

Gurewitch, Morton L. *Comedy: The Irrational Vision*. Ithaca: Cornell University Press, 1975.

Hill, Hamlin. *Mark Twain: God's Fool*. New York: Harper & Row, 1973.

Hoffman, Daniel G. *Form and Fable in American Fiction*. 1961. Reprint. New York: Norton, 1973.

Hymes, Dell. "Models of the Interaction of Language and Social Life." In *Directions in Sociolinguistics* ed. John J. Gumperz and Dell Hymes. New York: Holt, Rinehart & Winston, 1972.

Inge, M. Thomas, ed. *The Frontier Humorists: Critical Views*. Hamden, Conn: Archon Books, 1975.

Jones, Steven Swann. *Folklore and Literature in the United States*. New York: Garland Press, 1984.

Kenney, W. Howland, ed. *Laughter in the Wilderness: Early American Humor to 1783*. Kent, OH: Kent State University Press, 1976.

Kittredge, George L. *The Old Farmer and His Almanack*. Cambridge: Harvard University Press, 1904.

Leacock, Stephen Butler. *Humour and Humanity: An Introduction to the Study of Humor*. London: Butterworth, 1937.

Lemay, Leo. "The Text, Tradition and Themes of 'The Big Bear of Arkansas.'" *American Literature* 47(1975): 321–42.

Loomis, C. Grant. "A Tall Tale Miscellany." *Western Folklore* 6 (1947): 28–41.

Lynn, Kenneth S. *Mark Twain and Southwestern Humor*. 1959. Reprint. Westport, Conn: Greenwood Press, 1972.

———, ed. *The Comic Tradition in America: An Anthology of American Humor*. New York: Norton, 1968.

McKeithan, D. M. "Bull Rides Described by 'Scroggins', G. W. Harris, and Mark Twain." *Southern Folklore Quarterly* 17(1953): 241–43.

Major, Mabel, and T. M. Pearce. *Southwest Heritage: A Literary History and Bibliographies*. 3d ed. Albuquerque: New Mexico University Press, 1972.

Meine, Franklin Julius. *Tall Tales of the Southwest*. New York: Knopf, 1930.

Miles, Elton. *Southwest Humorists*. Austin: Steck-Vaughn Co., 1969.

Penrod, James H. "The Folk Hero as Prankster in the Old Southwestern Yarns," *Kentucky Folklore Record* 2(1956): 5–12.

———. "Folk Motifs in Old Southwestern Humor." *Southern Folklore Quarterly* 19(1955): 117–24.

Pilkington, William T. "The Comic Novel in the Southwest." In *My Blood's Country*, ed. William T. Pilkington. Fort Worth: Texas Christian University Press, 1973.

Rourke, Constance. *American Humor: A Study of the National Character*. 1931; Reprint. New York: Harcourt Brace & Jovanovich, 1959.

Rubin, Louis D., ed. *The Comic Imagination in American Literature*. New Brunswick: Rutgers University Press, 1973.

Schmitz, Niel. *Of Huck and Alice: Humorous Writing in American Literature*. Minneapolis: University of Minnesota Press, 1983.

Stahl, Sandra K. D. "The Personal Narrative as Folklore." *Journal of the Folklore Institute* 14(1977): 9–30.

———. "Studying Folklore in American Literature." In *Handbook of Ameri-*

can Folklore, ed. Richard M. Dorson. Bloomington: Indiana University Press, 1983.

———. "Style in Oral and Written Narrative." *Southern Folklore Quarterly* 43(1979): 39–62.

Stanley, David H. "The Personal Narrative and the Personal Novel: Folklore as Frame and Structure for Literature." *Southern Folklore Quarterly* 43(1979): 107–20.

Taylor, J. Golden, Thomas J. Lyon, George F. Day, Gerald W. Haslam, James H. Maguire, and William T. Pilkington, eds. *A Literary History of the American West*, Ft. Worth: Texas Christian University Press, 1987.

Thompson, Harold W., and Henry Seidel Canby. "Humor." In *Literary History of the United States*, ed. Robert E. Spiller, William Tharp, Thomas H. Johnson, Henry Seidel Canby, Richard M. Ludwig. 2d ed. New York: Macmillan, 1957.

Toelken, Barre. *The Dynamics of Folklore*. Boston: Houghton Mifflin, 1979.

———. "Folklore in the American West." In *A Literary History of the American West*, ed. J. Golden Taylor, Thomas J. Lyon, George F. Day, Gerald W. Haslam, James H. Maguire, and William T. Pilkington. Ft. Worth: Texas Christian University Press, 1987.

Thorp, Willard. *American Humorists*. Minneapolis: University of Minnesota Press, 1964.

Tulp, Margaret Chisholm. *Cowboy Humor: An Examination of the Humorous Side of the Rugged Men Who Helped Develop the American West*. El Reno, OK: El Reno Junior College, 1982.

Turner, Arlin. "Seeds of Literary Revolt in the Humor of the Old Southwest." *Louisiana Historical Quarterly* 39(1956): 143–51.

Welsch, Roger. *Catfish at the Pump: Humor and the Frontier*. Lincoln, NB: Plains Heritage, 1982.

———. *Shingling the Fog and Other Plains Lies: Tall Tales of the Great Plains*. Chicago: Sage Press, 1972.

White, Evelyn Brooks, and Katherine S. White, eds. *Subtreasury of American Humor*. New York: Coward-McCann, 1941.

Wilt, Napier. *Some American Humorists*. New York: T. Nelson and Sons, 1929.

Wyatt, P. J. "So-Called Tall Tales about Kansas." *Western Folklore* 22(1963): 107–11.